Fashion, Women and Power

Fashion, Women and Power

The Politics of Dress

EDITED BY

Denise N. Rall

Bristol, UK / Chicago, USA

First published in the UK in 2022 by
Intellect, The Mill, Parnall Road, Fishponds, Bristol, BS16 3JG, UK

First published in the USA in 2022 by
Intellect, The University of Chicago Press, 1427 E. 60th Street,
Chicago, IL 60637, USA

A catalogue record for this book is available from the British Library.

Copy editor: MPS Limited
Cover designer: Holly Rose
Production manager: Laura Christopher
Typesetter: MPS Limited

Print ISBN 978-1-78938-461-1
ePDF ISBN 978-1-78938-462-8
ePUB ISBN 978-1-78938-463-5

Printed and bound by POD

To find out about all our publications, please visit our website.
There you can subscribe to our e-newsletter, browse or download our current catalogue and buy any titles that are in print.

www.intellectbooks.com

This is a peer-reviewed publication.

*To the Honourable Julia Eileen Gillard AC,
first female prime minister of Australia.*

Contents

Foreword

Prudence Black

'Taking Clothes Out of the Equation': The Politics of Dress

Women are often judged by what they wear, and women in public office obviously have many more eyes on them. In the first quarter of the twenty-first century, the numbers are alarming, as only 57 countries of the 193 member nations of the United Nations have had a woman as either prime minister or president (Gillard and Okonjo 2020: 19). A graphic display of the male bias in world politics is seen in the photo of the G20 economic forum in 2010 (see Plate i). Women leaders when they do attain positions of power, have to negotiate their occupancy of these largely male spaces. As writer and historian, Rosemary Hill said about politics:

> It's never been arranged for us and our convenience [...] so if you want to stand out, or you want to fit in, or you want to appear authoritative, or you want to disappear in the background, your clothes are going to be incredibly important in the way that you negotiate that.
>
> (Hill 2018: n.pag.)

Women's clothing may need to stake their ground in a political world, but that means their appearance becomes open for criticism (Akou 2011; Allman 2004).

Is it possible to take clothes out of the equation? In October 2018, the official portrait of ex-Prime Minister of Australia Julia Gillard was unveiled at Parliament House, Canberra. Gillard was the first female prime minister in Australia (2010–13), and she made the conscious decision to have a facial portrait (see Plate ii). She said to Vincent Fantauzzo, the artist who

ix

painted the portrait: 'It'll be from the neck up, please'. Further, she noted this was,

> a really conscious discussion and choice. I mean one of the things that I think is frustrating for women in leadership roles at the moment, still, is that there is endless commentary about what they're wearing. For me, being the first female prime minister, there were times when it was just truly absurd. And so, I did, in this, want to entirely take *clothes out of the equation*.
>
> (Anon. 2018a: n.pag., emphasis added)

For women in public office, taking their dress out of the equation appears impossible. So impossible that the Australian Member of Parliament Nicolle Flint responded to media criticism over her wardrobe by wearing a plastic garbage bag over her garments. On her Twitter feed, she asked, 'What should a woman in politics wear? […] How about a garbage bag? To match your rubbish views' (Beikoff 2020: n.pag.). Ms. Flint challenged the media with her garbage bag dress and disrupted the norm of appropriate appearance, what dress theorist Michael Carter names a 'descent into unacceptability' (2018: 777). Female (and male) politicians appearing in public should dress to a certain standard, or look 'smart'. Carter then outlines some of the general features of smart dress, 'it should be clean, without creases (ironed), crisp, and at least approaching a condition of completion' (2018: 777). This 'smart' appearance is now expected by the public.

So, Julia Gillard chose to take clothes out of her portrait, and Flint 'called out' the media for their comments, but women in public office are routinely criticized more than men for their appearance. In 2018, US First Lady Melania Trump wore a green-hooded Zara jacket to the Texan border camp to visit Border Patrol Agents and the children of migrants who had been quarantined away from their parents under her husband's 'Zero Tolerance' policy. The world gasped as they saw the words, 'I really don't care, do U?', scrawled on the back of her jacket. Melania's overt display of unconcern for both the children (Llamas 2018: n.pag.) and their families was quickly countered by her communications director who responded, 'It's a jacket, there was no hidden message' (Superville 2018: n.pag.). Shortly after this photo received global approbation President Trump reversed his executive order on the 'family separation' policy (Collinson et al. 2018: n.pag.).

That said, clothing matters most when they disrupt. This is how the fashion system works. While men in power typically wear a suit, shirt and tie leaving little to discuss, women leaders can choose outfits from a range of styles, thereafter scrutinized by the media and the public. Fashion consistently relies on change, so changes in fashion communicate a message of instability. This is a risk for those in power who must appear stable and will be criticized by the media, especially if their appearance is orchestrated as self-promoting, a type of vanity. Emmanuel Kant, writing in the late 1700s noted:

> Fashion, accordingly, comes under the heading of *vanity*, since our purpose in following it has no intrinsic value, and also of folly, because it still involves a coercion to let ourselves be led slavishly by mere example – the example that the many in society give us.
>
> ([1797] 1974: 112, original emphasis)

In society, fashion presents as an ever-changing desire. Thorstein Veblen addressed this in his seminal book, *The Theory of the Leisure Class* where he outlined the dysfunctionality of conspicuous consumption through the example of women, who donned 'high fashions' that limited their movement or access to simple activities ([1899] 1928). Recently, the equation between women's fashion and change then-Senator Hillary Clinton estimated that she lost 24 working days in her 2016 presidential campaign due to time spent styling her hair and make-up, when she could have employed those lost hours on the campaign trail rather than 'enhancing' her appearance (Gillard and Okonjo-Iweala 2020: 141).

So primarily, the fashion system works by drawing attention to the body through changing styles. Specific garments are composed of colour, style and through what parts of the body are exposed, or covered up. As dress can also mask the body many women in western politics adopted the male's business suit. The suit coat envelopes one's body, constructing a superficial profile around the body; thus, reshaping the body through its structure. And historically, the suit suggests a relationship to work. The first suits were designed for the male shape (Hollander [1994] 2016) and it must be acknowledged that women have different bodies to men. Male leaders are criticized by the media, but rarely because of their actual body shape. For women, the suit may help to disguise their 'actual' body. But both women and men still face media criticism even when wearing the 'immunity' of a business suit.

While Julia Gillard typically wore a suit to work she was continually criticized for her appearance; the cut of her jacket, the colour and style of her hair. Malcolm Turnbull (Liberal Party Prime Minister 2015–18) described what Julia Gillard endured as 'off the charts' and he elaborated, 'there's an obsession with the appearance of women in politics. How often do people talk about [Prime Minister] Scott Morrison losing his hair? [...] You never read this stuff about men. Are the males in Parliament just one Adonis after another?' (Doreian 2020: n.pag). Today's sensationalist journalists take up the option to focus on female leader's clothing to make their political criticisms seem less *ad feminam*, that is, 'against the woman', thus leaving her policies unreported.

There are exceptions. Prime Minster of New Zealand, Jacinda Ardern (New Zealand Labour Party 2017–present) was elected as the third female prime minister of her country and acknowledges her predecessors for smoothing her path. It is also necessary to mention that Ardern presents as a younger female with a normative body size and shape that drew less commentary from the press. Currently, women leaders are still highly criticized for their body shape through their clothing: in Julia Gillard's jackets and Hillary Clinton's pantsuits the 'fit' is labelled a 'misfit'. Here, the fit of one's clothes becomes 'the point of balance around which the elegant and the awkward circle one another' where elegance itself becomes 'a state where there is a harmonious integration between what is being worn and the body of the wearer. Awkward is a condition where that point of balance, and so fit, is absent' (Carter 2018: 778).

A further imbalance occurs when a female politician becomes too fashionable, that is, moving beyond institutional boundaries. Both Prime Ministers Margaret Thatcher (Conservative Party 1979–90) and Theresa May (Conservative Party 2016–19) choose fashionable high heels to express their 'femininity' that were ridiculed by the media, particularly May's leopard-print kitten-heeled shoes (Gillard and Okonjo-Iweala 2020: 137; see Chapter 7). Elsewhere in the world, Asian women leaders must not appear overly fashionable, too masculine or even too 'westernized' (see Chapter 6).

In Australia, red jackets and red shoes have been used as a way of signalling an internal female faction within the Liberal Party. Some Liberal Party women wore red at a sitting of parliament to testify their disapproval to the resignation of their colleague Julia Banks in the Victorian State Parliament due to bullying, and the fact that female Liberal candidates were passed over for pre-selection for the seat of Wentworth (Wright 2018: n.pag.).

Julie Bishop (Deputy Leader, Liberal Party [2007–18]; Minister for Foreign Affairs [2013–18]) entered politics more than 20 years ago. Bishop is widely acknowledged as one of Australia's most successful woman leaders who also employed the colour red when she announced her decision to resign from her Cabinet position on 27 November 2018 (Bolger 2018). Her bright red, block-heel and rhinestone-studded Italian Rodo shoes were donated to the Museum of Australian Democracy in Old Parliament House, Canberra, Australia. They are displayed in the museum alongside a photograph of her at her final press conference. The photograph shows her bare legs from skirt length down, hands clasped behind her back (nail polish matching the shoes), standing in her red shoes against a backdrop of men wearing dark suits (Anon. 2018b). The Museum labelled her shoes as a 'bold statement and a symbol of solidarity among Australian women' dignifying this pair of fashion objects with an expression of feminist ideology. Despite her credibility as one of the most successful Foreign Ministers in Australia's history it is predictable that 'those red shoes' are destined to identify the most iconic image of her long career (Bolger 2018: n.pag.) (see Plate iv). Like Dorothy's red shoes in the *Wizard of Oz*, the headline offered that Julie Bishop was indeed 'going home' (Sams 2019: n.pag.).

Women as political leaders are caught as their fashion and its criticism cycle around each other. This author suggests that clothing can be metonymic, where a garment stands for the whole person, echoing the Barthes' words on fashion that contains 'such a network of meaning' ([1967] 1990: xi). Women leaders could choose an unambiguous uniform (but even then) how their garments are understood remains contingent on the day, the time, the hour, the place and their perception by the audience. Certainly, Bishop's shoes offered a performative utterance when she required her shoes to 'say something' in rebuttal to her male counterparts, but the wider audience might easily misinterpret such a message. As Carter notes:

> Description slides into judgement. However hard we try to stop passing sentence on our own appearance and that of others, the very words we use to engage with the clothes we wear are already infused with moral value.
>
> (2018: 781–82)

The portrayal of women in political leadership continues to have wider ramifications. Amanda Haraldsson and Lena Wängnerud describe the impact of 'media sexism' as a 'factor contributing to women's lack of nascent political ambition' (Haraldsson and Wängnerud 2019: 528). Here, media sexism exerts a 'bystander effect' that can deter women from entering politics, pre-empting women who might want to stand for office inhibited by presumed media reactions to their appearance (Haraldsson and Wängnerud 2019: 526).

To conclude, women in politics will receive different treatment because of their gender coupled with the scrutiny and subsequent judgements about what they wear (Le Marquand 2020). In 2019, only 24.3 per cent of all national parliamentarians were women and if women were to achieve parity with men; it is unlikely whether comments about women's dress will diminish (Anon. 2019). In an era composed of rapid response media bites, Twitter feeds and social media, women must manage and control the marginalization of their political effectiveness and deflect focus on their fashion where critical interpretations are given free reign (Ibroscheva and Stover 2012). Today, women in politics and their assistants must continue their vigilance, and swiftly call out unwanted attacks on their appearance and demeanour and return the focus to their policies. The more often women in leadership call out and block such demeaning language regarding their fashion could lessen such denigration in the future.

REFERENCES

Akou, Heather M. (2011), *Dress in Somali Culture*, Bloomington: Indiana University Press.

Allman, Jean (ed.) (2004), *Fashioning Africa: Power and the Politics of Dress*, Bloomington: Indiana University Press.

Anon. (2018a), 'Julia Gillard portrait unveiled in national parliament', *ABC News*, 24 October. https://www.abc.net.au/news/2018-10-24/julia-gillard-portrait-unveiled-in-parliament-house/10424304. Accessed 1 June 2020.

Anon. (2018b), 'Items with a story to tell', Museum of Australian Democracy, 6 December, https://www.moadoph.gov.au/blog/items-with-a-story-to-tell/. Accessed 5 August 2020.

Anon. (2019), 'Facts and figures: leadership and political participation', https://www.unwomen.org/en/what-we-do/leadership-and-political-participation/facts-and-figures. Accessed 1 May 2020.

Barthes, Roland ([1967] 1990), *The Fashion System* (trans. M. Ward and R. Howard), Berkeley: University of California Press.

Beikoff, Katrina (2020), 'Do we rate the policy or the shoes? Judging women in power by what they wear is actually getting worse', *In Queensland*, 30 July, https://inqld.com.au/opinion/2020/07/30/the-politics-of-fashion-will-our-female-politicians-ever-escape-power-dressing/. Accessed 13 August 2020.

Bolger, Rosemary (2018), 'Friends and foes alike have praised Julie Bishop's tenure as foreign minister after she stepped aside from the role she has filled for five years', https://www.sbs.com.au/news/our-finest-foreign-minister-end-of-an-era-as-julie-bishop-leaves-cabinet. Accessed 14 August 2020.

Carter, Michael (2018), 'Dressed in adjectives, Part 2 the lowly adjective', *Fashion Theory: The Journal of Dress, Body and Culture*, 24:5, pp. 775–82.

Collinson, Stephen, Westwood, Sarah, Jarrett, Laura and Kopan, Tol (2018), 'Trump reverses course, signs order to keep families together', *CNN*, 20 June, https://edition.cnn.com/2018/06/20/politics/trump-separation-action-immigration/index.html. Accessed 24 September 2021.

Doreian, Robyn (2020), '"What Julia Gillard endured was off the charts": Malcolm Turnbull talks women', *Sydney Morning Herald*, 4 July, https://www.smh.com.au/culture/books/what-julia-gillard-endured-was-off-the-charts-malcolm-turnbull-talks-women-20200701-p5582t.html. Accessed 8 July 2020.

Gillard, Julia and Okonjo-Iweala, Ngozi (2020), *Women and Leadership: Real Lives, Real Lessons*, Melbourne: Vintage Books.

Haraldsson, Amanda and Wängnerud, Lena (2019), 'The effect of media sexism on women's ambition: Evidence for a worldwide study', *Feminist Media Studies*, 19:4, pp. 525–41.

Hill, Rosemary (2018), interviewed by J. Green, *Blueprint*, ABC Radio National, 4 August, https://www.abc.net.au/radionational/programs/blueprintforliving/frock-consciousness/10065536. Accessed 10 July 2019.

Hollander, Anne ([1994] 2016), *Sex and Suits*, New York: Alfred A. Knopf.

Ibroscheva Elza and Stover, Maria (2012), 'The girls of parliament: A historical analysis of the press coverage of female politicians in Bulgaria' in Karen Ross (ed.) (2012), *The Handbook of Gender, Sex and Media*, West Sussex: John Wiley & Sons, pp. 35–52.

Kant, Emmanuel ([1797] 1974), 'On taste in fashion', *Anthropology from a Pragmatic Point of View* (trans. M. J. Gregor), The Hague: Martinus Nijhoff.

Le Marquand, Sarrah (2020), 'Julia Gillard', Stella section, *Sunday Mail*, 12 July, pp. 3–7.

Llamas, Tom (2018), 'First Lady Melania Trump on immigration, family separation and "the jacket"', *ABC Nightline*, 13 October, https://www.youtube.com/watch?v=4GOWjH9mT-M, Part One and Part Two. Accessed 20 October 2019.

Sams, Lauren (2019), 'Minister for fashion takes a bow', *Australian Financial Review [LUXURY]*, 6 September, pp. 1–2.

Superville, Darlene (2018), 'What was the message behind Melania Trump's jacket?', PBS, 21 June, https://www.pbs.org/newshour/politics/what-was-the-message-behind-melania-trumps-jacket. Accessed 17 April 2020.

Veblen, Thorstein ([1899] 1928), *The Theory of the Leisure Class*, New York: Vanguard Press.

Wright, Tony (2018), 'No handmaids here! Liberal party women launch their resistance', *Sydney Morning Herald*, 17 September, https://www.smh.com.au/politics/federal/no-handmaids-here-liberal-women-launch-their-red-resistance-20180917-p504bm.html. Accessed 5 August 2020.

Preface

Denise N. Rall

As never before, women have been thrust into positions of political power, and likewise into the maelstroms of mass media regarding their fashion, their deportment and their right to govern. These contributors will offer a wide set of perspectives on women and their roles, and their fashions when taking up powerful positions in Australia, New Zealand, Great Britain and the United States. From the United Kingdom, the historical issues surrounding the movement towards 'rational dress' for women seeking their rights to vote and exercise will be interrogated. The volume also explores viewpoints from East Asia, such as the constricting role for 'common' women upon entering the Imperial family in Japan. From the United States comes the troublesome media stories engulfing two significant American Democratic First Ladies, Hillary Rodham Clinton and Michelle Obama. From New Zealand, the media reports on Prime Minister Jacinda Ardern upon her motherhood while serving in the office and on her clothing during the recent Christchurch massacre comprise a much-needed contribution to the literature on women, politics and dress. Further, the role of dress in politics broadly as a form of resistance will be examined in Australia from recent skirmishes over 'appropriate dress' worn by ex-Prime Minister Julia Gillard and other Australian female politicians. The role of women and what their fashion selections mean continues via considerable debate during worldwide events. Finally, the theme of resistance and social media continues with an examination of protest dressing in the recent street battles in Hong Kong, to how young Asian women have been influenced by the social media campaigns to encourage wearing the veil in Indonesia, to prime ministers negotiating femininity in political dress.

Introduction: Theoretical approaches to women in leadership and political fashion

Denise N. Rall and Jo Turney

This introductory section explores a number of theoretical approaches to fashion that interplay with women, their identities and their political efficacy as they construct a suitable (pun intended) public persona when taking up political office and/or influential positions of leadership. Within fashion research, a number of theories have decoded women's adoption of specific types of dress and how fashion influences their roles in society. These theories run the gamut of perspectives from Goffman's theories of presentation, and how fashion works through 'branding', including power dressing, the significance of fashion for nation branding and the employment of sartorial diplomacy, alongside women who negotiate a personal political identity through their dress. Lastly, recent feminist approaches to power are summarized to explain the limitations to women's opportunities to take up authoritative positions through theories of role congruity and intersectionality.

Following the Introduction are three sections of case studies that survey selected global responses to women in leadership, their dress and comportment while in office, as well as challenges and resistance to the dominant male-oriented cultures regarding women in leadership and the politics of what they wear.

Part I: Gender, politics and identity: Lessons from past and present

Part I develops three narratives of women's performance of gender as it relates to significant social trends from the 1900s through to the twenty-first century. These chapters each offer a series of perspectives that challenged women's authority in the public sphere, in the workplace and how fashion trends affected women as they took up positions of influence and political life. At question is women and their ability to function as productive members of society or in politics, while negotiating the vexing matters of family life as affiliative or reproductive agents within their life partnerships, marriages and/or family obligations. Further issues arise in the chapter on Japan's royal family that details the responsibilities fostered on women's dress from enduring historical dynastic obligations.

Chapter 1: Rational dress 'as an expression of the fin-de-siècle *aspiration towards equality of the sexes*'

Madeleine Seys

Writing in *Aglaia: The Journal of the Healthy and Artistic Dress Union* in 1894, Lasenby Liberty described the dress reform movement as 'an expression of the *fin-de-siecle* aspiration towards equality of the sexes'. During the 1880s and 1890s proponents of the British women's liberation, suffrage and dress reform movements adopted androgynous ensembles of bloomers or divided skirts, waistcoats and jackets. In its rejection of the fashions and gender ideologies of male-dominated Victorian society, this politically motivated mode of dress was termed Rational Dress. Rational Dress afforded women both physical and political mobility. The invention of the bicycle and Rational cycling dress allowed women to negotiate public space in pursuit of equality and employment, challenging the Victorian ideology of 'Home-is-the-Woman's-Sphere'. Through its androgynous style, Rational Dress also represented both a symbolic and further, a real threat to patriarchal Victorian society by undermining its very foundations. This research drawn from nineteenth-century primary sources outlines the practical and symbolic use of Rational Dress by British women's rights and suffrage campaigners at the turn of the twentieth century.

Chapter 2: Prime Minister Jacinda Ardern: Fashion and performing gender

Sarah Baker

In September 1893, New Zealand became the first self-governing country in the world to give women the right to vote in parliamentary elections. Since then, New Zealand has had three women prime ministers, Jenny Shipley, Helen Clark and most recently Jacinda Ardern. These prime ministers all experienced the double standards associated with women's appearance and questions about their leadership while they were head of the country. For example, Helen Clark suffered many cruel comments about her appearance as 'masculine' while later, Ardern was famously quizzed by the media on whether she would have children while she served as prime minister. Ardern's role as a governor, and her ability to do her job potentially conflicts with the popular media portrayals of her as a woman, mother and fashion icon – requiring much negotiation between her public and private self. Recently, Ardern appeared on the September 2018 edition of *Vogue* to discuss her motherhood, a story which was edited by the Duchess of Sussex, Meghan Markle. Following the horrific Christchurch Massacre in early 2018, she famously donned a headscarf to show solidarity and received both praise and criticism by the media. These two examples highlight where Ardern's role as prime minister has been linked to fashion and further, to her ability to negotiate and deliver a normative gender performance. This discussion outlines the role of fashion and its ties to Ardern's performance of gender and delineates how slippery the climb up the political ladder becomes. The conclusion suggests that women as high-level politicians are still hindered by the constraints of fashion and gender.

Chapter 3: An empress's wardrobe unlock'd: Empress Masako and Japan's imperial fashions

Emerald L. King and Megan Rose

The story of Empress Masako's integration into the Royal Family in Japan highlights an interesting instance where a powerful woman in East Asia has struggled with her negotiation of the self. The public stories of women and their insertion into the imperial Japanese court focus on three life stages: the initial courtship, the assimilation into Royal court life and consequent pressures to produce a male heir. Before her marriage, Empress Masako was a highly accomplished woman and an aspiring diplomat who hesitated to marry into the royal family. She was 'heroed' in the western media as the 'next Lady Di' before failing to maintain her identity within the limitations of the Japanese court. Here, the analysis of Japan's court dress codes illustrates Empress Masako's 'princess lifestyle'. Focusing on three key movements in the Empress's presentation: her courtship by the crown prince, her life as a princess, and finally as Japan's empress; we demonstrate how the use of colour and style are codified. A careful selection of her ensembles worn across this time period is explored through a systematic review of news reportage (both eastern and western) alongside a semiotic analysis of the outfits in question. Further, the manner in which the empress is dressed evokes the occidental fantasy of the elegant woman, retaining strong visual parallels to the British Royal Family.

Part II: Making politics through fashion

Part II concentrates on women in political office at the highest level, as presidents, prime ministers as well as the influential role taken up by United State's First Ladies. These chapters outline how women leaders encountered enormous differences in governmental and political structures in Australia, the United States of America and throughout Asia. These female leaders were repeatedly challenged to adopt appropriate dress choices and afterwards to witness how their fashion choices dictated society's acceptance or blatant non-acceptance within their designated role. Here, the scrutiny of women's dress was first analysed in detail by the daily newspapers in Australia in the mid-1800s and elsewhere reported through other mass media, including print, radio, television and the rise of various social media that have dominated the expression of public opinion during the last two decades of the twenty-first century. In these three chapters, the media continued to regard women's fashion as an indicator of their ability to take up political power alongside family life and country-specific expectations of leadership.

Chapter 4: *Women politicians, fashion and the media in Australia: Enid Lyons to Julia Gillard*

Amanda Laugesen

Australian women politicians have been subjected to enormous scrutiny ever since they first entered parliament via Dame Enid Lyons in the 1940 federal election who served until 1951. She was the first female member of the House of Representatives, elected alongside the first female Senator, Dorothy Tangney. They are often held to higher standards and expectations, and they are watched closely lest they slip up and do something 'wrong'. This scrutiny has often included their fashion choices, ranging from hairstyles to the colours they choose to wear. Sometimes these choices are met with approval; other times they are torn to shreds. The media have frequently passed judgement on the attire of women politicians in a way that men are rarely subject to, and thus media commentary has played and continues today as a powerful force in shaping women's political careers, even shaping a political downfall in some instances. Australian women politicians have, nevertheless, exerted some agency across time in employing this media scrutiny, as well as gender stereotyping, to their own advantage.

Chapter 5: *'Dressing up' two Democratic First Ladies: Fashion as political performance in America*

Denise N. Rall, Jo Coghlan, Lisa J. Hackett and Annita Boyd

They influence American 'womanhood' and by 'their husband's elections' First Ladies become *sites* for the symbolic negotiation of female identity'. The process of negotiation in female identity appears in various forms after women assume political power, for example, Golda Meir in Israel, Margaret Thatcher in the United Kingdom, Indira Gandhi in India and most recently, Australia's first female Prime Minister Julia Gillard (2010–13). While the position of First Lady is unique to American politics, the ways in which Hillary Clinton and Michelle Obama each rejected a 'suitably feminine' image provides an important lesson for all women in power. Therefore, we argue here that this analysis of two Democratic American First Ladies and their employment or disregard of fashion informs the gender-based and race-based issues affecting women in political leadership through their choices in dress. When 'dressing up' both Hillary Clinton and Michelle Obama struggled with issues of individual identity, subjectivity and power and negotiated their First Lady roles through their fashion.

Chapter 6: Codes of power: Transforming the dress and appearance of female Asian politicians

Jennifer Craik and Anne Peirson-Smith

Women in politics have always faced challenges in matters of dress. Modern politics has largely been seen as the province – perhaps the playground of men – who have dressed primarily in either a (western) business suit or (less commonly) customary or ethnic dress. The former conveys connotations of authority, discipline, convention and formality associated with the ideals of democratic political systems, while the latter conveys a more colourful aesthetic and image of the exotic. By contrast, female Asian politicians have to negotiate complex interplays between professional credibility and subtle overtures of mainstream femininity. Yet, over the past decade, the wardrobe of female politicians in Asia has expanded to include more colourful fabrics, informal outfits and generally more mainstream garments, cuts and styles. However, female politicians must be careful to retain a vestimentary image that is credible, serious, capable and attractive. Thus, Asian dress codes – although increasingly relaxed – still require a strategic negotiation between professional and gender codes in the selection and combination of garments that can convey an acceptable balance of efficiency, legitimacy and believability while in office. The dress of female Asian politicians and their public appearance attracts more media and public attention than their policies, skills and achievements. Using paired examples of contemporary female politicians in South and East Asia it is suggested that dress codes are employed to change both the look and efficacy of female politicians in Asia.

Part III: Women and dress: Social media, politics and resistance

Part III includes the narratives of resistance offered in the sartorial choices of women, from the highest political office in the United Kingdom to the opening public sphere for young women adopting Instagram-promoted fashions in Indonesia, and finally within the recent street protests of Hong Kong. The overwhelming visual nature of dress speaks to its performative aspect and through performance, its impact on public opinion and mass media. From the more subtle wearing of high fashion shoes to the uptake of a particular style of veil, and through clothing worn of necessity during public political demonstrations, it is evident that women's clothing offers a resistance to the status quo and therefore performs its function as an indicator of resistance.

Chapter 7: Leopard in kitten heels: The Politics of Theresa May's Sartorial Choices

Rachel Evans

The British government has faced recent upheavals over the issue of British nationhood which came to the fore as the country faced dissolution from the European Union. Theresa May was placed squarely in the spotlight as a female member of parliament and as the second female prime minster of Great Britain. A conservative member of parliament and with a conservative background growing up as a Vicar's daughter and grammar school education, Mrs May's sartorial choices have evolved to conform with an understanding of women members of parliament as proxy men and to reflect British National dress as defined by tradition. However, within this conservative persona she struck a discordant note by her shoe selections. Here, her shoes provide a clear message of 'everyday resistance'. As her government faced increasing unpopularity, her employment of leopard-print kitten heels indicates a form of subaltern resistance.

Chapter 8: Felix Siauw, storyteller, preacher and profiteer: Fashioning a new brand of Islam in Indonesia

Rheinhard Sirait

The success of Felix Siauw is explored through his personal history and his role in utilizing Indonesia's online space to promote conservative Islamic ideas through clothing. He succeeded in his enterprise by marketing the hijab ('head covering or veil') to younger women as a pious fashion item. Siauw's narrative begins with a careful reconstruction of his persona, through his conversion to Islam from his former Christian Chinese minority ethnic family background. After his credibility as a popular online preacher or ustadz (digital preacher) was established, he became a so-called 'micro-celebrity' through his lessons via social media. This popularity allowed further development of his core commercial enterprises, including a range of his books and clothing, particularly 'proper' hijabs for young women. Siauw's business model for his products included his promotional materials that were designed to establish a khilafah (Islamic caliphate) in Indonesia. The reach of Felix Siauw's online persona through his celebrity status enabled him to market and commodify conservative Islamic ideas, by amplifying controversial fatwas ('Islamic ruling') about female Muslim piety. It is noted that some of these concepts are considered unlawful by Indonesian state policy, yet through their online distribution have gained considerable traction amongst young Indonesian men and women. Siauw's marketing strategies for the hijab, or female veil, tell the story of how his promotion of an item of clothing impacted on religious piety amongst young women in Indonesia. Finally, some of his prohibitions were not appreciated by Indonesian's young, Internet-savvy online audience.

Chapter 9: All dressed in black: The gendered appearance of protest

Anne Peirson-Smith and Jennifer Craik

The recent protests in Hong Kong, from 2017 to present highlight the symbolic aspects of protest gear in terms of its rationale, communicative impact and gender implications. Theories about embodied dress codes, identity presentation and liminality assist to examine female protestors. Here, dressing-up in a particular way transformatively and mimetically invests these women with individual agency based on their connections through wearing a shared uniform. This clothing provides discursive framework which can be viewed as radical or seditious in the public domain. Protest uniforms can enhance, neutralize or negate expressions of gender when operating in the liminal zones of a rebellion and signal their subversive relevance to a political cause or movement. For women, the strategic choice of dress and appearance become social representations and expressions of individual, collective and gendered power. The deliberate donning of black clothing and masks, and how these affect identity, emotion, behaviour and consequently elicit public responses to the women's embodied images are presented within Hong Kong's unique socio-cultural context.

Acknowledgements

I first thank both Prudence Black and Madeleine Seys for their co-led seminar, 'The Politics of Dress: "I really don't care, do U?"' at the University of Adelaide, South Australia on 26 October 2018. Their symposium was generously supported by the Faculty of Arts, University of Adelaide and the Fay Gale Centre for Research on Gender, where the speakers, including myself worked through the implications of the above theme and its political subtext. I thank them both for the seminar as well as the generous permission to use 'The Politics of Dress' as a subtitle. These discussions provided the impetus to continue this examination of the recent trends in women's political leadership along with the articulated, as well as the many latent requirements to solidify their political identities through dress.

My understanding editors at Intellect, especially Laura Christopher, during the COVID-19 pandemic meant that this book could emerge during a time of hardship felt around the world. The fashion scholars from five different countries and territories, Australia, New Zealand, the United Kingdom, Hong Kong and Indonesia all persevered while working under difficult conditions to deliver their chapters. The reviewers from the United Kingdom and the United States also offered useful assistance as the volume took shape, and any remaining errors are strictly my own.

The graphics and illustrations only came to fruition with the help of Emerald L. King, a Japanese language and fashion scholar par excellence, with a profound understanding of dress in the Asian context. This volume could not have been illustrated without her assistance.

I continually thank my family, Associate Professor J. Doland Nichols, Fran and Louis B. Rall and Alyse Rall Benjamin. All of them are writers, either as scientists or poets, and I am indebted to their support in all my endeavours.

The first and former prime minister of Australia, the Hon. Julia Eileen Gillard, AC, while unable to contribute personally to this volume, did so with co-author Ngozi Okonjo-Iweala, after publishing *Women in Leadership: Real Lives, Real Lessons* in 2020. I was lucky enough to purchase a copy from my local bookstore in Lismore, New South Wales. The eight lessons for women in leadership are often painful to read. I hope that future women and non-gendered officeholders can present their policies rather than their shoes in the world's political arenas.

Introduction

Theoretical Approaches to Fashion, Power and Women's Leadership

Denise N. Rall and Jo Turney

There are a number of theoretical approaches to fashion that interplay with women, their identities and their political efficacy as they construct a suitable (pun intended) public persona when taking up political office and/or influential positions of leadership. Within fashion research, a number of theories have decoded women's clothing and how it influences their roles in society. These theories run the gamut of perspectives, from Goffman's theories of presentation, what it means to 'brand' a type of clothing, power dressing and issues of political and personal female identity. The section concludes with a very brief discussion of feminist analysis of women's roles through theories of role congruity and intersectionality.

Following this Introduction are three sections of case studies or narratives that survey the issues for women leaders in both western and eastern cultures, their dress and comportment while in office, as well as highlighting challenges and resistance to the dominant male-oriented cultures regarding women and the politics of what they wear.

Introduction

> Vain trifles as they seem, clothes have, they say, more important offices than merely
> to keep us warm; they change our view of the world and the world's view of us.
> (Woolf [1928] 2004: 166)

The study of fashion, particularly women's dress, has dwelt in many houses composed of interactive disciplinary rooms: material culture, fashion design, textiles, craft, historical and contemporary costume as viewed through the lenses of economics, literature, art, photography, film, television and various social media.

1

Scholars of fashion include museum curators, cultural sociologists, post-colonialists feminists and queer theorists, anthropologists and art historians.

Our exploration of political fashion is 'well suited' to the field of popular culture, which explores scholarly interpretations of the social activities and the cultural meanings that are produced and circulated through the practices of everyday life. Further, 'clothing, as artefacts "create" behaviour through their capacity to impose social identities' (Crane 2012: 2) which become in themselves dynamic forces that shape societies. For women in leadership roles, these identities are changing and therefore, challenging. As never before in history more women have secured positions of political power, which has thrust them into the view of mass media as regarding their fashion, their deportment and their right to govern (Sreberny-Mohammadi and Ross 1996; Ross 2004). Women as leaders and what they wear reflect a series of fluctuating expectations in today's challenging political arena.

Note there are many ways that clothing signals a political stance. Colours and styles are employed by specific political parties, reformation or protest movements, such as the Orange 'revolution' in Ukraine (Wilson 2005) the yellow vests of France (Cigainero 2018) and women and their families donning pink 'Pussy Hats' as they marched on Washington DC following the inauguration of President Donald Trump in 2017 (see https://www.pussyhatproject.com. Accessed 3 August 2021). Recent protesters in London and within the globalized Black Lives Matter (BLM) movements are wearing black (see Plate xxiv). Even the Democratic Women's Caucus donned white outfits to match the garb of the suffragists in 1920 to recognize the centenary 'of the ratification of the US Congress's 19th amendment, and to demonstrate their solidarity with disenfranchised groups' (Lang 2020: n.pag.).

In fact, dress presents a rhetoric of its own that cannot be ignored.

Beyond an expressive emblem, clothing has shaped women as they have campaigned and sometimes succeeded in assuming positions in leadership around the world. Women in politics are subjected to commentary time and again on their looks rather than their governmental policies or political acumen.

This volume explores the complex and frequently uncontested preconceptions that govern the politics of dress, and for women in leadership, the everyday practice of 'getting dressed' exhibits and articulates far more than the clothing worn. Today, what political women wear dominates the media whereby their clothing is judged as equivalent to their professionalism and suitability for office.

Dress as a measure of women's political viability and strength varies throughout scholarly interpretations offered in this volume. When women take up a standard masculine 'uniform', they present an exercise of power or authority (Jansens 2019). A semiotic approach aligns the female body within a liminal space between being 'dressed' and 'undressed' as specific costumes test the appropriateness of 'how much to reveal' and how those choices limit women leaders and their ability to navigate within a given political landscape. As a European MP reflected:

> You have to be careful not to arrive in a too low cut shirt or too short skirt. It is also more noticed if a woman hasn't had her hair combed or if she swears. It is important to find the right balance as a woman. If you smile too much, you flirt and try to attract. If you don't smile enough, you're just a sulky cow.
>
> (interviewee cited in Moustgaard 2004: 27)

Both fashion and political scholars have assessed women leaders through their posts in social media, as the socials have become the default way to measure the effectiveness of women's clothing, their campaigns and their success in achieving political office (Fountaine et al. 2019; Mavin et al. 2010).

Thus, as in the cliché 'clothes make the man',[1] women's dress presents the conflict between the concept of the feminine as a predetermined set of moral obligations expressed through their sexuality, reproduction and motherhood versus a self-determined identity outside of these social restrictions. The feminist analyses on gender and power provide a well-established set of critiques that resonate through the contemporary fashion literature (see Hollander 1994; Smith 1990) and this volume offers further illustrations of gender as women have entered the political arena.

Appearance, performance and identity

From the earliest times, women in power have been challenged to perform effectively while in office. Erving Goffman, in his seminal *The Presentation of the Self in Everyday Life* (1959), introduced the notion of appearance as part of a staged presentation, as 'players' navigate between their appearances 'on stage' and 'off stage'. Some scholars suggest that managing a 'staged' appearance becomes a process of manipulation. As Efrat Tseëlon reports, 'the manipulative view was advanced by "impression-management" researchers [...] if persons attempt to present themselves in the best light, is it deceptive?' (2015: 157, see Schlenker 2012).

Here is the crux of the matter: while politicians seek to communicate authority and truthfulness through their political stance, their appearance can belie their statements. Dress becomes the most salient aspect of their 'performance' and draws the line between believable/trustworthy or false/untrustworthy.

To be a woman in leadership, she must look the part:

> There are two important functions to clothes in nonverbal communication. First, they help us to negotiate identities as we present our situated identities or roles, moods,

3

values and attitudes to one another. Second, they help us to define situations, that is, to socially construct the basis for our interactions.

(Kaiser 1997: 217, cited in Marzel and Stiebel 2015: 9)

Today's emphasis on the visual means politicians are critiqued on their appearance – through their dress, hairstyle, makeup, etc. – in order to create their political effectiveness. For women in politics, the emphasis on the visual display over political substance has dramatically escalated. All of this critique ties into the essence of impression management and the role it plays in contemporary politics.

Fashion as 'brand'

One of the guiding tropes within the field of fashion is the creation of the 'brand'. Certainly, brands, as labels for products 'derive their appeal from the story of origin, purpose and character of the consumer products they create' (Tseëlon 2018a and b: 3). Brands, as makers' names existed prior to the Industrial Revolution, but the rise of the factory system, through England's textile factories that exploited labour to serve the consumer 'commodity fetishism' inspired *The Communist Manifesto* from Marx and Engels to champion an alternative economy (Sullivan 2016: 34). The critiques of branding as a practice are likewise embedded in the process of rampant capitalism that privileges the consumer over the producer in the process called globalization (Lury 2004). Naomi Klein's seminal book, *No Logo* (2000) outlined much of the infrastructure within the fashion industry that remains in place today through ruthless practices by global enterprises to meet the demands of rapid turnovers in style. Georg Simmel noted this over 100 years ago as a 'nervousness' generated by the need for social differentiation amongst the upper echelons in large cosmopolitan cities – in his city of pre-war Berlin (Simmel 1957 [1904]: 547 cited in McNeil 2016: 74).

Much later, Gilles Lipovetsky elaborates on Simmel to suggest that fashion exists to offer women the potential to change, perhaps 'change for the sake of change', introducing concepts of fashion within his New French philosophy (1994) that elaborated narratives about women and women's bodies; their innate instability, expressed as movement, change, uncontrollability, lack of discipline and attention and ease of seduction. Fashion is ultimately defined by what women seek in appearance, '*seduction and metamorphosis*' (Lipovetsky 1994: 112, emphasis added). As Caroline Evans (2003, cited in O'Connor 2010: 936) noted, since the birth of the mass market women and clothing have been linked, or rather chained together in a fashion system driven by constant change. These changes became pronounced through frivolous detailing deemed as 'feminine': unnatural shaping of body, complex construction and over-decorativeness, exploiting gender assumptions of childlike characteristics apportioned to women as seductive, decorative and effectively without reason, substance or purpose. However, theorists then suggested that women, through this constant reassignment of dress will acquire individual *agency* (as an expression of power) through the consumption, wearing and performing through clothes as individuals (Lipovetsky 1994; Smith 1990).

Therefore, how women employ a fashion as 'brand' provides the narrative of her 'personal presentation of the self' and provides a marker of her individual agency, as defined through the theories of identity politics. But 'branding' in terms of women's political leadership can be more or less successful when acted out on the world stage. More discussion on branding will follow.

Fashion branding and personal agency

Note that agency – the ability to act – for women in leadership splits into two dimensions. The individual expression of agency through one's dress is the basis of one's social identity. Recently, as Efrat Tseëlon emphasizes and others have said, fashion stands in for the self,

> objects, fashion and other material possessions increasingly function in consumer culture as shorthand summaries of the self. Whether we see ourselves represented in certain brands, or use them as props or boosters not only to project who we are, but to actually *be* these persons […] the magic of fashion, nation or brand share a similar type of identity politics that is bound up with the quality of the story we fabricate through word and material.
>
> (2018a: 3, original emphasis)

Fashion itself depends on – at least the myth – that clothing empowers one's personal agency, or as Tseëlon indicates clothing dresses bodies through 'summaries of the self'. This has become central to the style blog where the garments on display 'gives bloggers a means to express who they are, to share this with readers […] to engage with the conventions of modern fashion […] that is, to assert a fashionable and specific presence through visual representation' (Findlay 2012: 201, see Findlay 2017). While this speaks specifically of amateur fashionistas and their online 'outfit posts' the point is taken that visual representation in digital space offers a place for individual women to express their agency through what they wear. Or rather, what they are *seen* to wear.

For women in politics, an expression of personal agency challenges the norms of leadership, the masculine oeuvres of rationality, competition, leadership and power that are referenced as 'corporate masculinity' or 'corporatized masculinity' (see Maier 1999; Mavin et al. 2016; Jansens 2019). Here, fashion also serves to craft identities: where fashion 'plays a seminal role in the creation of political identities, from the crafting of national identity to various iterations of individual forms of subjectivity' (Shinko 2017: 46). And Rall et al. (2018: 276) add that dress is important in communicating a political point of view and/or allowing the wearer to take up an authoritative stance in the press and public opinion (see Chapter 5).

In 1994, to disrupt this cultural stereotype in the political arena, a five-day workshop once called the Women's Campaign School (now the Campaign School) is hosted by Yale University each year in New Haven, Connecticut:

> The Campaign School at Yale University is a nonpartisan, issue-neutral leadership program, whose mission is to increase the number and influence of women in elected and appointed office in the United States and around the globe. The Campaign School at Yale University has been inspiring and training women to lead for over twenty years.
>
> (Anon. 2020: n.pag.)

While there are a number of workshop options, in 2013, the five-day course acknowledged the scrutiny that women in politics face by introducing a new session called 'Dress to Win' (Friedman 2018: n.pag.). While some women protested at the requirement to 'fashion' their image, 'the campaign school is trying to teach [prospective candidates] to see dress not as a liability to overcome, but as a weapon, women are lucky enough to wield' and 'even if you are being judged [...] it does not mean that you should fall back on the safety net of banal dressing' (Friedman, quoting Sonya Gavankar, the lecturer in charge of 'Dress to Win' 2018: n.pag.). Julia Baird, writing about women in politics in Australia, suggests that female politicians have 'exploited the stereotypes and superficiality of press coverage for their own gain', a strategy that has not always worked well (Baird 2004: 8).

Further commentary on the divisiveness of the American political scene and now seen globally is the rule of women dressing for 'safety' where 'the pantsuit – and its cousin, the stewardess skirt suit – is the Garment Least Likely to Offend Any Interest Group, and thus the garment of choice. All else is a risk', noting:

> In the end, Ms. Gavankar said, 'they [the prospective candidates] are not playing it safe with their views. So why should they play it safe with their clothes? When we tell women to wear the same suit, that is doing a disservice to women. They are, and should be, different'.
>
> (Friedman 2018: n.pag.)

This sounds more like hopeful rhetoric for the future rather than today's political reality. But there remain some lessons from the past.

The question of female–male

The portrait of Queen Elizabeth I (reigning from 1558 –1603) bedecked in an elaborately designed costume, composed of sumptuous and pearl-encrusted fabrics with her left hand clutching a sieve to indicate her virginity (Jordan 1990). Opposed on all sides by political enemies, research on Queen Elizabeth I suggests that her gender was the most controversial part of her rule. One solution to her right to rule came after Nicholas Heath, Archbishop of York 'describes Elizabeth as having two identities simultaneously, one male and the other female' (Levin 2013: 121). The 1554 Act Concerning Regal Power, after much verbiage about the word 'kinge' and the properties assigned to it, ultimately 'split her body into two parts, while physically she is a woman, 'politically she is a man' (Jordan 1990, cited in Levin 2013: 121). While this sounds absurd today, Queen Elizabeth I successfully out-manoeuvred both the precariously based religious authority of the new Church of England as well as a fraught parliament to manage to declare herself both male and female; in order to avoid marriage and relinquish her throne to her husband, she styled herself 'The Virgin Queen'. This is hardly a strategy for today's political women: but only as a pointer that out of necessity, Elizabeth I, and her adroit 'branding' of herself as a Virgin Queen, afforded her the first and longest reign as head of state (and religion) in Great Britain until Queen Victoria (reigning from 1837 until her death in 1901).

Today, to adopt a male identity in order to bolster a woman's authority to rule is absolutely out of the question. Yet, assumptions of female and/or male are quickly becoming irrelevant as a non-binary gendered personae becomes normalized in many societies. Recently, six 'openly transgender' candidates have won political office in the US mid-term elections in 2017 (Eltagouri 2017). In liberal democracies, this trend is likely to continue, while in other cultures gender ambiguity remains unacceptable, but that may change over time.

The 'dress for success' movement

Timewise, the 'dress for success' movement (Molloy 1975) followed the counter-culture upheavals and experimental fashions in the aftermath of the 'hippie chic' paradigm (Lobenthal 1990, 2010: 417–18) and the Twiggy-style and psychedelic-influenced fashions of Carnaby Street in London. In 1966, Mary Quant was even awarded for 'jolting England out of its conventional attitude toward clothes' (1966: 96).

The cover of John Molloy's later offering, *Women's Dress for Success* (1977) depicts two women side by side. The woman on the left wears a pastel-coloured dress, with a modest neckline, chunky but not overly large necklace, a gold bangle, and most notably, holds a glass of wine. Her auburn hair is coiffed in a winsome semi-flip, curled up on one side to reveal a modest hoop earring, as she converses with a seated male dinner companion. On the right side, her female counterpart is wearing a navy trench coat, with her coat collar outlined by a white open scarf, revealing no neck skin, holding a business report while her other hand rests on a brown square briefcase. Her auburn hair is a shade darker, and much longer, and tucked behind one ear, without earring, and she presents her written report to two seated businessmen, one who takes notes on a legal pad.

These sexy images of American women dressed for 'work' were introduced by the image of the sexualized office 'girl' popularized by *Sex and the Single Girl* (Brown 1962). This motif was developed through popular magazines such as *Cosmopolitan* (published in the United States as a woman's magazine since 1965) and in Australia, *Cleo* (published from 1972–2016, Anon. 2016: n.pag.). The call for 'power dressing' for women became enmeshed with self-help narratives that empowered the career woman but likewise emphasized how to attract men (Brown 1964). As a sign of the times, this unfortunately remains divisive for women seeking leadership today, 'whether they should be feminine or "business like"; babes or bitches' (Mavin 2009 cited in Mavin et al. 2010: 556).

The issue of how women in politics can brand themselves as both strong and successful, yet appropriately 'female' through their attire still remains problematic. As outlined in the following three sections of case studies women's political dress and the male–female equation invites controversy around the world.

The pantsuit

Dressing the female body for utility and strength, or as 'male' – from 'Bloomers' to trousers – is not without its perils. However, workplace mobility for women increased when they adopted elements of male work attire, demonstrating how the split-skirt or trouser offers not only power, but freedom to travel to move around on a new technology, the bicycle (see Chapter 1). So, the mobility of women required their liberation from restrictive clothing (Miller 2000). Grant McCracken's (1988) argument is summarized by Lynch and Strauss, when they conclude, 'women were motivated to assimilate male vestiges of power through fashion change and simultaneously to drop symbolic liabilities, thus on balance they acquired symbolic advantages and gained status in the workplace' (2007: 65).

Women in leadership are told that changeability or whimsey in their clothing presents a liability, even though some stylists suggest otherwise. However, adopting the ubiquitous jacket and trousers with crisp shirt and some kind of neckwear, worn by male politicians and businessmen from the 1920s onwards would become problematic for their female counterparts, even after 'power dressing' entered the social norms for business wear. In a 2019 interview with *Die Zeit*, German Chancellor Angela Merkel noted, 'It's no problem at all for a man to wear a dark blue suit for a hundred days in a row, but if I wear the same blazer four times in two weeks, that leads to letter-writing from citizens' (Mischke 2019: n.pag.).

Many female prime ministers and other governmental figures, such as the American First Lady, later senator and Secretary of State, Hillary Clinton has adopted the men's suit, either with matching or contrasting jacket and trousers, labelled the 'pantsuit' (see Plate iii). An unremarkable garment for men in politics, it became a sensible outfit for women to meet the unceasing demands of political office. However, the 'predictability' of male prime ministerial dress did not apply equally to women (Gillard 2014: 282), and as the first female prime minister Gillard had no predecessors in Australia:

> Undoubtedly a male leader who does not meet a certain standard will be marked down. But that standard is such an obvious one: of regular weight, a well-tailored suit, neat hair, television-friendly glasses, trimmed eyebrows. Being the first female prime minister, I had to navigate what that standard was for a woman.
>
> (Gillard 2016: n.pag.)

Finally, the requirement to adopt a 'male' uniform of a business suit to present political authority while in office should not be necessary. A woman should be (and is) capable of governing in her own right, no matter what she wears. The difficulty then lies in the public's perception of a woman 'dressed as a man' as outlined in the Campaign School's 'Dress to Win' session. Fashion styling can manipulate the female body into models of 'power' (wide shoulders, double-breasted suits and through cut, fit, etc.). While a suit coat and trousers cut to fit a woman's body may accentuate natural or create artificial curves, an ensemble devoid of these features can imitate a male body and create a sense of artifice (Binkley 2008: n.pag.).

The dilemma remains – there seems to be no middle ground. While 'your clothes should not speak for you' says 'Rosana Vollmerhausen, the founder of DC Style Factory [...] [who dresses] both female and male politicians' but amongst the more media-savvy women leaders there comes 'a growing belief [...] that says that clothes should absolutely say something about who you are and what makes you different' (Friedman 2018: n.pag.).

Fashion branding to express both personal identity and political efficacy is only one lens through which to view women in leadership and their dress. Clearly, fashion's interplay with politics is more than a personal dress sense, but influences political identity. Oh writes that fashion can be a strategic tool used by female politicians 'to increase their credibility as leaders', usually when they mimic the fashion of men (2019: 376). Shinko adds that dress 'impose[s] identities', but it can also 'subvert those identities'. She continues: 'dress has not just been central to hardcore politics; it has also been the instrument of underground movements and everyday forms of resistance' (2017: 46). The last section of this volume deals with how clothing can challenge political systems.

Sartorial diplomacy as political agency

American First Lady Michelle Obama and her clothing are explored later, but it is noted that her ability to express agency through her fashion choices became labelled as 'sartorial diplomacy',

> like the first ladies from Jacqueline Kennedy to Nancy Reagan, Mrs. Obama understood that fashion was a means to create an identity for an administration. But unlike any other first lady, instead of seeing it as part of a uniform to which she had to conform, with the attendant rules and strictures that implies, she saw it as a way to frame her own independence, add to her portfolio [of talents] and amplify her husband's agenda.
>
> (Friedman 2017: 3)

That said, some women in leadership positions have located a way to 'brand their look' that has worked well; others have tried similar techniques that have crashed and burned. No one approach is perfect, but some have been more successful than others. Anna Murphy offers successful branding by women in leadership as exemplified by both the conservative Australian Julie Bishop (Deputy Leader, Liberal Party [2007–18]; Minister for Foreign Affairs [2013–18]) and Theresa May (Prime Minister of the United Kingdom; Leader of the Conservative Party [2016–19]) (2016: 16). Both were noted as wearing strong colours and in particular, making a fashion statement through their shoes; Theresa May's selection of 'kitten heels' was reminiscent of Margaret Thatcher's wearing of designer high heels (see Chapter 7).

Prime Minister Margaret Thatcher is a special case as her attire has been extensively reviewed for how clothing exemplifies the gendered aspects of politics, including a body of analysis of how she used fashion to her advantage. Daniel Conway (2016: 174) argues that Thatcher was able to encourage and manipulate the media to present her policies in a favourable light. She regarded dress as a 'tool of the job', and, argues that '[d]ress and politics were intertwined in Thatcher's daily life' (Conway 2016: 180, 188). Thatcher chose to 'look British' on the international stage and used fashion to project her image as a powerful and successful leader (Conway 2016: 189). Her clothes also communicated her politics, for example, wearing anti-Communist colours while in Poland near the end of the Cold War (Conway 2016: 192). Conway's conclusion was that 'Thatcher's agency as a woman and politician was both enabled and constrained by dress and constructions of dress' (Conway 2016: 194).

Murphy concludes that women in leadership should 'wear efficiency chic: clothes that foreground rather than grandstand [...] they're not out to make a fashion statement, rather a statement of intent: I am modern, I am together, I am a safe – but not dull – pair of hands' (2016: 16).

Julie Bishop, with an extremely fit profile, stressed 'fashion diplomacy' [...] 'in person she always presents in trim and tailored fashion, helped along by her long time love of [designer Giorgio] Armani' (Murphy 2016: 16). Ms. Bishop also adopted a strategic use of the salient colour red (see Plate iv), arguably the most powerful colour in the fashion lexicon:

> Red is one of my favourite colours. It evokes power, passion and fashion. In power I always noted that many nations have red in their flags and that's because it symbol-ises courage and freedom. Passion, well, you know, red hearts, red roses. And fash-ion – that's why they call it a red carpet – and red lipstick, red nail polish, red shoes.
> (Peatling 2018: n.pag.)

Ms. Bishop made her point by wearing red-stacked sparkle-studded high heels, standing out from the 'men in blue suits' as she resigned as Minister for Foreign Affairs on 27 November 2018 (Bolger 2018: n.pag.). But the use of bright colours by women leaders such as Julia Gillard, Australia's first female prime minister (2010–13), who was criticized for her 'inappropriate' use of brightly coloured jackets (see Jansens 2019) (see Chapter 4). Another press put-down states, 'while it's understood the PM favours bold colours, her penchant for the white jacket has earned its own Twitter hashtag: #awj, for another white jacket' (Caldwell and Stead 2011: n.pag.). This only demonstrates how social media can whip up a frenzy over a woman leader's fashion when they should be commenting on her policies. The reality is that clothing becomes an essential part of any politician's identity, image and appearance, a way to communicate consistently who they are, and what they represent in terms of their personal branding (Scammell 2015, [1995] 2016).

Andreas Behnke notes that fashion is 'part and parcel of the performativity of the political' (2017: 19). Further, gender is 'not a fixed attribute; rather, it is a constant, reiterative performance of gender roles as defined and expected by soci-ety' (Behnke 2017: 20). Fashion goes beyond gender, he argues: '[i]t is involved also in the performative constitution of political subjectivities, of power and authority, as well as of the subjects and victims of such power' (Behnke 2017: 21). Further, dress can be understood as a means by which identity can be performed and affirmed, and therefore, 'becomes *a site of political struggle*' (Conway 2016: 178, emphasis added).

11

Brands and the nation-state

Brands are part and parcel of the fashion system, but also play into the machinery of the nation-state. Simon Anholt had introduced the concept of the 'nation brand' initially in 1996, later expressed as follows:

> My original observation was a simple one: that the reputations of countries (and by extension, of cities and regions too) behave rather like the brand images of companies and products, and that they are equally critical to the progress, prosperity and good management of those places.
>
> (2011: 289)

This concept is grounded in historical events as some nations aspired to power through adopting another nation's brand. This process of adoption presented a solution for Japan's leadership in the mid-1850s to the 1870s as 'they struggled to work out what it was that made the West so much richer and stronger', looking for answers in the West's political and educational systems, 'or the way they dressed?' 'as they shed their samurai garb and kimonos in favour of replica European suits and dresses':

> Unsure, the Japanese decided to take no chances, They copied everything [...] from the Prussian constitutional system to the adoption of the British gold standard [...]. The army drilled like Germans; the navy sailed like Britons. An American-style system of state elementary and middle schools was also introduced.
>
> (Ferguson 2011: 221)

Thus, for nineteenth-century Japan, the connection between western prosperity and power became concentrated in wearing westernized costume (King and Rall 2015: n.pag.). This concept of the nation brand as generating a certain kind of power through dress has migrated throughout the world, as most male politicians wear the western business suit. There are exceptions such as the Saudi Arabian leaders who continue to wear their traditional robes, or military leaders such as Libya's 'Colonel Gaddafi' and Cuba's Fidel Castro who retained their battle dress (see Norton 1988). Likewise, Vladimir Putin, Russia's President (1999–2008, 2012–present), who has also served repeated terms as Russia's prime minister, often posed bare chested as he engaged in athletic outdoor activities. Putin's 'bare chest' images were splashed all over the media prior to his 2018 re-election campaign, presenting a strong nation brand that links national power with personal athleticism (Oliphant 2017: n.pag.). It is noted that his 'machismo' brand does not seem likely to be emulated by other male politicians around the world, and certainly not by women in leadership.

Fashion as soft power

Simon Anholt's (2011) nation brand was derived from the field of advertising, and how the dissemination of commercial brands and their uptake through the marketplace could export national ideologies as a kind of brand. Scholars who work in geopolitics took a slightly different approach to the brand where nations influence each other through uptake of their policies as products (see Lury 2011). This concept of 'soft power' was defined as a form of diplomacy that would allow a western political position, for example, a free market system to influence other nations rather than subjugation through military force (Nye 2009, 2004).

In the 1960s and 1970s, during the Cold War period between the West and the Soviet bloc, this soft power took on a special force in the case of blue jeans, as Ferguson reports, 'such was the desirability of this article of clothing that Soviet law-enforcement officials coined the phrase "jeans crimes" which referred to "law violations prompted by a desire to use any means to obtain articles made of denim"' (2011: 244 quoting an interview with Stefan Wolle in 2009).

So the wearing of blue jeans as a symbol of western influence was identified a primary example of soft power, as denim jeans spread throughout the world (Sullivan 2006; Ferguson 2011). Particularly, wearing a fashion that reflected one's patriotism when engaging with other nations has become an act of 'sartorial diplomacy' (Friedman 2017: 1). In Asia, wearing traditional clothing such as the Chinese *qipao* meaning banner gown or *cheongsam* meaning long dress in Cantonese suggest nationality (Mears 2010: 548) (see Chapter 6).

Feminist theories and women's leadership

This scoping study of fashion, power (as access and agency) and women's identities seeks to only summarize some of the theories that connect fashion and women in politics. Generations of feminist scholars have provided significant contributions to current analysis of the problematic roles for women in the workplace, and specifically women in leadership or executive positions. Note that the word executive originates from execute, meaning to enact. Today's women in politics must achieve a platform in which to 'enact' that is – to exercise of power from a position of authority – which is continually called into question by their fashion. Therefore, two final theories should be mentioned that are crucial to the analysis of how women as leaders achieve political efficacy while in office.

Role congruity theory

Early feminist theory from Rosabeth Moss Kantor's study, *Men and Women of the Corporation* (1977) and often revised (1993, 2008) laid the groundwork for workplace analysis and how it challenges women's authority and delivered a whole new literature on masculinity and patriarchal assumptions in the modern workplace. Conversational analysis also came to the fore to analyse how men and women communicate at work, and as the subtitle of linguist Deborah Tannen's book suggests, 'how women's and men's conversational styles affect who gets heard, who gets credit, and what gets done at work' (1994). This trend has proliferated in the popular press, including bestsellers such as *Lean In*, authored by the Chief Operating Officer (COO) of Facebook (Sandberg with Scovell 2013). As could be anticipated, the literature on women and leadership has proliferated in the last decade.

Most recently, those who research women and leadership in the workplace have introduced the concepts behind role congruity theory (Dzubinski et al. 2019). This theory pulls together the ongoing research in gender inequity, to argue that women in executive positions are forced to take up 'gendered self-constraint' to achieve their leadership goals (2019: 233) and relieving women of the necessity for self-constraint though a more diverse workplace culture would aid their capacity to take up leadership roles. Role congruity theory is based on gender-role stereotypes that 'are deeply embedded in both society and organizations, with women expected to be "communal" and men expected to be "agentic"' (Eagly and Karau, 2002: 574). It is not too difficult to assess the requirements of the communal role offered to women in the workplace: women are expected to be 'affectionate, helpful, kind, sympathetic, interpersonally sensitive, nurturing, and gentle' whereas the 'agentic' persona expected from men requires behaviours that are 'aggressive, ambitious, dominant, forceful, independent, daring, self- confident, and competitive' (Eagly and Johannesen-Schmidt 2001: 783). Here, the role congruity analysis provides the conundrum for leadership in the workplace because leaders need to take care of their staff as well as to act with agency, to 'get the job done' (Dzubinski et al. 2019: 233). In the end, these scholars conclude that today's organizations overwhelmingly stress 'getting the job done' which skews the workplace to promote men as more suitable for leadership rather than women, 'an effect which has persisted for decades' (Dzubinski et al. 2019: 234).

While this may seem obvious, role congruity theory offers a model for re-aligning the workplace with more diverse values, essentially a process of de-gendering the roles of leaders to include all types of leaders, to effectively champion 'a woman's way of leading' (Dzubinski et al. 2019: 233). However, de-gendering is only the start of rebuilding women's authority and their potential for leadership.

There are other factors that greatly influence how women can enter politics and remain in important political roles.

Intersectionality

It has been stated that the theories behind intersectionality arose during the second-wave movement of feminism, usually roughly labelled as 'the 1960s', where gender, race and overall social disadvantage, such as poverty of women contributed to their oppression. Since then, a great deal of feminist literature has opened up the conversation from leading postcolonialists such as the creative writer and scholar, Mexican American Gloria Anzuldúa's contribution to boundary analysis in her ground-breaking book *Borderlands/La Frontera* ([1987] 2012). Here, the dilemma of women in modern society undergoes a racially explicit and geopolitical layer that forcefully impacts an already gendered landscape, which set the foundations of modern theories of intersectionality (see Anzaldúa 2009; Cho, Crenshaw and McCall 2013; Collins and Bilge 2016; and many others).

While the importance of intersectionality is evident, it is not always so clear how the theory can be applied in any given context. Collins and Bilge note that,

> intersectionality as an analytical tool [is used] in many different ways to address a range of issues and social problems [...] intersectionality's core insight [is] useful: namely that major axes of social divisions in a given society at a given time, for example, race, class, gender, sexuality dis/ability, and age operate not as discrete and mutually exclusive entities, but build on each other and work together.
>
> (2016: 27)

Collins and Bilge, and many other feminists, argue that intersectionality can be promoted as a 'heuristic' or 'problem-solving tool' to explain disadvantage through an interconnecting nexus of conditions, rather than relying on single-term analysis such as racism or sexism. Other forms of 'outsider' presentations, including non-binary sexuality, dis/ability and ageism have also come to bear on the assessment of women's ability in politics.

Why intersectionality is well placed to understand the conundrum of women in politics becomes clear through the following case studies, as women in different regions of the world face interconnecting and overlapping challenges to their authority. These challenges derive from culturally driven notions of identity and femininity, complicated by race, class, non-binary sexuality and patriarchal dynastic rule (see Carastathis 2014). Women's role in their own family that is, their personal affiliations plus their role in taking control of a national 'family' means that any woman in political leadership faces a barrage of complications.

Finally, how fashion choices communicate or fail to establish an authoritative presentation for women in politics should provide another 'vector' to place within the well-established theory of intersectional dynamics.

Conclusion

Today, women in politics must walk a tightrope between the expectations of their office, the political goals of their party and nation and overall must rely on what Margaret Maynard calls 'the politics of recognition' (2004: 53). George Packer states that 'in politics, identity is an appeal to *authority*' (2019: 66, emphasis added). Women in office find their 'appeal to authority' becomes quickly undermined through their fashion choices and their representation in the press and social media. For women in leadership positions, their success depends on communicating a powerful presence: at the level of an effectiveness in their role through their personal agency and the higher level of political authority for the nation-state they represent. However, fashion can be successful in 'challenging social norms and creating empowerment for individuals and groups advocating for transformation and change' (Lynch and Medvedev 2018: 3). Ultimately, the expectations of taking office alongside a considered semantics of dress becomes fluid and constantly under review by both social media and political analysis. As this volume puts forward, political dress is a form of consolidation, a means of joining traditions, histories, affiliations, the nation, the party, together. It is not about 'fashion' per se, but it is clear that fashion movements can and do generate global change.

Finally, the recent book, *Women and Leadership: Real Lives Real Lessons* (2020) co-authored by Australia's first female prime minster Julia Gillard (Australian Labor Party 2010–13) and Ngozi Okono-Iweala contains a series of sobering conclusions in their final chapter. And for women in politics this vexing issue of physical appearance is labelled 'Lesson One',

> Leadership isn't 'all about the hair,' but sadly judgements about women [in office] are still based more on their appearance than is true for men [...] do not be surprised or discomfited when there is commentary about how you look. *Expect it.*
>
> (2020: 274, emphasis added)

Women, as they enter the arena of politics and dress for leadership do so in a sartorial minefield.

NOTE

1. 'Clothes make the man. Naked people have little or no influence on society' (*More Maxims of Mark* by Mark Twain, edited by Merle Johnson, 1927).

REFERENCES

Anholt, Simon (2011), 'Beyond the nation brand: the role of image and identity in international relations', in A. Pike (ed.), *Brands and Branding Geographies*, Cheltenham and Northampton: Edward Elgar, pp. 289–303.

Anon. (2016), 'Cleo magazine to close after 44 years in print, Bauer Media Group confirms', 20 January, https://www.abc.net.au/news/2016-01-20/cleo-magazine-to-close-bauer-media-group-confirms/7100808. Accessed 6 August 2020.

Anon. (2020), 'TCS, the campaign school at Yale university', https://tcsyale.org/about-us/. Accessed 14 August 2020.

Anzuldúa, Gloria (2009), *The Gloria Anzaldúa Reader*, Durham: Duke University Press.

Anzuldúa, Gloria ([1987] 2012), *Borderlands/La Frontera: The New Mestiza*, 4th ed., San Francisco: Aunt Lute Press.

Baird, Julia (2004), *Media Tarts: How the Australian Press Frames Female Politicians*, Melbourne: Scribe.

Behnke, Andreas (2017), 'Introduction', in A. Behnke (ed.), *The International Politics of Fashion: Being Fab in a Dangerous World*, Milton Park: Routledge, pp. 1–18.

Binkley, Christina (2008), 'Women in power: Finding the balance in the wardrobe', *The Wall Street Journal*, 24 January, https://www.wsj.com/articles/SB120112420869611063. Accessed 21 January 2020.

Brown, Helen Gurley (1962), *Sex and the Single Girl: The Unmarried Woman's Guide to Men*, New York: B. Geis Associates.

Brown, Helen Gurley (1964), *Sex and the Office*, New York: B. Geis Associates.

Caldwell, Anna and Stead, Laura (2011), 'Prime Minister Julia Gillard's penchant for the white jacket', *CourierMail*, (24 September), https://www.couriermail.com.au/lifestyle/fashion/pm-fashions-variations-on-a-theme/news-story/b27ef0f300a744befd24d17ce5aaf686?sv=ef42f908014f10f52065bc7433f86251. Accessed 16 August 2020.

Carastathis, Anna (2014), 'The concept of intersectionality in feminist theory', *Philosophy Compass*, 9:5, pp. 304–14.

Cho, Sumi, Crenshaw, Kimberlé Williams and McCall, Leslie (2013), 'Toward a field of intersectionality studies: Theory, applications, and praxis', *Signs: Journal of Women in Culture & Society*, 38: Summer, pp. 785–810.

Cigainero, Jake (2018), 'Who are France's yellow vest protesters, and what do they want?', *National Public Radio*, 3 December, https://www.npr.org/2018/12/03/672862353/who-are-frances-yellow-vest-protesters-and-what-do-they-want. Accessed 14 August 2020.

Collins, Patricia Hill and Bilge, Shirma (2016), *Intersectionality*, Cambridge: Polity Press.

Conway, Daniel (2016), 'Margaret Thatcher, dress, and the politics of fashion' in Andreas Behnke (ed.), *The international politics of fashion: Being fab in a dangerous world*, London: Routledge, pp. 161–86.

Crane, Diana ([2000] 2012), *Fashion and Its Social Agendas: Class, Gender, and Identity in Clothing*, Chicago: University of Chicago Press.

Dzubinski Leanne, Diehl, Amy and Taylor, Michelle (2019), 'Women's ways of leading: The environmental effect', *Gender in Management: An International Journal*, 34:3, pp. 233–50.

Eagly, Alice H. and Johannesen-Schmidt, Mary C. (2001), 'The leadership styles of women and men', *Journal of Social Issues*, 57:3, pp. 781–97.

Eagly, Alice H. and Karau, Steven J. (2002), 'Role congruity theory of prejudice toward female leaders', *Psychological Review*, 109:3, pp. 573–98.

Eltagouri, Marwa (2017), 'Transgender people have been elected before. But they can finally let the voters know', *The Washington Post*, 9 November, https://www.washingtonpost.com/news/retropolis/wp/2017/11/08/transgender-people-have-been-elected-before-but-they-can-finally-let-the-voters-know/. Accessed 15 August 2020.

Evans, Caroline (2003), *Fashion at the Edge: Spectacle, Modernity and Deathliness*, Newhaven: Yale University Press.

Ferguson, Niall (2011), *Civilization: The West and the Rest*, London: Penguin.

Findlay, Rosie (2012), 'At one remove from reality: Style bloggers and outfit posts', *Australasian Journal of Popular Culture*, 1:2, pp. 197–208.

Findlay, Rosie (2017), *Personal Style Blogs: Appearances that Fascinate*, Bristol: Intellect.

Fountaine, Susan, Ross, Karen and Comrie, Margie (2019), 'Across the great divide: Gender, Twitter, and elections in New Zealand and the United Kingdom', *Communication Research and Practice*, 5, pp. 226–40.

Friedman, Vanessa (2017), 'How clothes defined the First Lady', *The New York Times*, 18 January, pp. 1–3.

Gillard, Julia (2014), *My Story*, North Sydney: Knopf.

Gillard, Julia (2016), 'Julia Gillard speaks in London in memory of Jo Cox MP', *JG*, https://www.juliagillard.com.au/julia-gillard-speaks-in-memory-of-jo-cox-mp/. Accessed 7 February 2020.

Gillard, Julia and Okono-Iweala, Nogozi (2020), 'The stand-out lessons from eight lives and eight hypotheses', *Women and Leadership: Real Lives, Real Lessons*, Melbourne and Sydney: Vintage, pp. 274–301.

Goffman, Erving (1959), *The Presentation of the Self in Everyday Life*, London: Penguin.

Hollander, Anne ([1994] 2016), *Sex and Suits*, 2nd ed., New York: Alfred A. Knopf.

Jansens, Freya (2019), 'Suit of power: Fashion, politics, and hegemonic masculinity in Australia', *Australian Journal of Political Science*, 54:2, pp. 202–18.

Jordan, Constance (1990), 'Representing political androgyny: More on the Siena portrait of Queen Elizabeth I', *The Renaissance Englishwoman in Print: Counterbalancing the Canon*, pp. 157–76.

Kaiser, Susan (1997 [1990]), *The Social Psychology of Clothing: Symbolic Appearances in Context*, New York: Fairchild Publishing.

King, Emerald and Rall, D.N. (2015), 'Re-imagining the Empire of Japan through Japanese schoolboy uniforms', *M/C Media Culture*, 18:6, http://journal.media-culture.org.au/index.php/mcjournal/article/viewArticle/1041. Accessed 15 June 2020.

Lang, Cady (2020), 'Why democratic Congresswomen wore white again to send a message at the state of the union', *Time Magazine*, 4 February, https://time.com/5777514/women-wearing-white-state-of-the-union/. Accessed 14 June 2020.

Levin, Carole (2013), *The Heart and Stomach of a King: Elizabeth I and the Politics of Sex and Power*, 2nd ed., Philadelphia: University of Pennsylvania Press.

Lipovetsky, Gilles (1994), *The Empire of Fashion: Dressing Modern Democracy*, Princeton: Princeton University Press.

Lobenthal, Joel (1990), *Radical Rags: Fashions of the Sixties*, New York: Abbeville Press.

Lobenthal, Joel (2010), 'Hippie Style', in V. Steele (ed.), *The Berg Companion to Fashion*, Oxford: Berg, pp. 417–18.

Lury, Celia (2004), *Brands: The Logos of the Global Economy*, London and New York: Routledge.

Lury, Celia (2011), 'Brands: Boundary method objects and media space', in A. Pike (ed.), *Brands and Branding Geographies*, Cheltenham and Northampton: Edward Elgar, pp. 44–56.

Lynch, Annette and Medvedev, Katalin (2018), *Fashion, Agency, and Empowerment Performing Agency, Following Script*, London: Bloomsbury.

Lynch, Annette and Strauss, Mitchell (2007), *Changing Fashion: A Critical Introduction to Trend Analysis and Meaning*, Oxford: Berg.

Maier, Mark (1999), 'On the gendered substructure of organization: Dimensions and dilemmas of corporate masculinity', in G.N. Powell (ed.), *The Handbook of Gender and Work*, Thousand Oaks: Sage, pp. 69–94.

Marzel, Shoshana-Rose and Stiebel, Guy D. (2015), *Dress and Ideology: Fashioning Identity from Antiquity to the Present*, London: Bloomsbury.

Mavin, Sharon (2009), 'Gender stereotypes and assumptions: Popular culture constructions of women leaders', Paper presented to the *10th International Conference, HRD Development, Research 567 and Practice across Europe: Complexity and Imperfection in Practice*, Gdansk, 10–12 June.

Mavin, Sharon, Bryans, Patricia and Cunningham, Rosie (2010), 'Fed-up with Blair's babes, Gordon's gals, Cameron's cuties, Nick's nymphets: Challenging gendered media representations of women political leaders', *Gender in Management: An International Journal*, 25:7, pp. 550–69.

Mavin, Sharon Anne, Elliott, Carole, Stead, Valerie and Williams, Jannine (2016), 'Women managers, leaders and the media gaze: Learning from popular culture, autobiographies, broadcast and media press', *Gender in Management*, 31:5&6, pp. 314–21.

Maynard, Margaret (2004), *Dress and Globalisation*, Manchester: Manchester University Press.

McCracken, Grant (1988), *Culture and Consumption: New Approaches to the Symbolic Character of Consumer Goods and Activities*, Bloomington: Indiana University Press.

McNeil, Peter (2016), 'Georg Simmel: The 'Philosophical Monet', in A. Rocamora and A. Smelik (eds), *Thinking through Fashion: A Guide to Key Theorists*, London: I.B. Tauris, pp. 63–80.

Mears, Patricia (2010), 'Orientalism', in V. Steele (ed.), *The Berg Companion to Fashion*, Oxford: Berg, pp. 546–49.

Miller, Leslie Shannon (2000), 'The many figures of Eve: Styles of womanhood embodied in a late-nineteenth-century corset', in J. D. Prown and K. Haltman (eds), *American Artifacts: Essays in Material Culture*, East Lansing: Michigan State University Press, pp. 71–92.

Mischke Judith (2019), '"For a woman, projecting authority is something you have to learn" says German chancellor', 23 January, https://www.politico.eu/article/german-chancellor-angela-merkel-clothing-criticism-reveals-double-standards/. Accessed 21 July 2020.

Molloy, John T. (1975), *Dress for Success*, New York: P. H. Wyden.

Molloy, John T. (1977), *The Woman's Dress for Success Book*, New York: Follet Publishing.

Moustgaard, Ulrikke (2004), *The Handbag, the Witch and the Blue-eyed Blonds: Mass Media in (re)distribution of Power*, n.p.: Ministry of Welfare of the Republic of Latvia.

Murphy, Anna (2016), 'Efficiency chic: the new power dressing', *The Australian*, 10 August, p. 16.

Norton, Anne (1988), *Reflections on Political Identity*, Baltimore: Johns Hopkins University Press.

Nye, Joseph S., Jr. ([2004] 2009), *Soft Power: The Means To Success In World Politics*, New York: Public Affairs.

O'Connor, Karen (2010), *Gender and Women's Leadership: A Reference Handbook*, vol. 1, Oxford: Sage, p. 936.

Oh, Youri (2019), 'Fashion in politics: What makes Korean female politicians wear "the suit" not a dress?', *International Journal of Fashion Design, Technology and Education*, 12:3, pp. 374–84.

Oliphant Vickiie (2017), 'VLADIMIR Putin stripped bare chested as he enjoyed a summer holiday diving and fishing in Siberia', 5 August, https://www.express.co.uk/news/world/837333/Vladimir-Putin-strips-off-bare-chest-holiday-Siberia-fishing-diving-Russia-election-2018. Accessed 8 August 2020.

Packer, George (2019), 'When the culture war comes for the kids', *The Atlantic*, October, pp. 56–71.

Peatling, Stephanie (2018), '"A comfortable work boot": Julie Bishop on her resignation red shoes', 27 November, https://www.smh.com.au/politics/federal/a-comfortable-work-boot-julie-bishop-on-her-resignation-red-shoes-20181127-p50iks.html. Accessed 26 July 2020.

Quant, Mary (1966), *Quant by Quant*, London: Cassell and Company.

Ross, Elsabeth Moss ([1977] 1993), *Men and Women of the Corporation*, New York: Basic Books.

Ross, Elsabeth Moss (2008), *Men and Women of the Corporation*, 2nd ed., New York: Basic Books.

Ross, Karen (2004), 'Women framed: The gendered turn in mediated politics', in K. Ross and C.M. Byerly (eds), *Women and Media: International Perspectives*, London: Blackwell, pp. 60–80.

Sandberg, Sheryl with Scovell, Nell (2013), *Lean In: Women, Work, and the Will to Lead*, New York: Alfred A. Knopf.

Scammell, Margaret (2015), 'Politics and image: The conceptual value of branding', *Journal of Political Marketing*, 14:1&2, pp. 7–18.

Scammell, Margaret ([1995] 2016), *Designer Politics: How Elections are Won*, London: Palgrave Macmillan.

Schlenker, Barry R. (2012), 'Self-Presentation', in M.R. Leary and J.P. Tangney (eds), *Handbook of Self and Identity*, New York: Guilford Press, pp. 542–70.

Shinko, Rosemary (2017), 'This is not a mannequin: Enfashioning bodies of resistance', in A. Behnke (ed.), *The International Politics of Fashion: Being Fab in a Dangerous World*, Milton Park: Routledge, pp. 19–40.

Simmel, Georg (1904), 'Fashion', *International Quarterly*, X, pp. 130–55.

Smith, Dorothy E. (1990), *Texts, Facts and Femininity: Exploring Relations of Ruling*, London: Routledge.

Sreberny-Mohammadi, A. and Ross, K. (1996), 'Women MPs and the media: Representing the body politic', *Parliamentary Affairs*, 49:1, pp. 103–16.

Sullivan, Anthony (2016), 'Karl Marx: Fashion and capitalism', in A. Rocamora and A. Smelik (eds), *Thinking through Fashion: A Guide to Key Theorists*, London: I.B. Tauris, pp. 28–45.

Sullivan, James (2006), *Jeans: A Cultural History of an American Icon*, New York: Gotham.

Tannen, Deborah (1994), *Talking from 9 to 5: How Women's and Men's Conversational Styles Affect Who Gets Heard, Who Gets Credit, and What Gets Done at Work*, New York: William Morrow and Co.

Tseëlon, Efrat (2018a), 'Fashion Tales: How we make up stories that construct brands, nations, and gender', *Critical Studies in Fashion and Beauty*, 9:1, pp. 3–33.

Tseëlon, Efrat (2018b), 'The emperor's new clothes revisited: On critical fashion, magical thinking and fashion as fiction', in A. Peirson-Smith and H. Joseph (eds), *Transglobal Fashion Narratives: Clothing Communication, Style Statements and Brand Storytelling*, Bristol: Intellect, pp. 141–56.

Wilson, Andrew (2005), *Ukraine's Orange Revolution*, New Haven: Yale University Press.

Woolf, Virginia ([1928] 2004), *Orlando: A Biography*, 2nd ed., Oxford: Oxord University Press.

PART I

GENDER, POLITICS AND
IDENTITY: LESSONS FROM
PAST AND PRESENT

1

Rational Dress 'As an Expression of the *fin-de-siècle* Aspiration Towards Equality of the Sexes'

Madeleine Seys

Introduction

In 1894, Arthur Lasenby Liberty described the emergence of a new style in women's dress as 'an expression of the *fin-de-siècle* aspiration towards equality of the sexes' (28). During the 1880s and 1890s, members of the British women's dress reform, liberation and suffrage movements adopted tailored ensembles of divided skirts or knickerbockers, waistcoats and jackets. These garments rejected the prevalent fashions and gender ideologies of dominant Victorian society. This politically motivated mode of dress was labelled Rational Dress.

At the *fin de siècle*, Rational Dress both facilitated and represented women's increased physical and political mobility. To prioritize physical comfort and practicality in middle- and upper-class women's dress was radical and inherently political in the nineteenth century. Rational Dress allowed women to traverse public space and pursue employment and political equality, challenging Victorian gender ideologies, as shown in *Punch* magazine's lampoon of women's rational dress (see Figure 1.1). In Rational Dress, women could 'climb the hills, or run, or ride a [bicycle]' (Hall 1895: 39), or, as Ouida (a pseudonym of Maria Louise Ramé), they could' [clamour] for franchise' (1894: 613). The androgyny of Rational Dress also threatened patriarchal Victorian society by undermining the conflation of biological maleness with the social and sartorial construction of men's authority. Therefore, Rational Dres became a political response to the position of women in *fin-de-siècle* Britain. In the media and literature, Rational Dress was further politicized as an icon of the women's rights and suffrage campaigns at the turn of the twentieth century (Seys 2020).

FIGURE 1.1: John Tenniel, 'Woman's Emancipation. (Being a Letter addressed to Mr Punch, with a Drawing, by a strong-minded American Woman)', in *Punch* magazine, 1851, p. 3. Source: TopFoto, Topham Partners, LLC, UK.

In contemporary sources and subsequent scholarship, Rational Dress is closely connected with other anti-fashion movements that emerged in British at the *fin de siècle*, such as the healthy, artistic, hygienic and aesthetic dress movements. These movements are united in their rejection of elaborate, tight and physically restrictive women's fashion in favour of loose-fitting garments, including ankle-length skirts, divided skirts, flowing princess-cut gowns, knickerbockers, tunics and tailored ensembles. In the nineteenth century, the idea that women should dress for comfort and health rather than social status or beauty was radical and inherently political. Thus, the Rational Dress movement and the use of the terms Rational (as adjective) and Rationals (as noun) are unique as they directly politicize this style of dress. In adopting Rational Dress, women protested against the physical and political restrictions placed on them in Victorian patriarchal society. As well as giving women bodily freedom, Rational Dress became a recognizable expression of their beliefs and their work towards realizing gender equality. British Rational Dress was an ideological, if not a stylistically distinct movement at the end of 1800s (*fin de siècle*) that was associated with the women's rights movement. There were similar movements in the United States and throughout the British Empire. However, each of these movements differed in their geographic and political context, depending on issues of racial inequality and the status of women's rights in each jurisdiction. Here, the focus is on the British movements.

Rational Dress

In Grant Allen's 1897 novel *The Type-Writer Girl*, the heroine Juliet describes her brown tweed suit as 'like all else about me (I trust) [...] rational' (2004: 42). Juliet plays on the use of 'rational' as meaning sensible. She indicates that her 'pretty brown cycling suit belongs to the politically motivated style of Rational Dress (Allen ([1897] 2004: 42).

In the 1880s and 1890s, women's rights activists argued that physically restrictive contemporary fashions were both a cause and effect of women's political subjugation. Instead of fashionable corsets, long skirts and cloaks, they promoted the adoption of tailored 'bloomers' or a divided/bifurcated skirt; a waistcoat and a Norfolk jacket (De Blaquière 1895: 14). Many late-Victorian sources use the term 'bloomers' as synonymous with knickerbockers to refer to 'loose breeches gathered or pleated into buckled band at knee' (Calasibetta and Tortora 2003: 299). The term 'Bloomers' originated in the Bloomer costume, first developed and named by American dress reformer Amelia Jenks Bloomer in the 1850s. Bloomer's version comprised full-length trousers gathered at the ankle which closely resembled Turkish trousers (Calasibetta and Tortora 2003: 34). 'Bloomers' were promoted as a reform to the burdensome long skirts as a 'healthful' garment by American women's rights campaigners Bloomer and Libby Miller from the 1850s onwards. By the 1890s, the term 'bloomers' was applied to a calf-length garment, that reconfigured men's mid-Victorian hunting breeches. By then, 'bloomers' had shed its capital letter and became synonymous with Rational styling.

In the late nineteenth century, Rational Dress described a form of clothing that was healthy, sensible and practical, and allowed women freedom of physical movement outside the home (see Figure 1.2). The style and construction of *fin-de-siècle* Rational Dress were influenced by women's riding habits (David 2002) and traditional men's tailoring (Taylor 1999: 33). The prioritization of health in styling women's clothing was then coupled with radical political sensibilities, meaning that the *fin-de-siècle* Rational Dress movement emerged as something entirely new. Rational Dress became the expression of and tool for 'the *fin-de-siècle* aspiration towards equality of the sexes' (Liberty 1894: 28) and became associated with the 'Woman Question' and the figure of the New Woman.

The Woman Question is answered by the New Woman

The British *fin de siècle* was a period of unprecedented upheaval in understandings, politics and practices of gender. Throughout the Victorian period (1837 to 1901), the ideology of 'separate spheres' defined and policed gender roles. The public

FIGURE 1.2: George Rose (*c*.1895), 'Rational Dress Picnic, Fernshaw, Victoria, Watts River', Stereograph, State Library of Victoria, H4118. Private collection of Madeleine C. Seys.

sphere of business and politics belonged to men, while home was the woman's sphere; here, she was wife, mother, nurse, household manager as well as the moral custodian of the Victorian family. This model was challenged towards the close of the 1800s by the rise of the New Woman and the 'Woman Question'. The so-called 'Woman Question' was called forth by many forces in society: the rise of girls' education, the 'surplus' of women in Britain, women's increasing participation in the workforce and a developing understanding of gender as a social construct distinct from biological sex (Richardson 2002: xxxvi).

The 'Woman Question' became a topic of vehement debate in literature, such as novels and poems, and in the periodical press in the 1880s–90s. The 'Woman Question' was not singular as the phrase suggests, but rather queried a series of ideas about the role and nature of woman and femininity: what constitutes a woman? What are a woman's status and role outside of marriage and the family? How is her role connected to education, work, citizenship and enfranchisement? (Richardson 2005: xxxvi). It was prompted, in part, by what was termed the 'surplus' of women in Britain at the time (Richardson 2002: xxxvi). In the second half of the nineteenth century, the number of women in Britain exceeded that of men by approximately 400,000 (Richardson 2005: xxxvi). This imbalance necessarily challenged the idea that a woman's primary roles were as a wife and mother, and that women should not seek employment outside the home. Angelique Richardson states that 'previously, middle-class women had been largely engaged in charitable works, but now bread-and-butter considerations were forcing them into the workforce' (2005: xxxvi). It is noted that previously, some roles for unmarried women, such as household servant, 'ladies companion' and governess, were considered suitably domestic, while public roles had been decried as indecent (see Jordan 1999). At the *fin de siècle*, the 'surplus' single women were obliged to seek education and paid work to survive. At the same time, new understandings of biological determinism challenged the social norms concerning race and class, and these intersected with questions of gender equality (Richardson 2005: xxxvi). As a result, the figure of the New Woman was constructed to address the 'Woman Question'. The New Woman represented new forms of womanhood and femininity at the *fin de siècle* (Richardson and Willis 2001: 1). As Sally Ledger states, she 'was a discursive construct of the late-nineteenth century women's movement and the periodical press' (1997: 1).

The term 'New Woman' was coined by Sarah Grande in her article 'The new aspect of the "woman question"' in *The North American Review* in 1894. Grande characterizes the New Woman as one who 'proclaimed for herself what was wrong with Home-is-the-Woman's-Sphere, and prescribed the remedy' (1894: 271). The term 'New Woman' was used to describe the various new configurations of femininity and womanhood that emerged in the 1890s (Richardson and Willis 2001: 1). The New Woman appears in multiple guises; she is a feminist, a writer, a poet, a social reformer and a suffrage activist (Ledger 1997: 1).

The New Woman's dress expresses her role as an agent of social change at the *fin de siècle*. Popular novelist Ouida satirized the New Woman, writing that fashionable dress 'is one of her pet aversions' (1894: 217) and that her rational dress announces her rejection of conventional Victorian femininity. In popular literature and the press, the New Woman is embodied by her Rational Dress, and evidence shows that the two developed in tandem. These side-by-side movements shared a radical goal of challenging Victorian gender politics as a route to women's equality. Rational Dress allowed women freedom of movement outside the home; the attire was then further politicized in the appearance of the iconic New Woman. As Richard Heath states in his 1889 essay 'Politics in dress', the 'fashion of expressing political sentiments in dress, though doubtless provoking, has sometimes been a guide to the true bent of thing' (402).

The development of Rational Dress

As a style and political movement, Rational Dress originated in the middle and upper classes in Britain in the 1880s. Contemporary working- and serving-class women always dressed for practicality, and their clothing allowed the relatively free movement of their bodies while at work. They lacked the liberty to reform their wardrobes as a political act (see Jordan 1999). Women in the middle- and upper classes could choose practical Rational Dress to signal their radical and deliberate political departure from the established modes of femininity and womanhood. From its origins in the work of the Rational Dress Society, Rational Dress was designed and theorized as political. Later, these garments would disseminate from this more privileged group to merge with British fashions of the day, a process noted by sociologist Georg Simmel (1904).

The Rational Dress Society was established by Briton Lady F. W. Harberton and New Zealander Emily M. King in 1881 (Kortsch 2009: 78). *The Rational Dress Society's Gazette* defined their aims as follows:

> To protect against the attempt to introduce any fashion in dress which either deforms the figure, impedes the movements of the body, or injures the health.

> To protect against corsets or tight-fitting bodies of any kind, and high and narrow-heeled boots and shoes, as injurious to health; against heavily-weighted skirts, as rendering healthy exercise almost impossible; and all 'tie-down' cloaks or other garments which impede the movements of the arms; also crinolettes and crinolines of any kind or shape, as deforming, indecent and vulgar. To recommend that the maximum weight of underclothing (without shoes) should not exceed 7 lbs.
>
> ('The Rational Dress Movement' 1888: 128)

Therefore, Rational Dress was developed as a direct response to contemporary women's fashion as well as the conditions of women's rights in Britain at the *fin de siècle*.

Costume and body shape

Throughout the 1800s, women's bodies were shaped by continually changing fashions, as: 'Waists, moulded by constricting corsets, rose and fell; busts were forced in and up, and silhouettes straightened and curved anew. Shoulders dropped and were raised, and sleeves lengthened and shortened, broadened and narrowed' (Seys 2018: 6–7). In the 1880s, women's fashionable dress was defined by long-line 'cuirass' bodices, heavily draped skirts and excessive embellishment (Byrde 2003: 898). The fashion for the bustle[1] skirt was revived between 1883 and 1887 and was at its most exaggerated, with the skirt having a 'heavy, sculptural quality, being made in richly coloured and patterned fabrics with plenty of folds and drapery' (Byrde 2003: 898). As a result, these gowns were extremely heavy. After 1887, the bustle skirt was replaced with a full A-line skirt, the hem equal in width to the broad puff sleeves of the bodice, forming an X-shaped silhouette (Byrde 2003: 898). These gowns were worn with heavily boned corsets that, although they supported the weight of the skirts, could impair a woman's movement (Byrde 2003: 898).

Dress reformers argued that these fashions resulted in ill-health, especially for young girls and pregnant women (Anonymous 1889: 2). In January 1889, an article in *The Rational Dress Society's Gazette* stated that: 'the deterioration of the [human] race [...] is being stealthily affected by [...] unwholesome dress' (2). *Fin-de-siècle* feminists and dress reformers associated the physical restrictions that fashionable dress exercised on the female body with women's social and political subjugation. Writing in *The Woman's World*, Emily Crawford declared that 'liberation will be found in [...] the general agreement that each should be free to dress as she is minded' (284). The Rational Dress Movement advocated for women's clothing that allowed freedom of bodily movement and freedom from patriarchal standards of beauty and femininity. Consequently, these garments represented the politics and ideals of the *fin-de-siècle* women's movement. There were three distinct styles of Rational Dress that emerged during the 1880s and 1890s: the 'tailor-made'; the cycling skirt; and cycling knickerbockers or 'bloomers'. During the same period, the artistic and aesthetic dress movements also came to the fore. Rather than tailored wear, they promoted a light muslin tea gown as healthy and elegant (Byrde 2003: 282); however these styles fell outside of the purview of Rational Dress.

The tailor-made

The 'tailor-made' was a simple application of the principles of Rational Dress. From the 1880s, women were increasingly taking up visible public roles in the workforce and as political activists so the 'tailor-made' was popular daywear for this new class of urban women (Anderson 2006: 172–73). As the name suggests, it was a tailored ensemble, consisting of a matching jacket, waistcoat and skirt in tweed or woollen broadcloth (Byrde 2003: 898).

Tailor-made skirts were narrow and ankle length. Rather than being gathered or draped like contemporary fashion, these skirts used side gores to create sufficient fullness for ease of movement, but avoiding the bulkiness of full skirts (De Blaquière 1895: 14). Dora De Blaquière described this style in 1895, stating that:

> Many skirts open, and button down the entire left side; but the best tailors button them down half way, on either side of the front. [...] The skirts are sometimes stiffened, and also weighted; and are always well lined. But no rule can be given about the width, as each skirt, if made by a tailor, is fitted and cut with the utmost care.
>
> (14)

An anonymous author published in *Cornhill* in 1894 described the 'tailor-made' as 'always close-fitting [...] and wholly simple' (217). The same principle applies to the jackets of the 'tailor-made' to allow free movement of the wearer's arms. In *The Cult of Chiffon*, Mrs. Eric Pritchard describes the style of these: double-breasted and with exaggerated revers, collars and cuffs (Pritchard 1902: 67). De Blaquière states that the favoured style is the Norfolk jacket, a hip-length jacket with box-pleats extending from the shoulders to the hem (Calasibetta and Tortora 2003: 99). The jacket is belted with 'skirts extending over the hips' (De Blaquière 1895: 14).

The 'tailor-made' is illustrated in Ella Hepworth Dixon's 1894 novel *The Story of a Modern Woman*. The character Alison Ives wears a bespoke Rational 'tailor-gown' made by the British couturier Charles Frederick Worth. The narrator enthuses that this ensemble is designed so Alison can travel 'on the top of those charming trams' (1894: 76), affording her independence when traversing London. Alison assists destitute women in London's East End, putting into practice her belief that 'all we modern women [...] [should] help each other' (1894: 164). Such contemporary examples demonstrate how Rational Dress, such as the 'tailor-made', became integral to the work of the late-nineteenth-century women's movement. Alison's 'tailor-gown' allows her to work in public spaces, and her Rational Dress becomes symbolic of her politics. The association between Rational Dress and feminist politics were strengthened through the popular publications by *fin-de-siècle* writers such as Dixon.

Practicality and health

The two principles of practicality and health dictated all aspects of Rational Dress and governed even the choice of cloths. In 1893, Margaret Booth Scott emphatically wrote that 'nothing but wool should be worn', as it is lightweight and breathable and suited to the tailored style of Rational Dress (31). In fact, *fin-de-siècle* cloth manufacturers and retailers marketed fine woollen tweeds, broadcloths, checks and plaids directly to the Rational Dress market (Taylor 1999: 30). In December 1897, Manchester cloth retailers Lewis's advertised their range of 'New Bicycle Tweeds' and 'New Amazon Habits' (420). Note that the use 'New' to describe these textiles emphasizes their novelty, and likewise, implies an association between their goods and the persona of the New Woman. The naming of the 'New Amazon Habit' explicitly connects Rational Dress and the New Woman with the mythical Greek figure of the female Amazon: a symbol of strong, independent and resilient womanhood. These advertisements show that even the public newspapers and periodical press politicized the role of Rational Dress for women. In 1896, *The Illustrated Queen Almanac* listed *ensembles* of Bannockburn tweed, covert coating and natural homespun as the 'Latest Bicycling Costumes' (62–63). Cycling-wear quickly emerges as the most innovative and iconic form of Rational Dress. The act of cycling represented a significant challenge to the Victorian gender ideology of separate spheres – both literally and figuratively. The invention of the bicycle provided the New Woman with the physical mobility necessary to negotiate both the physical and political landscape, to both pursue employment or when protesting for gender equality. In turn, the female cyclist became an icon of the *fin-de-siècle* campaign for women's equality.

Cycling

John Kemp Starley's invention of the Rover Safety Bicycle in 1885 was revolutionary for British women. Writing in 1895, De Blaquière stated that 'the bicycle seems to have come as a great emancipation to women' (12). Cycling gave women unparalleled freedom of 'movement and equality' (Richardson 2005: lv); with a bicycle, women could travel independently and at low cost for work and leisure. The bicycle crossed the boundaries of the gendered ideology delineating separate spheres for men and women. Contemporary commentators noted, with enthusiasm or concern (in almost equal measure), that cycling would 'collapse' the traditional gender roles in British society (Richardson 2005: lv). The female cyclist's ease of physical movement became directly linked to the swift pace of social change for British women. Charlotte Oates (1902: 248) in her poem warns readers of the challenges this New Woman poses to the political status quo:

> BEHOLD! the 'new woman' is coming apace!
> Athletic in figure, with resolute face;
> In rational dress, is she coming to stay?
> With firmness of purpose she's pushing her way.

Her practical garb indicates that the female cyclist is 'pushing her way' towards equality (Oates 1902: 248). In literature and the popular press in the 1890s, the woman cyclist in Rational Dress appears both as a New Woman and an icon of feminism (Seys 2020). In H.G. Wells's 1896 novel, *The Wheels of Chance* when the hero viewed a female cyclist approaching, he muses that 'probably, she was one of these here New Women' (42).

Cycling 'revolutionised the whole idea of [women's] dress' (Pritchard 1902: 72). Throughout the 1890s, female cyclists became inundated with clothing advice from doctors, experts in etiquette, advocates for women's sport, and women's liberation groups. As with other forms of Rational Dress, cycling-wear was informed by these guiding principles: comfort, practicality, ease of physical mobility and safety. The physical demands of cycling meant that the garments must 'allow of the necessary play of the knees when pedalling' (De Blaquière 1895: 14); 'a trailing skirt would, of necessity, be incongruous as well as dangerous', Pritchard explains (1902: 72). Margaret Booth Scott wrote in *Aglaia: The Journal of the Healthy and Artistic Dress Union* that,

> an ideal cycling costume should allow of free easy movement of limbs and body; it should be light in weight, of sufficient substance to guard against cold, and at the same time sufficiently porous to admit free passage of air so as to carry off the moisture and exhalation of the skin.
>
> (1893: 31)

Further, Mrs. Pritchard states that cycling-wear 'should be of the tailor order of things' (1902: 72). In 1893, T.H. Holding in London advertised a 'natural wool' 'Ladies' Rational Cycling Dress'. The ensemble includes the: 'bodice, skirt, knickers, cape, cover coat and knickerbocker breeches' (see Figure 1.2, *Aglaia* 1893: 32). There were two distinct types of cycling-wear available for women at the *fin de siècle*: the divided or bifurcated skirt and knickerbockers or bloomers, some disguised by button-on overskirts (De Blaquière 1895: 14). These ensembles were worn with 'ribbed stockings, elastic garters and gaiters', 'a small hat of straw simply trimmed with ribbon, and an *aigrette*,[2] and kid gloves' (De Blaquière 1895: 14).

W.D.F. Vincent reports that,

> the popularity of cycling has created quite a large demand for suitable garments, and whilst the controversy on the subject of knickers and skirts has raged in a portion of the Press, the trade has done well [to] design suitable cycling skirts.
>
> (1898: 136)

British tailors, habit-makers and clothing manufacturers competed to patent the safest cycling costumes. Vincent includes a pattern for a cycling skirt in the 1898 third edition of *The Cutters' Practical Guide to the Cutting of Ladies' Garments*. Vincent describes the 'C.P.G. Cycling Skirt' as,

> designed with a fork at the back forming a seat, and consequently a division at the back; but as this was hidden in the folds of the pleats when working it was no way objectionable, and it has this great advantage, that it distributed the material on either side of the wheel.
>
> (1898: 136)

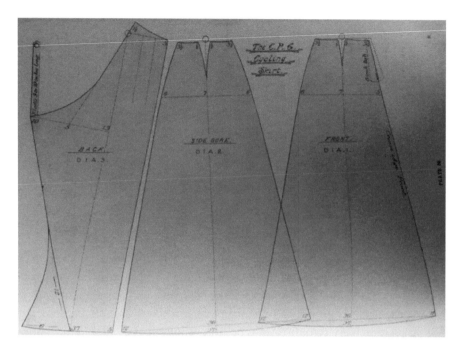

FIGURE 1.3: W.D.F. Vincent (1898), 'C.P.G. Cycling Skirt', *The Cutters' Practical Guide to the Cutting of Ladies' Garments*. Plate 56, page 137. Private collection of Madeleine C. Seys.

The design has three pieces: front, side gore, and back, as shown in Figure 1.3 (Vincent 1898: 137). The back pieces have a deep fork and are very full, having 'two broad [box] pleats, that separate when the wearer is seated' (De Blaquière 1895: 14). Further, Vincent gives instructions for the skirt to have a deep waistband, wherein the peak of the fork is attached via elastic and a button to an 'Italian cloth tab'[3] that inserts into the inside of the waistband at the skirt's front (Vincent 1898: 139). This design pulls the seat of the skirt between the wearer's legs, ensuring that the legs are fully covered while providing a full range of movement. The two back panels of the skirt fall over the bicycle's rear wheel. Vincent's 'Hint's on Making' include other instructions for making the garment practical and comfortable: such as a glissade lining to 'prevent the skirt from riding up', 'a inseam pocket on the right side' and 'reinforcing the seat seam and facing the hem with leather to prevent wear' (Vincent 1898: 138–39).

Such cycling garments presented a compromise between practicality and the appearance of respectable Victorian femininity, so that when the rider dismounts, the bifurcation disappears, resembling a conventional skirt. Writing for *Aglaia* in 1893, however, Scott argued that 'for comfort and health' in cycling attire this disguise would be better removed, so 'the more nearly it approached, except in mere detail, to that of her brother-rider, the better' (31). Knickerbockers, variously called Rationals and bloomers, most closely approximated both the form and functionality of menswear. For this reason, they emerged as the most iconic and controversial type of Rational Dress.

Knickerbockers

In 1895, George F. Hall's *A Study in Bloomers, or The Model New Woman* declared bloomers to be 'the most sensible idea in woman's dress that has been advanced in centuries' (36). Like the divided skirt, knickerbockers allowed female cyclists to move freely without the danger of entangling their clothing in the bicycle's wheels. Knickerbockers are loose breeches gathered or pleated into a waistband and cuffs below the knees (Calasibetta and Tortora 2003: 299). De Blaquière stated that,

> the knickerbockers or 'bloomers' of this year are not full [...] They are put on a yoke, which fits smoothly over the hips, and buttons at the back; expand over the knees or a greater fullness, and are gathered just below them into a band, with buckles and strap, or else buttons and button-holes.
>
> (1895: 14)

Knickerbockers were first introduced for men's sporting wear in the 1860s (Calasibetta and Tortora 2003: 299). When they were adopted as Rational Dress by women in the 1890s, they were a radical and political choice, a challenge to the Victorian gender binary. Knickerbockers were the most iconic form of Rational Dress; in the 1890s, writers began to use the noun 'Rationals' to refer to knickerbockers (see Figure 1.2).

In H.G. Wells's *The Wheels of Chance*, the protagonist Mr Hoopdriver meets a female cyclist. As they approach each other on the road, the narrator remarks that 'strange doubts possessed [Hoopdriver] as to the nature of her nether costume' (1896: 33). When he realizes 'the things were – yes! – *rationals!*'(Wells 1896: 34, emphasis in original), Hoopdriver reflects: 'probably, she was one of these here New Women'(Wells 1896: 42). Here, Hoopdriver infers the heroine's aspirations for freedom and equality from her 'nether costume' (Wells 1896: 33). The novel then confirms his assumption as the heroine Jessie says: 'I want to struggle, to take me place in the world. I want to be my own mistress, to shape my own career' (Wells 1896: 193). Her cycling attire at once enables and symbolizes this desire for freedom and autonomy.

As well as being the most iconic and radical form of Rational Dress, knickerbockers were also the most controversial. In her satirical description of a female cyclists in 'rationals', Charlotte Oates' poem continues:

> If she and a male-friend are out for a round,
> The one with the other we nearly confound!

The 'new woman's' dress now has reached such a pitch,
'Tis difficult often, to tell which is which!

(1900: 248)

Contemporary critics of Rational Dress argued that Rational Dress signaled the collapse of gender roles alongside the disintegration of Victorian family and societal structures (Richardson 2005: lv). However, the androgynous appearance of Rational Dress is central to its radical political function as an expression of the aspiration towards British women's equality at the *fin de siècle*.

Androgyny in dress

Dora De Blaquière wrote that female cyclists in Rational Dress 'affect a mixture of masculine and feminine costume' (1895: 14). This description is the very definition of androgyny, stemming from the Greek cognates of anthro (man) and gyne (woman). The design, cloth, colour, cut and styling of *fin-de-siècle* Rational Dress closely resembled contemporary menswear, and when women adopted these garments they radically challenged the established division between the genders in the late 1800s and early 1900s. Oates' satirical poem demonstrates that the New Woman threatened the Victorian patriarchy *because* her androgynous dress made her indistinguishable from her male counterpart (1900: 248). This forced Victorians to the realization that 'it was the costume, not the body, which inscribed gender and assigned social power to the wearer' (Heilmann 2000: 83 and elsewhere).

Fashion and gender

During the nineteenth century, fashion was highly gendered. Men's fashion was characterized by simple tailoring, straight lines and neutral colours. The lines of women's clothing were more fluid, and the garments heavily embellished and richly coloured. These starkly differentiated styles reflected Victorian sensibilities; they also inscribed them onto the wearer's body. In *Sex and Suits*, Anne Hollander argues that during the 1700s and 1800s, men's clothing became increasingly plain and practical, while women's garments became more embellished and colourful, emphasizing gender differences. As a result, the simplicity and practicality of the black three-piece suit constructed modern masculinity as respectable, capable and rational (Hollander 1995: 72–79). These characteristics, and the social and political power they represented, were ascribed to Victorian men. For the middle and upper classes, fashions for women restricted their movement and prevented strenuous manual labour. For those who could afford it, their dress fostered notions of frailty, demureness and gentility – the ideals of Victorian femininity. These characteristics were then projected onto Victorian women's bodies, rationalizing their political disempowerment as a natural effect of their biological sex. This logic conflates sexual differences with socially, culturally and sartorially constructed gender categories. At the *fin de siècle*, both scholars and social activists challenged this logic and worked to redefine gender. The figure of the woman in androgynous Rational Dress was at the forefront of this change; she challenged late-Victorian patriarchal authority by drawing into question the conflation of biological maleness, with masculinity and hegemonic power (Heilmann 2000: 83).

The colour, cloth and cut of Rational Dress closely resembled contemporary men's tailoring. Contemporary sources describe women's Rational Dress as 'manly' (Anon. 1889: 217), 'like a man's' (Pritchard 1902: 67) and, in the case of cycling attire, close 'to that of her brother-rider' (Scott 1893: 31). This androgyny was achieved in the fundamental ways in which Rational Dress was tailored and in the more subtle and playful ways that women styled these garments.

The rise of wool

Scott had advised members of the Healthy and Artistic Dress Union that 'nothing but wool should be worn' (1893: 31) because it is robust, breathable, waterproof and light-weight (Anderson 2005: 287). De Blaquière is more specific still in her advice, stating that Rationals should be tailored in serge or tweed, preferably in grey, black, brown or dark green (1895: 14). In the second half of the 1800s these textiles and colours defined menswear, particularly sportswear, so when used for Rational Dress, they communicated stalwart masculinity. It is noted that tweed originates in Scotland, but became fashionable for menswear during the 1820s and 1830s, influenced by celebrity Scotsmen Sir Walter Scott and Lord Brougham (Lord Chancellor of Great Britain) (Anderson 2005: 284). Fiona Anderson suggests that tweed was the 'characteristic cloth' of modern masculinity and 'manly worth' (2005: 171); for other scholars, wool reflects intelligence, modesty, probity, rationality and restraint (Hollander 1995: 72–79). When proponents of Rational Dress chose wool and tweed, they challenged this gender coding of garments (Anderson 2006: 180). The popular literary representations of the New Woman also depict her as strong, intellectual, brave, capable and independent. A discussion of the history of tweed and the significance of its use in the New Woman's cycling dress is offered elsewhere (see Seys 2018). As above, the cuts and styles of garments from men's tailoring contributed to the effect that Rational Dress was androgynous.

The role of accessories

Further, in their choice of accessories *fin-de-siècle* feminists could conjure the image of the androgyne and appropriate some of the sartorial signifiers of masculinity. Rationals were worn with collared 'shirts of silk or muslin'; a sailor, bowler or top hat (De Blaquière 1895: 14); and a bowtie or four-in-hand-tie. In Figure 1, a cabinet photograph shows a young woman in a double-breasted jacket, a collared shirt with a bar pin and a bowtie. On her hatband, she wears a second pin, displaying a cyclist and bicycle. These accessories are not practical – they are purely symbolic, representing the wearer's politics. Her shirt, bowtie and hat indicate her conscious challenge to the gendered strictures in Victorian fashion. The cyclist hatpin clearly reveals her as a sympathizer to the aspirations of the New Woman and the movement towards gender equality at the *fin de siècle*.

First-wave feminism and suffragettes

During the late 1880s and through the 1890s, a woman in Rational Dress offered the iconic image of a first-wave feminist. Her radical androgynous dress made her conspicuous on the streets of Britain and on the pages of British literature. The portrayal of these garments made a bold statement for women's rights to occupy public space and participate in political life on an equal footing with men. As Cally Blackman argues, in their dress *fin-de-siècle* feminists deployed a strategy of resistance by refusal (2015). Rational Dress indicated their complete rejection of contemporary fashion and gender politics.

However, by 1900, the 'radical' characteristics of Rational Dress – of health, mobility and practicality – were becoming standard in women's fashion in Britain. These garments once signalled comradeship with an elite social and political movement, but women's tailor-made garments had become popular and ordinary: sourced from tailors and high-street clothing retailers and available to women across the classes. Simultaneously, women's athleticism, physical mobility and employment became more socially accepted. (see Brooke and Laver 2000). Having achieved its aims for women as individuals, the Rational Dress Movement shifted its attention towards collective equality for women and the campaign for suffrage. After 1900, the image of the androgynous New Woman was replaced in the popular press with the figure of the suffragist (in the United States, suffragette) as the icon for first-wave feminism.

In her 1894 essay in *The North American Review*, Ouida describes the New Woman's dress in the following terms: 'she wears an inverted plate on her head, tied with strings under her double chin; she has balloon-sleeves' (1894: 612–13), and she laments: 'why cannot this orator learn to gesticulate and to dress, instead of clamouring for franchise?' (Ouida 1894: 613). Here, the popular British authoress Ouida accuses women who are gender-nonconforming in their attire of being badly dressed. Rational Dress did not result from women who lacked in taste or education, but from the New Woman's deliberate rejection of contemporary dress codes and gender politics. On the other hand, suffragists,

> sought to effect change not by challenging contemporary fashion and ideals of femininity, but by conforming to them. Haunted by the stereotypical image of the 'strong-minded woman' in masculine clothes, pebble-thick glasses and galoshes created by cartoonists, they chose instead to present a fashionable, feminine image.
>
> (Blackman 2015: n.pag.)

The radical clothing of Rational Dressers made them conspicuous, but often the Suffragettes preferred to be hidden in plain sight. As Cally Blackman reports, those who sold copies of *The Suffragette* in the early 1900s were requested to 'dress themselves in their smartest clothes' (2015: n.pag.) and to be 'dainty and precise' in their dress (2015: n.pag.). Contemporary photographs show suffrage campaigners in the 'tailor-made' developed by the Rational Dress Movement in the 1880s and 1890s. No longer radical, the 'tailor-made' was now fashionable and allowed these radical campaigners to blend into the crowd wearing conventional Edwardian dress. It can be argued whereas the New Woman matched her radical politics with radical dress, the suffragettes delivered their radical ideas wearing the conventional dress of the day. In today's political dress, women's tailored suits are part of the landscape even as they continue to attract critique as masculinized. However, it can be argued that Rational Dress persists as a radical and politicized attitude towards women's clothing, particularly the belief that clothing is always political: expressed in the enduring catchphrase, 'the personal is the political'. Clearly, dress indicates our adherence or challenge to the political status quo.

Rational Dress in the twenty-first century

In her 1889 novel *New Amazonia: A Foretaste of the Future*, Mrs George (Elizabeth Burgoyne) Corbett uses the feminist iconography of Rational Dress to illustrate a future utopia where gender equality exists. In this utopian meritocracy all citizens, regardless of gender, wear a uniform of bloomers and tunic, resembling the portrayal of *fin-de-siècle* Rational Dress in the United Kingdom. Corbett's radical image for a future where uniform dress represents universal human rights is revisited in the twenty-first century by the company, Rational Dress Society.

In New York City, the company Rational Dress Society was launched in 2015 on Kickstarter by New York-based visual artist Maura Brewer and Chicago-based fashion designer Abigail Glaum-Lathbury as reported by Baxter Barrowcliffe (2015: 1). Like the Victorian movement detailed above, the company set out to challenge contemporary fashion's gender binary and wasteful consumerism. They created variations of a jumpsuit designed for 'functionality and practicality' (Rational Dress Society 2019: n.pag.). 'Since the advent of the *prete-a-porte* industrialized system of garment manufacture', Brewer and Glaum-Lathbury explain, 'we have witnessed the slow ebb of well-fitting garments. As a result, we are left adrift, wallowing in a sea of Lycra® imbued jersey' (Rational Dress Society 2019: n.pag.). As a solution to this problem, the Rational Dress Society make androgynous jumpsuits designed in the following way:

> For increased range of movement through the arms and upper body, a raglan sleeve design was used. A standard convertible collar and front-fly closure with a heavy-duty zipper provides ease of use and a sensible style. Two diagonal-seamed pockets and two back-patch pockets allow for convenient storage.
>
> (Rational Dress Society 2019: n.pag.)

As well as selling ready-made garments, Rational Dress Society provide patterns for download from their website, free of charge. In ethos and practice, this is a radical approach to ethical and gender-free dress that creates community through equality and uniformity of attire. Rather than combining characteristics of gendered dress, they reject gender in clothing entirely. Consequently, Rational Dress Society, 'developed a comprehensive sizing system that can accommodate 248 body types, using gender-neutral terminology' (Rational Dress Society 2019: n.pag.). They have fitted and unfitted variations in styles, and their sizing appears in names such as 'tango', 'orion', 'companion', 'cactus' and 'bogotá'. Co-founder Maura Brewer said that, 'JUMPSUIT is both a garment and an apparatus that produces a conversation about our relationship to dress' (Barrowcliff 2015: 1). The Rational Dress Society is designed to create politically radical communities through the adoption of uniform clothing:

> What alliances might be formed between JUMPSUIT-wearing individuals? Just as we reject the mini-mansion in favor of the city, refuse the automobile in favor of the train, JUMPSUIT offers a way to forego the insular logic of self-expression in favor of forming communal bonds. We embrace our neighbors. We reject the signs of class, race and gender that are inscribed into our daily interactions. In the future, we will be brothers and sisters together in JUMPSUITS.
>
> (Rational Dress Society 2019: n.pag.)

Although the jumpsuit differs substantially in style to tweed Rationals, the principles of the Rational Dress Society are fundamentally the same as those of the Rational Dress movement at the turn of the twentieth century: to challenge contemporary power structures of gender and class through reconsidering the relationship between the clothed body and politics.

Conclusion

At the *fin de siècle*, writers of fiction and periodical journalism politicized Rational Dress, connecting its practical and androgynous style with the contemporary crisis in gender and with the rise of the women's equality and suffrage movements. Grant Allen, Ouida, H.G. Wells and Ella Hepworth Dixon represented Rational Dress as the garb of the New Woman, an icon of first-wave feminism. However, it was not simply the case that Rational Dress became political because of the associations made by such writers. The Rational Dress Society and their publication, the *Rational Dress Society Gazette*, promoted dress reform as fundamental to achieving gender equality. Rational Dress was designed as a response to the political and social conditions of women in late nineteenth-century Britain; its style, construction and cloth all reflect its feminist politics. For middle- or upper-class Victorian women to dress for comfort and practicality was inherently political as it indicated their rejection of contemporary fashion and gender constructs. Practical bloomers, divided skirts, shirt and jackets allowed freedom of movement and labour, challenging the Victorian dictate that 'Home-is-the-Woman's-Sphere' (Grand 1894: 271). The woman in Rational Dress could cycle, work and participate in political activism. The Rational Dress movement revealed how Victorian fashion worked to inscribe gender, and therefore gendered political power, onto a wearer's body. Their androgynous style of dress represented women's political power.

In Britain (and elsewhere) the Rational Dress movement grew throughout the 1890s alongside the New Woman, first-wave feminist and suffrage movements. By virtue of its radicalism, Rational Dress was only politically effective while it remained new and shocking. As such, it had a short lifespan within the progressive political climate of the *fin de siècle*. The end of Rational Dress was indicated by the integration of androgynous-tailored clothing into women's fashion; then the movement had achieved its goal of reforming attitudes towards women's clothing and 'protect[ing] against the attempt to introduce any fashion in dress which either deforms the figure, impedes the movements of the body, or injures the health' ('The Rational Dress Movement' 1888: 128). The *Rational Dress Society Gazette* published their final issue in 1889 and dress reformers began to shift their attention to suffrage as the next step towards gender equality. In the twentieth

41

century, the tailor-made ensembles of the Rational Dress Movement became standard daywear, and the introduction of trousers for woman-rendered bloomers obsolete. Nevertheless, the *fin-de-siècle* Rational Dress movement sustained a lasting impact on women's dress culture.

Rational Dress is a radical and political approach to dress, one that redefines the relationship between the clothed body and the social and political world it inhabits. This radical sensibility persists in the twenty-first century, where the legacies of *fin-de-siècle* Rational Dress are more broadly evident in the ongoing reassessment of how a gender binary is produced, reproduced and policed within the fashion industry.

Dress is the interface between the intimate body and the political world and, therefore, reforming the way we cloth ourselves is a powerful political act. In the twenty-first century, dress remains a crucial part of political activism and protest – be it in an iconic garment, a colour or a slogan on a t-shirt. We still wear our politics on our sleeves.

NOTES

1. The bustle is a fullness protruding from the back waist of a skirt to the hem. This was created with a pad or a wire cage (Calasibetta and Tortora 2003: 48).
2. An 'aigrette' is a headdress consisting of a tuft of feather, usually a white egret's feather.
3. Italian cloth is 'a cloth of botany [Australian wool] weft and cotton warp, having a glossy face' and commonly used for linings (Cumming et al. 2017: 323).

REFERENCES

Allen, Grant ([1897] 2004), *The Type-Writer Girl*, Peterborough: Broadview Press.

Anderson, Fiona (2005), 'Spinning the ephemeral with the sublime: Modernity and landscape in men's fashion textiles, 1860–1900', *Fashion Theory*, 9:3, pp. 283–304.

Anderson, Fiona (2006), 'This sporting cloth: Tweed, gender and fashion 1860–1900', *Textile History*, 37:2, pp. 166–86.

Anon. (1889), 'A gossip on dress reform', *The Rational Dress Society's Gazette*, January, pp. 2–3.

Anon. (1894), 'Character note: The New Woman', *Cornhill* XXIII:136, pp. 365–68.

Barrowcliff, Baxter (2015), 'Rational Dress Society's JUMPSUIT jumps up new kickstarter campaign', *University Wire*, 23 February, pp. 1–3.

Blackman, Cally (2015), 'How the suffragettes used fashion to further the cause', *The Guardian*, 8 October, https://www.theguardian.com/fashion/2015/oct/08/suffragette-style-movement-embraced-fashion-branding. Accessed 20 April 2020.

Brooke, Iris and Laver, James (2000), *English Costume from the Seventeenth through the Nineteenth Centuries*, Mineola: Dover Publications.

Byrde, Penelope (2003), 'Dress: The industrial revolution and after', in D. Jenkins (ed.), *The Cambridge History of Western Textiles*, vol. 2, Cambridge: Cambridge University Press, pp. 882–909.

Calasibetta, Charlotte Mankey and Phyllis Tortora (2003), *The Fairchild Dictionary of Fashion*, 3rd ed., London: Fairchild Publisher.

Corbett, Mrs. George [Elizabeth Burgoyne] (1889), *New Amazonia: A Foretaste of the Future*, London: Tower Publishing.

Crawford, Emily (1889), 'Women wearers of men's clothes' in O. Wilde, (ed.), *The Woman's World*, January, pp. 283–86.

Cumming, Valerie, Cunnington, C.W. and Cunnington, P.E. (2017), *The Dictionary of Fashion History*, 2nd ed., London: Bloomsbury.

David, Alison Matthews (2002), 'Elegant Amazons: Victorian riding habits and the fashionable horsewoman', *Victorian Literature and Culture*, 30:1, pp. 179–210.

de Blaquière, Dora (1895), 'The dress for bicycling', *The Girl's Own Paper*, XVI, October, pp. 12–14.

Dixon, Ella Hepworth ([1894] 2004), *The Story of a Modern Woman*, Peterborough: Broadview Press Limited.

Grand, Sarah (1894), 'The new aspect of the woman question', *The North American Review*, 158:448, pp. 270–76.

Hall, George F. (1895), *A Study in Bloomers, or The Model New Woman*, Chicago: American Bible House.

Heath, Richard (1889), 'Politics in dress', in O. Wilde (ed.), *The Woman's World*, 8, pp. 399–405.

Heilmann, Ann (2000), '(Un)masking desire: Cross-dressing and the crisis of gender in New woman fiction', *Journal of Victorian Culture*, 5:1, pp. 83–111.

Hollander, Anne (1995), *Sex and Suits: The Evolution of Modern Dress*, New York: Kodansha.

Jordan, Ellen (1999), *The Women's Movement and Women's Employment in Nineteenth Century Britain*, London: Routledge.

Kortsch, Christine Bayles (2009), *Dress Culture in Late Victorian Women's Fiction: Literacy, Textiles and Activism*, Farnham: Ashgate Publishing.

Ledger, Sally (1997), *New Woman: Fiction and Feminism at the Fin de Siècle*, Manchester: Manchester University Press.

'Lewis's in Market St., Manchester' (1897), '[Advertisement] now is the new season for velveteens', *The Young Ladies' Journal*, 1753:L, p. 420.

Liberty, Arthur Lasenby (1894), 'On the progression of taste in dress III: In connection with manufacture', *Aglaia: The Journal of the Healthy and Artistic Dress Union*, Autumn, pp. 26–31.

Oates, Charlotte (1900), *Miscellaneous Poems, Songs, and Rhymes*, Bradford: J. S. Toothill.

Ouida [Maria Louise Ramé] (1894), 'The new woman', *The North American Review*, 158:450, pp. 610–19.

Pritchard, Mrs. Eric (1902), *The Cult of Chiffon*, London: Grant Richards.

Rational Dress Society (2019), 'Counter-fashion as critical practice', *Design and Culture*, 11: 3, pp. 345–53.

Richardson, Angelique (2005), 'Introduction', in A. Richardson (ed.), *Women Who Did: Stories by Men and Women 1890–1914*, London: Penguin, pp. xxxi–lxxxi.

Richardson, Angelique and Willis, Chris (2001), 'Introduction', in A. Richardson and C. Willis (eds), *The New Woman in Fiction and in Fact:* Fin de Siècle *Feminisms*, Houndsmill: Palgrave, pp. 1–38.

Scott, Margaret Booth (1893), 'Cycling costume', *Aglaia: The Journal of the Healthy and Artistic Dress Union*, 1: July, pp. 31–32.

Seys, Madeleine C. (2018), *Fashion and Narrative in Victorian Popular Literature: Double Threads*, New York: Routledge.

Seys, Madeleine C. (2020), 'Rational dress', in L. Scholl (ed.), *The Palgrave Encyclopedia of Victorian Women's Writing*, Melbourne: Palgrave Macmillan, n.pag.

Simmel, Geog (1904), 'Fashion', *International Quarterly*, 10, pp. 130–55.

Taylor, Lou (1999), 'Wool cloth and gender: The use of woollen cloth in women's dress in Britain 1865–1885', in A. de la Hay and E. Wilson (eds), *Defining Dress: Dress as Object, Meaning and Identity*, Manchester: Manchester University, pp. 30–47.

Vincent, W. D. F. (1898), *The Cutters' Practical Guide*, vol. 2, London: The John Williamson Company Limited.

Wells, H. G. (1896), *The Wheels of Chance: A Holiday Adventure*, London: Macmillan and Co., Ltd.

2

Prime Minister Jacinda Ardern: Fashion and Performing Gender

Sarah Baker

Introduction

New Zealand has an enviable history in the representation of women in politics with three New Zealand women: Dame Jenny Shipley (National Party leader, 1997–99), Helen Clark (New Zealand Labour Party leader, 1999–2008) and more recently, Jacinda Ardern (New Zealand Labour Party leader 2017, re-elected 2020–present) taking office as prime minister. New Zealand was also the first country in the world to offer the franchise for eligible women, moving in Parliament to award them the vote on 19 September 1893, outstripping its antipodean neighbour Australia's enactment of the Commonwealth Franchise Act in 1902.

From this promising beginning, New Zealand appears as an enlightened country. However, the role of the women in political life, and most notably in the role as the foremost leader of the country, has been heavily constrained by both media's representation and the public opinion generated by their attire. The trend continues to see female leaders as fashion consumers that should display their bodies as either feminine and/or as leaders, but not both. These female prime ministers have all experienced criticism from the press associated with their public appearance. Naomi Wolf, in her seminal work, *The Beauty Myth*, wrote many years ago: 'the more legal and material hindrances women have broken through, the more strictly and heavily and cruelly images of female beauty have come to weigh upon us' (1991: 10).

Jacinda Ardern, New Zealand's third woman prime minister, came into office during a time of increased media presence: the relentless 24/7 news cycle and the dominance of social media commentary on women and their clothing. The current New Zealand's electoral system is a Mixed Member Proportional (MMP) model where Ardern was a List Member of Parliament from 2008 to 2017 and Member of Parliament for the electorate of Mount Albert (2017–present) and the leader of the New Zealand Labour Party from (2017–present). Achieving this position at age 37 in October 2017 as the elected prime minister meant she became the country's youngest elected prime minister in the electoral history of New Zealand's government of 150 years. Her image as a young and vibrant-looking prime minister earned her popularity with the electorate, especially with the international media.

Fashion and political style

It is worth repeating that political leaders rely on their access to power, and a female leader poses the question 'is she man enough?' to take up the challenge of a higher political office (e.g. in the United States, see Meeks 2012).

In the world of politics, women in leadership must maintain their power and authority in order to rule effectively. Pamela Golbin, an international fashion critic states, 'whether they acknowledge it or not, all political figures partake in the act of power dressing from the first time they stand before an audience seeking a leadership role' (2011: 8). Today's media demands on one's physical appearance are considerable, while 'there is often widespread uneasiness about the importance of politicians in contemporary times, and yet public performance is necessary for the practice of politics' (Craig 2016: 11). With this emphasis on performance for politicians, the focus becomes their physical 'looks', their attire and deportment.

No one escapes (except the rare nudist) the role of clothing to reinforce the divide between the sexes as expressed in gendered ideas and behaviour. Drawing on concepts from anthropology, Joanne Entwistle states:

> Dress is a basic fact of social life and this, according to anthropologists is true of all human creatures that we know about: all cultures 'dress' the body in some way, be it through clothing, tattooing, cosmetics or other forms of body painting.
>
> (2015: 31)

Clearly, clothing is particularly associated with gender. 'Fashion, particularly as it is laid out in the fashion magazine, is "obsessed with gender"' (Wilson [1985] 2020: 117) and therefore, fashion becomes a boundary issue, constantly shifting and negotiating the limits of clothing amongst today's complicated array of genders. While binary-gendered roles have changed in many societies, there is no escaping the fact that fashion is never neutral or removed from gender-based theoretical perspectives (Reilly and Barry 2020).

Of course, gender plays its role in political elections, as the reporter Max Ufberg comments, in 2014, psychologists at Dartmouth College found that people were less likely to vote for women candidates' if there was even a tiny amount of hesitancy in assigning their gender. This dynamic was not found for the male politicians [...] women politicians who couldn't be instantaneously categorized as female receive fewer votes.

(2017: n.pag.)

Gender and its performance deeply impact on how female politicians are represented in the media, after the rise of social media and the 24/7 news cycle changed the political landscape since the mid-1990s. Rose Weitz summarizes the argument 'that gender rests not only on the surface of the body, in performance and doing, but becomes embodied part of whom we are physically and psychologically' (Weitz 2010: 29, referencing Young 1990; Connell 2005). From other scholars comes the viewpoint that 'this body/dress awareness is gendered': as Tseëlon notes, concluding that 'women's sense of self (and self-worth) is frequently a "fragile" one' (1997: 61). Dress can either bolster a political woman's confidence or make her acutely self-conscious and uncomfortable.

The rise of women in national politics in the United States, notably first ladies Hillary Clinton and Michelle Obama indicated a turning point in continuous media scrutiny (see Chapter 5). Fashion editor Vanessa Friedman notes this transition as follows:

The twin conditions of the historic nature of this [Obama] presidency and the rise of social media, which turned every public second into a sharable, comment-worthy moment, combined to create a new reality where every appearance mattered.

(2017: 3)

This new, and even unwelcome scrutiny to the dress of the world's female politicians or women in leadership roles also influenced the media 'down under' in Australia and New Zealand. In Australia, the media evaluations on political women's fashion were notorious after Julia Gillard became the nation's first and – so far – only female prime minister (see Chapter 4).

New Zealand women in politics

New Zealand Prime Ministers Dame Jenny Shipley vs. Helen Clark

Jenny Shipley (National Party leader, 1997–99) and Helen Clark (New Zealand Labour Party leader, 1999–2008) were each judged by their looks and fashion choices as female prime ministers and politicians in New Zealand. Entire news stories from a wide range of critics and commentators explored the details of these two prime ministers from their bodies to their chosen ornamentations. These commentators included hairstylists, fashion designers and image consultants who passed judgement on the two former prime ministers' physical appearance and clothing as image consultants became part of the new reality for women in political roles.

The feminist sociologist Linda Trimble, in her article entitled 'Melodrama and gendered mediation television coverage of women's leadership "coups" in New Zealand and Australia' (2014) outlined the complexity of appearance for both Jenny Shipley and Helen Clark during their successful runs to win the New Zealand prime ministerships. During the leadership campaign when Helen Clark defeated Jenny Shipley, the media became obsessed with their differences in dress, for example, stating 'Miss Clark was drab in olive' while Shipley was 'resplendent in National [Party's] royal blue' (2014: 129). Further, Shipley's feminine appearance caused the stylists to comment 'image gurus say it won't take a lot to get Shipley shipshape' (2014: 129). Sporting the party colour appeared as an appropriate choice for the National leader, but when Helen Clark suited up in the Labour Party red this was broadcast as 'going too far'. In her 2002 campaign, Clark took 'a few knocks for her clothes sense', 'including a bright red number [...] which some commentators compared to a walking Labour billboard' (Trimble 2014: 129).

New Zealand's first elected female Prime Minister Helen Clark served as Labour Prime Minister for three terms (Shipley had inherited the office). Although highly successful in her political career, Clark was also constantly attacked for her appearance and her lack of bearing children. As Brian Edwards explains during an interview:

> Although he has known Clark for years, it was only in 1996 that her minders called in Edwards and his wife, Judy Callingham, to look at her media performance. This was three years after Clark had become Leader of the Opposition and just after Michael Cullen's attempted takeover. Many others had tried to change the perception, but Clark, with her deep, gruff voice and taciturn manner, seemed doomed to be the bridesmaid forever [rather than Prime Minister].
>
> (du Chateau 2001: n.pag.)

As Trimble reported, one news item focused entirely on 'Ms. Clark's swept-up glamorous image'. For Clark, 'a gal who once didn't wear lipstick' came to recognize 'cosmetics as a girl's best friend' (2014: 129, 132). The pressure for Clark to conform to feminine expectations was intense. When the 2002 election campaign came around, Clark's transformation 'from ugly duckling to media darling' was said to be complete and completely convincing. 'The severe, aloof figure of yesteryear has been replaced by a confident, polished politician', who 'looked comfortable as she took the microphone' and 'looked good in the debates' (Trimble 2014: 136).

The persistence of the focus on Helen Clark's fashion choices throughout her time as prime minister continued, and one example shows the level of pettiness in the media coverage. In 2002, Helen Clark was criticized by British media for her costume while attending a state dinner for the visit of Queen Elizabeth II. Clark hit back via an interview on television by suggesting that the British Broadcasting Corporation (BBC) were 'out of date and out of line' (TVNZ 2002: n.pag). Later, Clark accompanied the British monarch during her walkabout around Auckland's Viaduct Harbour, attired in another designer trouser suit that was not dissimilar to the one worn during the State dinner. Clark's trousers came in for further criticism when they reported, 'New Zealand's Prime Minister [...] She's the one wearing trousers', sniffed the broadcaster's voice-over to the BBC's international television audience (TVNZ 2002: n.pag.).

During the 2005 elections, even the makeup she wore attracted criticism, where 'Miss Clark, decked in red with matching lipstick, was aggressive' thereby linking her lipstick colour and look with an over-the-top political demeanour (Trimble 2014: 128). During the 2008 campaign, two articles characterized Clark's 'makeup regime as 'professionally applied war paint' and 'here we see a discursive disjuncture because Clark was viewed as complying with the conflicting norms of exaggerated femininity and warrior masculinity' (2014: 128). New Zealand's media continued to emphasize that women prime ministers should portray feminine stereotypes in fashion, grooming and in their demeanour.

There was much commentary on the continuing transformation of Clarke with pundits' perspective on the restyling of Clark as a media-savvy politician:

Ms. Clark's rise in the past few weeks of the campaign has been spectacular and has been based – as much as she hates it – on smartening up her television image. For so long the victim of television she is – for the first time – its master.

(Trimble 2014: 136)

In contrast, Prime Minister Jenny Shipley did not experience the same attacks as Helen Clark as she projected a firmly articulated identity as a wife and mother. She was consistently referred to as 'Mrs Shipley', and placed her husband and children as key figures in her political persona. Here, the press regarded Shipley's gender as female, and presented within the sanctity of heteronormative marital relationships, while Clark's heterosexual marriage was open to debate and questions about her gender remained an easy target.

Ironically, Helen Clark was a very strong supporter of the New Zealand fashion industry, and leading designers came forward to defend her. International designer

Denise L'Estrange-Corbet said 'I think she looks very smart and casual; I don't see any reason why she shouldn't be wearing pants – it's the age of equality and all that. I think she's very slim and got great legs and why not?' (2005: n.pag.). Clark also signed an exclusive contract in 2008 with the Newmarket Business Association to 'dress, accessorise, and style Prime Minister Right Honourable Helen Clarke for the 2008 election campaign', and the contract was reported to have a retail value of up to a quarter of a million dollars (Scoop 2008: n.pag.).

This transformation showed that Helen Clark was first and foremost, a good politician who undertook a strategic and comprehensive makeover of her political image to win leadership. Her successful role as an international leader was recently bolstered by this announcement on New Zealand Radio (RNZ):

> Former Prime Minister Helen Clark has been given the job of jointly leading an investigation into the response of the World Health Organization, and that of governments, to Covid-19. She will share the role with the former president of Liberia, Ellen Johnson Sirleaf.
>
> (Hill 2020: n.pag.)

Jacinda Ardern's key fashion moments

Jacinda Ardern became New Zealand's third female prime minister on 26 October 2017 (New Zealand Labour Party leader, 2017–present). Her political career is illustrated here through several key fashion choices. Cressida Heyes (2007: 134) states that 'a refusal on the part of the feminist subject to style herself in any way – to be uninvolved, neutral or natural – is impossible', thus making a woman's appearance 'loaded' in a way a man's dark suit does not. Further, Sehra suggests that a big part of fashion in politics remains 'women playing by rules that the men formulate and participating in structures of power that men monopolize, rather than questioning power itself' (2019: n.pag.).

In Ardern's case, it can be argued that she simultaneously experiences the scrutiny that other prominent female politicians have endured while also deploying fashion as a way to promote her political brand. Pamela Golbin entwines the fashionable and political representation together by saying:

> It is therefore quite natural that fashion is used to convey gender and power, respect and authority, modernity and authenticity, making it a sartorial billboard that disseminates clear-cut messages to an array of audiences, from intimate to global.
>
> (2011: 7)

In November 2019, Jacinda Ardern appeared in a pre-recorded segment on *The Late Show with Stephen Colbert* when host Stephen Colbert visited New Zealand in October. The segment had an estimated 3.5 million viewers in the United States, which excited the tourism sector of New Zealand. This broadcast was estimated to be worth $5.5 million in New Zealand's tourist revenue (Molyneaux and McRae 2019: n.pag.).

This overall enthusiasm for her freshness has not gone without the usual criticism and double standards about the appropriateness of women as leaders that the previous female prime ministers of New Zealand have experienced. The critique of her appearance was broadcast in Australia when the television host Steve Price took the offensive stance on her saying that, 'Jacinda is too emphatic, she's just too young, she dared to have a baby in office, she's too polite and cap it off her teeth are too big' (Dickens 2020: n.pag.). Andrew Dickens reported that *The Project* host Steve Price provided the perfect case of 'irrational misogyny' and continues to report that many voters have qualms about women in politics and therefore perceptions of their abilities coalesce around their appearance (2020: n.pag.).

Jacinda Ardern – in contrast to the previous female New Zealand prime ministers – has recognized the significance of her appearance. She has curated her fashion choices to articulate her own political brand. In 2018, Jacinda was reported as 'making a splash in New York, not just with her many media appearances and attendance at the United Nations but for her fresh fashion choices' (Black 2018: n.pag.). Eleanor Black reported on her approachable style matched with a 'what you see is what you get personality'. So, Ardern's fashion and her stated small-l liberal political stance have been directly linked. Similarly, Ardern was praised by *Vogue Fashion* as the 'anti-Trump' (Lester 2018: n.pag.). Later in September 2019, Ardern received criticism when she met the United States' President Donald Trump after she did not discuss climate change with him; and reflected positively on their meeting in the White House (Edwards 2019).

Jacinda Ardern: Mother in office

Shortly after winning the election in 26 October 2017, Jacinda Ardern announced that she was pregnant and would continue to work as prime minister and have her child. She met with world leaders, in this case German Vice Chancellor Angela Merkel, while visibly pregnant (see Plate v). When Ardern gave birth to her daughter on 21 June 2018 she became the first world leader to give birth in almost 30 years. The previous politician giving birth while in office was Pakistani Prime Minister Benazir Bhutto (see Chapter 6). In New Zealand, Ardern's pregnancy was viewed as a mark of progressiveness that is still rare amongst developed nations (Steger 2018). In a further deviation from the maternal role, her partner

Clarke Gayford would be taking the main parenting role while Ardern chose to continue her duties as prime minister.

Recently, the impact of the maternal role in politics is hotly contested (Bauer 2020: 170 citing Deason et al. 2015). An emphasis on motherhood can be viewed as a gesture of appeasement for taking on an unpopular role, as suggested in the case of First Lady Michelle Obama (see Chapter 5). In the United States, motherhood is symbolized within the nationalistic style of patriotism, as in the American catchphrase 'motherhood and apple pie', as it is further amended to 'motherhood and apple pie and the flag' meaning the three things that all Americans ascribe to their country. Elsewhere, scholars have found that 'voters rate childless female candidates substantially lower than childless male candidates, mother candidates and father candidates', which in New Zealand relates back to the childless Prime Minister Helen Clark (Stalsburg 2010: 273).

Ardern's cover on *British Vogue*

Jacinda Ardern's cover photo appeared in *British Vogue's* September issue (2018). September, as indicated in the popular movie, is *Vogue's* most prestigious month for publication (Cutler 2009) and comprised another first for a New Zealand leader. The magazine *Vogue* has long appropriated the title, 'fashion Bible' after it was founded in the United States in 1902, and published for the first time in the United Kingdom in 1916. Previously, *Vogue* has featured politicians' wives, including Michelle Obama, who appeared on the cover of the magazine three times, Hillary Clinton appeared as First Lady, and even Melania Trump was featured on the cover when she married the United States's past President Donald Trump (Hawkes 2017). Likewise, Theresa May, the female British prime minister was photographed by Annie Leibovitz for *British Vogue* where she sat in a seated pose at Chequers in front of a fireplace (Trevett 2017).

Ardern's photoshoot for *Vogue's* September 2018 edition was part of a collection of covers, curated by Meghan Markle, Duchess of Sussex, which she entitled 'Forces for Change' and included fifteen women from the world of politics, sport and the arts. Markle describes her project in glowing terms:

> These last seven months have been a rewarding process, curating and collaborating with Edward Enninful, *British Vogue's* editor-in-chief, to take the year's most-read fashion issue and steer its focus to the values, causes and people making impact in the world today [...] Through this lens I hope you'll feel the strength of the collective in the diverse selection of women chosen for the cover [...] I hope readers feel as inspired as I do, by the 'Forces for Change' they'll find within these pages.
>
> (Markle cited in Barr 2019: n.pag.)

It was reported that the selection of women was a highly personal process, from young (Greta Thunberg) and older (Jane Fonda) activists alongside many women of colour, but Jacinda Ardern was the only sitting political leader of her country. Perhaps the most unusual part of the 'photo shoot' was that photographer Peter Lindbergh shot her cover during a live video link from Auckland, New Zealand, representing another 'first' for both New Zealand politicians as well as for the magazine (Barr 2019). Ardern was described as a,

> 37-year-old with a beaming smile. She was photographed at West Auckland's Bethells Beach in a pair of sage green Herriot pants and a flowing trench coat from Harmin Grubisa [...] [she's] young, dynamic, forward looking and unabashedly liberal. The shoot also represents a major break for the Wellington designer Bron Eichbaum, whose label was just a year old at the time.
>
> (Black 2018: n.pag.)

After this positive portrait circulated around the world, the young New Zealand prime minister and mother would face the greatest challenge of her tenure in office.

The Christchurch Massacre and the hijab/headscarf

On 15 March 2019, there was an unprecedented terrorist attack in Christchurch, New Zealand. It is called unprecedented because New Zealand had largely escaped being a site of terrorist activity unlike many other countries around the world.

In an online forum at 1.28 p.m., an anonymous post appeared with links to a Facebook livestream and a document to a poster named 'manifesto'. The reporter Colleen Hawkes has collected the minute-by-minute unfolding of the tragedy in a timeline of the 'darkest day' (to date) in New Zealand's history (2019: n.pag.). As she reports, Prime Minister Jacinda Ardern was in New Plymouth, New Zealand to open the WOMAD music festival when her office received an unusual e-mail. Written in the past tense, it referred to an attack that had already taken place, and the e-mail was sent to 29 other recipients including media and other politicians. The scale of the assault at two Christchurch Mosques during Friday prayers was horrific. According to the final report from New Zealand Police Commissioner Mike Bush, the shootings began at the Al Noor Mosque in the suburb of Riccarton at 1.40 p.m. and continued at Linwood Islamic Centre at 1.52 p.m. In total, 51 people were killed and another 49 injured (Hawkes 2019). New Zealand had never experienced this magnitude before and clearly, the country needed strong leadership at this moment. In the aftermath of the massacre, Jacinda Ardern went to the scene of the crime to talk to survivors and responders. She was famously photographed wearing a headscarf, draped as a hijab that covered her hair, while she consoled a congregation of Muslim worshippers (see Plate vi).

This image circulated around the world, with Ardern described as a strong leader. The wearing of the headscarf by the prime minister was viewed by many to signal tolerance and compassion for a group of people celebrating their faith on an important day. For some, the wearing of the hijab was a powerful message of tolerance while others saw it as deeply problematic. Her donning of the headscarf was a strong, heartfelt message of 'cohesiveness between the attacked parishioners and their fellow Kiwis [New Zealanders]. It was an act of empathy rather than an endorsement of any particular religious symbol' (Shakir 2019: n.pag.). Ardern's headwear inspired Alice Sowerby to start a Facebook page 'Headscarf for Harmony' that then led to the hashtag #headscarfforharmony trending across the world, which inspired many Kiwi women to march in their hometown streets on 21 March and cover their hair with scarves. On the other hand, some criticized this as merely a political 'performance' (Ensor 2019). An unforeseen consequence for this was that many of her women friends 'cried their eyes out' as Ali Shakir reported:

> For the zillionth time, they were made to witness their faith being politicised and reduced to a piece of cloth. Even worse, they felt their new homeland was robbing them of their spiritual identity, declaring them not Muslim enough because they refused to cover.
>
> (2019: n.pag.)

This illustrates the problematic messaging that is communicated by others towards Muslim women and their choice of wearing/not wearing the hijab as a symbol of their religious faith. For further discussion of the hijab and its religious significance amongst young Muslim women, see Chapter 8.

In February 2020, Ardern was pictured serving up a Barbeque breakfast before giving her speech at Waitangi for 'Waitangi Day' celebrations. This depiction of her cooking in shirt sleeves is reminiscent of other world leaders who have been photographed serving food to ordinary people. Later in the day, Ardern also wore a traditional Maori cloak to finish off her formal ceremonies for Waitangi Day. Jacinda Ardern continues to employ fashion and her physical appearance to project her image of compassion and leadership.

Conclusion

The connection between women's political goals and their dress is more complicated than the clothing they wear, and thus connects deeply with the performance of gender. As Claire Trevett (2017: n.pag.) reported:

[*Vogue*] magazine says Ardern, who does not have a stylist, can wear a Juliette Hogan maxi dress and a faux fur jacket from a Hastings SaveMart on the red carpet, or be photographed on election night in a bespoke Maaike ensemble paired with Ugg boots in her living room. Her relatability, authenticity – and style – is part of her appeal.

Women, as political leaders have been criticized for their attire, and it has changed the public's perception of them as both women and leaders. While Jacinda Ardern has not been immune, she continues to use fashionable dress as a device that reinforces her place as a world leader. During the international controversies that arose during her tenure as prime minister, including the recent disastrous shootings in Christchurch mosques, she appears not to suffer much criticism in the media, and her handling of COVID-19 caused a journalist to suggest that she's become 'the most effective leader on the planet' (Friedman 2020: n.pag.).

The date 15 March 2020 marks the one-year anniversary of the Christchurch terrorist shootings and Jacinda Ardern appeared on the cover of the United States' *Time* magazine. Here, Ardern's fashion received coverage such that the 'Kiwi designers of the years-old silk top Prime Minister wore on the cover of *Time* magazine are considering another run of the blouse' (Sivignon 2020: n.pag.). This emphasis on her blouse is a bit surprising when the overall significance of this terror-driven anniversary is considered. Jacinda Ardern has been praised for her expression of so-called 'soft power', as she garnered praise 'for her empathic leadership following the mass shooting' (Luscombe 2020: n.pag.). This edition of *Time* magazine announces on its cover, 'Know us by our deeds', with Ardern's photograph taken during her prime minister's recent address at the Big Gay Out, an LGBTQI+ festival in Auckland that she has attended regularly for more than a decade (Roy Ainge 2020: n.pag.).

Arden's positioning of her political identity through her fashion choices ties her directly to the media, and their response to her dress. This was summed up by former Prime Minister Helen Clark, in an interview with former Prime Minister Jenny Shipley: 'When you look at the political scene when we first started out, could you ever have envisaged a 37-year-old woman, living with a partner and having a baby could be a successful Prime Minister?' (Women's Weekly 2018: n.pag.). Indeed, society has changed but also the personal and political requirements for prime ministerial leadership have altered since the late 1990s. In her story for *Time*, Belinda Luscombe writes that 'Ardern's real gift is her ability to articulate a form of leadership that embodies strength and sanity, while also pushing an agenda of compassion and community' adding that Ardern has 'infused New Zealand with a new kind of soft power' (cited in Ainge Roy 2020: n.pag., see also the Introduction to this volume).

It is evident that Jacinda Ardern, a young, vibrant and intelligent prime minister presents as a 'cover girl' for women as effective leaders, where her facilities in governance as well as her fashionable appearance have come alive in her political identity.

REFERENCES

Barr, Sabrina (2019), 'Meghan Markle honours female trailblazers as she guest edits British Vogue', *Independent*, 28 July, https://www.independent.co.uk/life-style/fashion/meghan-markle-british-vogue-september-thunberg-jamil-ardern-fonda-a9024066.html. Accessed 20 March 2020.

Bauer, Nichole M. (2020), *The Qualifications Gap: Why Women Must Be Better Than Men to Win Political Office*, Cambridge: Cambridge University Press.

Black, Eleanor (2018), 'Jacinda Ardern's Vogue Fashion shoot praises her as the anti-Trump', *Stuff*, 15 February, https://www.stuff.co.nz/life-style/fashion/101460272/jacinda-arderns-vogue-fashion-shoot-praises-her-as-the-antitrump. Accessed 2 February 2020.

Chateau, Carrol du (2001), 'The Transforming of Helen', *The New Zealand Herald*, 16 November, https://www.nzherald.co.nz/nz/news/article.cfm?c_id=1&objectid=228707. Accessed 3 January 2020.

Connell, R.W. (2005), *Masculinities*, 2nd ed., Cambridge: Polity Press.

Craig, Geoff (2016), *Performing Politics: Media Interviews, Debates and Press Conferences*, Cambridge: Polity Press.

Cutler, R.J. (2009), *The September Issue*, USA: Roadside Attractions.

Deason, Grace, Greenlee, Jill S. and Langner, Carrie A. (2015), 'Mothers on the campaign trail: Implications of politicized motherhood for women in politics', *Politics, Groups, and Identities*, 3:1, pp. 133–48.

Dickens, Andrew (2020), 'The Project host Steve Price's Jacinda Ardern criticism a little irrational, misogynistic', *The New Zealand Herald*, 15 January, https://www.nzherald.co.nz/nz/news/article.cfm?c_id=1&objectid=12300639. Accessed 17 January 2020.

Edwards, Bryce (2019), 'Ardern was supposed to be the anti-Trump, but she failed to speak truth to power', *The Guardian*, 25 September, https://www.theguardian.com/commentisfree/2019/sep/25/ardern-was-supposed-to-be-the-anti-trump-but-she-failed-to-speak-truth-to-power. Accessed 22 February 2020.

Ensor, Jamie (2019), '"I think it was overdone": Katie Hopkins criticises Jacinda Ardern for putting Muslims first', *Newshub*, 26 April, www.newshub.co.nz/home/politics/2019/04/i-think-it-was-overdone-katie-hopkins-criticises-jacinda-ardern-for-putting-muslims-first.html. Accessed 1 January 2020.

Entwistle, Joanne (2015), *The Fashioned Body: Fashion, Dress and Modern Social Theory*, 2nd ed., Cambridge: Polity Press.

Friedman, Uri (2020), 'New Zealand's prime minister may be the most effective leader on the planet', *The Atlantic*, 19 April, https://www.theatlantic.com/politics/archive/2020/04/jacinda-ardern-new-zealand-leadership-coronavirus/610237/. Accessed 21 April 2020.

Friedman, Vanessa (2017), 'How clothes defined the First Lady', *The New York Times*, 18 January, pp. 1–3.

Golbin, Pamela (2011), 'Forward' in R. Young (ed.), *Power Dressing: First Ladies, Women Politicians & Fashion*, London: Merrell, pp. 7–8.

Hawkes, Colleen (2017), 'Prime Minister Jacinda Ardern to star in March issue of US Vogue magazine', *Stuff*, 9 December, https://www.stuff.co.nz/life-style/fashion/99700366/prime-minister-jacinda-ardern-to-star-in-march-issue-of-vogue-magazine. Accessed 2 February 2020.

Hawkes, Colleen (2019), 'New Zealand's darkest day: A timeline of the Christchurch terrorist attacks', *Radio New Zealand*, https://shorthand.radionz.co.nz/NZ-DARKEST-DAY/index.html. Accessed 2 February 2020.

Heyes, Cressida J. (2007), *Self-Transformation: Foucault, Ethics, and Normalized Bodies*, New York: Oxford University Press.

Hill, Kim (2020), 'Helen Clark appointed joint lead of WHO investigation', *Radio New Zealand*, 10 July, https://www.rnz.co.nz/national/programmes/morningreport/audio/2018754340/helen-clark-appointed-joint-lead-of-who-investigation. Accessed 10 August 2020.

Lester, Amelia (2018), 'New Zealand's prime minister, Jacinda Ardern, is young, forward-looking, and unabashedly liberal – Call her the anti-Trump', *Vogue*, 14 February, https://www.vogue.com/article/jacinda-ardern-new-zealand-prime-minister-vogue-march-2018-issue. Accessed 15 March 2020.

L'Estrange-Corbet, Denise (2005), 'The many faces of Helen Clark', *New Zealand Herald*, 1 July, https://www.nzherald.co.nz/nz/news/article.cfm?c_id=1&objectid=10333670. Accessed 20 April 2020.

Luscombe, Belinda (2020), 'A year after Christchurch, Jacinda Ardern has the world's attention: How will she use it?', 20 February, https://time.com/5787443/jacinda-ardern-christchurch-new-zealand-anniversary/. Accessed 3 February 2020.

Meeks, Lindsey (2012), 'Is she "man enough"? Women candidates, executive political offices, and news coverage', *Journal of Communication*, 62:1, pp. 175–93.

Molyneaux, Vita and McRae, Tom (2019), 'The impact Jacinda Ardern's appearance on *The Late Show* with Stephen Colbert will have on New Zealand', *Newshub*, https://www.newshub.co.nz/home/travel/2019/11/the-impact-jacinda-ardern-s-appearance-on-the-late-show-with-stephen-colbert-will-have-on-new-zealand.html. Accessed 13 February 2020.

Reilly, Andrew and Barry, Ben (eds) (2020), *Crossing Gender Boundaries: Fashion to Create, Disrupt and Transcend*, Bristol: Intellect Books.

Roy Ainge, Eleanor (2020), '"A new kind of soft power"': Jacinda Ardern appears on cover of *Time* magazine', *The Guardian*, 21 February, https://www.theguardian.com/world/2020/feb/21/a-new-kind-of-soft-power-jacinda-ardern-appears-on-cover-of-time-magazine. Accessed 23 February 2020.

Scoop (2008), 'Newmarket signs fashion contract with Helen Clark', 1 April, https://www.scoop.co.nz/stories/BU0804/S00007.htm. Accessed 14 March 2021.

Sehra, Rohina Katotch (2019), 'For women in politics, personal style is a game of chess with the patriarchy', *Huffington Post*, 3 October, https://www.huffpost.com/entry/women-politics-dress-code-patriarchy_l_5d8ba3d6e4b01c02ca627f9c. Accessed 14 March 2020.

Shakir, Ali (2019), 'Don't let Jacinda Ardern's headscarf send the wrong message', *Stuff*, 2 October, https://www.stuff.co.nz/national/christchurch-shooting/116195738/dont-let-jacinda-arderns-headscarf-send-the-wrong-message. Accessed 3 January 2020.

Sivignon, Cherie (2020), 'Kiwi designer thrilled to see PM Jacinda Arden wear years-old silk shirt on *Time* cover, *Stuff*, 22 February, https://www.stuff.co.nz/life-style/fashion/119728693/kiwi-designer-thrilled-to-see-pm-jacinda-ardern-wear-yearsold-silk-shirt-on-time-cover. Accessed 20 February 2020.

Stalsburg, Brittany L. (2010), 'Voting for mom: The political consequences of being a parent for male and female candidates', *Politics and Gender*, 6:3, pp. 373–404.

Steger, Isabella (2018), 'Jacinda Ardern just became the first world leader to give birth in office in almost 30 years', *Quartz*, 21 June, https://qz.com/1311054/new-zealand-pm-jacinda-ardern-is-the-first-leader-to-give-birth-in-office-in-almost-30-years. Accessed 12 January 2020.

Trevett, Claire (2017), 'Strike a pose: PM Jacinda Ardern to feature in *Vogue*', *New Zealand Herald*, 9 December, https://www.nzherald.co.nz/nz/news/article.cfm?c_id=1&objectid=11956079. Accessed 13 January 2020.

Trimble, Linda (2014), 'Melodrama and gendered mediation: Television coverage of women's leadership "coups" in New Zealand and Australia', *Feminist Media Studies*, 14:4, pp. 663–78.

Tseëlon, Efrat (1997), *The Masque of Femininity*, London: Sage.

TVNZ (2002), 'PM's pants prove problematic', *ONE News*, 26 February, http://tvnz.co.nz/content/83922/2591764.xhtml. Accessed 8 January 2020.

Ufberg, Max (2017), 'The sexism behind the Hilary Clinton pantsuit jokes', *Pacific Standard*, 3 May, https://psmag.com/news/quit-it-with-the-hillary-pantsuit-jabs. Accessed 8 January 2020.

Young, Iris Marion (1990), *Justice and the Politics of Difference*, New Haven: Princeton University Press.

Weitz, Rose (2010) (ed.), *The Politics of Women's Bodies: Sexuality, Appearance, and Behaviour*, Oxford: Oxford University Press.

Wilson, Elizabeth ([1985] 2020), *Adorned in Dreams: Fashion and Modernity*, London: Bloomsbury Academic Press.

Woman's Weekly (2018), 'Dame Jenny Shipley and Helen Clark talk about their incredible friendship', *Now to Love*, New Zealand edition, 19 August, https://www.nowtolove.co.nz/lifestyle/career/dame-jenny-shipley-and-helen-clark-talk-about-their-friendship-38775. Accessed 3 January 2020.

Wolf, Naomi (1991), *The Beauty Myth*, New York: Harper Perennial.

3

An Empress's Wardrobe Unlock'd: Empress Masako and Japan's Imperial Fashions

Emerald L. King and Megan Rose

Introduction

In November 2019, the Reiwa emperor and empress ascended to the Chrysanthemum throne, completing the third stage in a series of public, semi-public and private ceremonies and events that, 'in some form or another' can be 'traced back to the seventh century' in Japan (Breen 2019: 6). This event was internationally recognized and attended by the world's modern royal families and other dignitaries and also heavily covered across social media and in the tabloids. The enthronement ceremony alone has been viewed via over 745,461 downloads since it was first streamed on YouTube October 22 (Global News 2019). In addition to the history and brief background that was given for each event, attention was also paid to the garments worn by the women of the imperial family – both western-style gowns and suits and traditional Japanese garments.

In many ways, these ceremonies, reimagined by the Meiji emperor (1852–1912) for his own accession ceremonies in 1868 (Breen 2019) showcase the essence of modern-day Japan – a perfect marriage between traditions dating back to nearly 1500 years and the modern day as viewed through the live streaming of accession's public events on YouTube. The Meiji period (1868–1912) comprised a rapid period of modernization, which took Japan from a feudal backwater to a modern player on a global stage, first by securing an alliance with Britain in 1902 and then wielding influence over an empire that spanned the Japanese archipelago including the Ryukyu Islands, Taiwan, southern Sakhalin and the Korean peninsula by the end of the era (see Tucker 2013; Tipton 2016). As the historian Niall Ferguson reports: 'The west shrank the world' through 'railways, steamship lines and telegraphs' but the true impact of this 'first globalization was sartorial'; 'With extraordinary speed, a mode of dressing that was distinctly western swept the rest

59

of the world' (2011: 218, 219). During the Meiji period, Japan leaned heavily on western ideology, deciding to 'copy everything' from the American-style schooling systems to British naval practices, to German-styled school-boy garments (see King and Rall 2015).

From the late 1880s, western styles of clothing were adopted by Japanese wealthy aristocrats as part of the Meiji Restoration (see Figure 3.1). As with any kind of fashion or trend adopted by the upper classes, these fashions eventually trickled down to those below. By 1927, 797 of the 1151 men who passed by the Ginza Shiseido gallery in one hour were observed in western-style clothing (Isa and Kramer 2003: 60), and by the advent of World War II, Japanese women aged between 20 and 40 years owned an average of 40 dresses, nearly double that of women in America (Dees 2009: 19). Thus, Japan adopting western clothing in the nineteenth century was not on its own a performative or meaningful act but reflects this 'first globalization' by the West (Ferguson 2011: 219). However, in the twenty-first century, the sartorial choices made by the Japanese imperial family during this time of accession provide a moment to examine the expressions of western dress becoming a performative tool in the silk glove of world diplomacy. The imperial family, especially Empress Masako, used their clothing to both toe the traditional line enforced by the Imperial Household Agency (*Kunaicho*) and navigate what it means to be a modern royal in, quite literally, a new era.

FIGURE 3.1: The Meiji emperor, empress and Crown prince resplendent in European fashions on an outing to Asukayama Park. *Illustration: Toyohara Chikanobu, circa 1890.* https://commons. wikimedia.org/wiki/File:Y%C5%8Dsh%C5%AB_Chikanobu_Asukayama_Park.jpg. Accessed 24 September 2021.

This chapter outlines Empress Owada Masako's public appearances since her entrée into public life as a royal bridal candidate in 1986, her wedding in 1993 and her rise to empress in 2019 (Sanz 1993; Anon. 2012). We evaluate the Japanese and English language popular press surrounding these appearances, including the advent of 'Royal Twitter'. By treating these clothes as texts (Dode 2012) and through close readings of these garments, it is clear that colour and costume choice are used to convey rank, power and position. While men's clothing in Japan has become more sedate and restricted – business suits for work; jeans and t-shirts for leisure – women's clothing has thrown off many previous restrictions on cut, colour and age appropriateness. Women's clothing of the Japanese imperial family reveals a special encoding of class and rank, layered by western styles adopted during the Meiji period and later refined to modern royal women's dress.

Methodology: Unlocking an empress's wardrobe

The volume entitled *Queen Elizabeth's Wardrobe Unlock'd* (Arnold 1988) presents one of the most cogent studies of the garments worn by Elizabeth I, the Queen who successfully forged a commanding public identity by emphasizing the extravagance of her dress. In fact, the expression of power through one's costume plays out in politics today (see the Introduction). To unlock Empress Masako's wardrobe, we have taken an inductive qualitative approach, drawing on a textual analysis of three key moments in the evolution of Masako's style – her ministry wardrobe, her clothing as a young princess filled with promise and her gowns as a crown princess/empress-to-be. A close reading continues of three key ensembles worn during the various Reiwa (the current era) accession ceremonies and events held throughout 2019. A visual analysis of the potential sartorial significance of these garments communicates Masako's position as a woman of power. We also conducted a content analysis of Japanese and English news reportage from 1980 to 2019, as well as a scoping review of public hashtags on Twitter to glean what the publicized narrative of these outfits might include, and the contents were then interpreted by thematic analysis.[1] This study suggests that there are correlations between the visual meaning of Masako's clothing and public reactions to its appearance and her corresponding life events, rather than overtly expressed causal links.

Dressing for the public: The Imperial Family in Anglophone and Japanese popular press

In English language reportage (including Wikipedia and similar online repositories), the principal chronicle of the Imperial family, even with its emphasis on

Masako, is Ben Hill's 2006 *Princess Masako: Prisoner of the Chrysanthemum Throne*. Initially, a Japanese language translation was proposed in the same year, but this was reportedly pulled under pressure from the Imperial Household. *Princess Masako* features the delightful description of a young Masako studying in America as 'chunky' and the previous Empress Michiko as a 'stick-thin, grey-haired wraith' and posits that Masako's only daughter was conceived after fertility treatments. It was later published in over seven languages, including Japanese, with a companion book in Japanese by Noda Mineo, *Purinsesu Masako no shinjitsu: kenetsu sareta Masako hime jyōhō no nazo* (*Princess Masako: The Censorship of True Story of Japan's Crown Princess* 2007). This publication re-offers Hill's reading of Masako as an unfortunate victim of the imperial household. While Masako has suffered from very public (and publicized) illnesses related to her constrained status in the imperial household, in this chapter, we suggest that there is far more at play than a simple narrative of a woman consumed by the imperial system.

Japanese public's ideas about the necessary balance between tradition and modernity are negotiated through the clothed figure of the modern empress. First, the *kisha* ('reporter') clubs govern all reportage on the imperial family in the same way that the British Royal family has the Royal Rota system in place with the British press (see sussexroyal.com 2020). Although the *kisha* clubs aim to author and shape all public narratives, in the climate of free engagement on social media as well as academic research on the empress and her role in Japanese society, we will see that there are dissenting voices – not only in official publications but also across social media – in both Japanese and Anglophone press.

As empress, Masako has provided a more successful negotiation of the duality between traditional/modern aesthetics proscribed for Japanese women, particularly the *ryosai kenbo* ('good wife, wise mother') female social roles from 1899 onwards (Bardsley 1998; Seaman 1995). However, Masako's vulnerability to illness means she has been scrutinized as lacking the qualities of an ideal empress. This media reportage is also swayed by Japan's hyper 'masculine society' (Kanayama and Cooper-Chen 2005: 23). Themes of Japanese tradition, modernity and vulnerability can be explored through Masako's clothing during key public appearances and likewise empower her to express her stance as a modern and well-educated woman.

Any study of Japanese imperial dress inevitably will include study of kimono; in the same way that the emperor is linked to rice growing, the empress has a similar link to sericulture (Kunaicho.go.jp 2014). While the kimono has attracted serious scholarship in Japanese and in English (see Dalby 2001; Monden 2014; Cliffe 2017), there are fewer works that focus on both the formal gowns and traditional robes worn by imperial princesses. Sally Hasting's 1993 work, *The Empress' New Clothes*, and David Howell's work on looking modern in the Meiji period are of particular use, even while these texts focus on pre-war culture and society (2009). In Japanese language scholarship, historian Osakabe Yoshinori's work on Meiji clothing and uniform reform provides an overview of clothing edicts, while the Japanese Costume Museum's *Nihon fukushoku-shi josei-hen* ('History of Japanese women's clothing') and *Nihon fukushoku-shi dansei-hen* ('History of Japanese men's clothing') provide visual glossaries for these garments. In the imperial context, formal kimono and regalia are deployed to justify and perpetuate the 'Mandate of Heaven' as expressed in Latin, *Per me reges regnant* – the divine right of kings.

In the royal context, the feminine self must appear presentable as a beautiful woman and ideal wife to best represent the nation (see Chapter 5). While the agency is accorded through a presentation of self, it still operates within the confines of gender norms. Rather than desirability, the royal and public figure Masako employs a feminine 'discourse' to cleverly construct outfits that reflect the public narratives of her life and, likewise, negotiate her identity as both a traditional and modern woman. The premise holds that before, during and after her wedding in 1993 to Naruhito (then the Crown prince, now Reiwa emperor from 1 May 2019) Masako had some influence over the clothing she wore in public. The literature suggests that women have agency to act creatively, as Dorothy Smith (1990: 120–55) indicates in 'Femininity as Discourse' in *Texts, Facts and Femininity: Exploring the Relations of Ruling*. Here, Smith maps the image-desire-shopping circuitry that encompasses and controls femininity, as women exercise agency through their fashion and beauty product selections. Women seek to mediate the social relations that play out in their daily lives, according to the premise that 'people's actual activities as participants give power to the relations that "overpower" them' (1990: 61). When acting as creators, women carefully plan their presentation of self, demonstrating skills and refined knowledge of the 'rules' of femininity to express their female competence (1990: 197). Further, Smith reminds us that these meanings implicit in exercises and performances are 'established by discursive texts outside her control', thus limiting women's full expression outside of patriarchal norms (1990: 182). While the presentation of the feminine self is a performance carried out by the woman-as-expert, it still operates within society's broader locus of desirability and attractiveness, shaped by a heteronormative male gaze.

The empress's new clothes: Owada Masko in the public press

From our survey of news reportage on Empress Masako, three key moments in her life – her engagement and marriage to then Crown Prince Naruhito in the late

1980s and early 1990s; her gradual withdrawal from public life in the early 2000s following a miscarriage – suffering from an 'adjustment disorder' termed by the Imperial Household followed by the birth of her daughter, Princess Aiko in 2001. Last in this sequence, the press signals her triumphant return to the public stage as empress in 2019. During her time as a princess, much of this narrative is sequestered by a 'silent' princess, 'straight jacketed' and suffering (Kato 2019: n.pag.; Bhat and Kang 2019: n.pag.). In keeping with the public demand for a sweeping, romantic narrative, the romance became heightened after Masako reportedly refused Naruhito's proposal – not once, but multiple times. Note that much of this reportage does not quote Masako, rather offers statements from Naruhito. Two more proposals later, Masako relented and agreed to take on what was promised to be the most important diplomatic post of her career.

When Masako is directly quoted, it is primarily drawn from her 2002 press conference about the birth of her daughter, Aiko, where she expresses gratitude towards the mystery of creating a new life (see Nikkei Shimbun 2019). The most salient theme in the media remains the engagement and wedding, which took place in the early 1990s, and in particular Naruhito's promise to protect Masako for the rest of his life (Anon. 2019b; Anon. 2019e; Anon. 2018a; Anon. 2018b). This promise is framed not only as highly romantic but also seems to foreshadow Masako's eventual breakdown and withdrawal from the public. Throughout this reportage, Masako is characterized as highly intelligent, with her graduation from Harvard University in 1985 often cited. Her potential to fulfil the role of 'wise mother' is further highlighted by the focus on maternal joy after the birth of her daughter in 2001 and the grief over her miscarriage in 1999 when Japan anticipated a male heir to the imperial throne (see Nikkei Shimbun 2019).

More broadly, Masako is depicted as gentle, benevolent and kind during her re-commencing of public engagements in the lead up to the 2019 coronation by making appearances with Crown Prince Naruhito during times of crisis, visiting children in hospitals and smiling and waving in parades (see Anon. 2018a). This is significant, as there was much anxiety and dismay over her lack of public appearances as a result of her 'adjustment disorder' after her highly publicized miscarriage. As the 2019 coronation date drew nearer, the press promoted a more sympathetic and compassionate account now that Masako has 'recovered' and is appearing in public again.

The responses in the press highlight Masako's emergence as soon-to-be-princess and the recent soon-to-be empress show her during bright, optimistic and joyous occasions, and her vulnerable break-down episode becomes brushed over. These events are carefully orchestrated because Masako is not presented through her own words in the media; however, her clothing, whether selected by the *Kunaicho* or not, offers subtle visual cues that allow her some agency to bypass the reportage that otherwise frames her.

Owada Masako's diplomatic suiting: Echoes of the past, visions of the future

In the mid-1980s, Owada Masako was a rising star in the Ministry of Foreign Affairs. After a childhood spent in Russia, America and Japan, she graduated from Harvard University in 1985, returning home to enter Tokyo University in order to prepare for extremely difficult entrance exams necessary for entrance to the Ministry of Foreign affairs in 1987 (Anon. 2020). She was a well-known and very visible figure in the ministerial offices, who handled the demanding hours with grace and enthusiasm. Masako seemed destined to climb to heights within Japanese bureaucracy never before reached by a woman in Japan in the late 1980s (Sanger 1993). Indeed, royal reporters at the time thought her marriage to the Crown prince was completely 'out of the running' when she accepted a posting in England to study at Oxford University (Fumio 2019: n.pag.). In a public address at the 'Gender, media and Japan's imperial succession' symposium on the start of the Reiwa era held at Monash University in 2019, the Consul-General of Japan Matsunaga Kazuyoshi recalled that 'Owa' seemed to be the only member staff who would appear without a hair out of place each morning – even if she had left the offices only two or three hours before (Matsunaga 2019: n.pag.).

Dressing in a masculine manner was popularized as 'power dressing' in America in the 1970s (Molloy 1975) and became more prominent around the world in the early 1980s with the 'increasing visibility of women in previously male-dominated professions' (Entwhistle 2015: 172). In 1993, after she entered the Japanese parliament, the current Governor of Tokyo, Koike Yuriko noted that '[Japanese] politics and kabuki are a lot alike, [the key roles are still] passed down from men to their sons' (Sanger 1993: n.pag.). In this era of male dominance, Masako began navigating the public sphere. She soon adopted the power dressing uniform: 'tailored skirt suit in navy blue with smart blouse and something "feminine" around the neck, such as a scarf or ruff' (Entwistle 2015: 172–73). During this time, Masako seemed to favour double-breasted suits in blues and whites, teamed with boxy, oversized coats (see, e.g. Anon. 2019c). Her oversized 'Sloane' style garments are designed to take up physical space, a necessary tool for a promising young woman in an all-male environment. This echoes Smith's argument that 'women encode their presentation with masculine touches to signal their ability and savviness of institutional norms within male-dominated work environments' (which in turn reinforces the structural paradigms in place; 1990: 182). Her business outfits show how Masako successfully negotiated the hypermasculine space of the Japanese office while still preserving her identity as a young woman. She chose masculine suits with a hint of feminine flair, indicating her ability to read the room and negotiate her space. We suggest that these garments of her own selection are arguably the one time that Masako, as 'Owa', had full control over her public presentation.

Imperial ensemble 1: A golden sun burst

There is a stark difference between Masako's ministry attire and the demure suits with nipped-in waists and matching hats she wore in her early years as an active royal. Her early 'royal outfits' seemed to play with bright colour blocking and pillbox or bumper hats (Anon. 2019c: n.pag.). Colour blocking is a strategy often used by royals; Queen Elizabeth II reportedly chooses bright colour blocks so that those in the crowd are able to say 'I've seen the queen!' (Hallemann 2018a: n.pag.). At first glance, this shift from the power suiting of her Ministry days to this highly feminized version might be considered as regressive and a sign of Masako relinquishing the mobility of her self-determined career for wifely servitude to the Crown prince (Sanger 1993). Here, the audience for this presentation-of-self – which Smith (1990) refers to 'interpretive circles' – had radically shifted. While at the Ministry, Masako presented a 'self' for a masculine workplace, as princess and empress she is scrutinized by the Japanese and world audience as a pleasant, even cheerful feminine leader.

For her official engagement photos in 1993, Owada Masako donned a lemon yellow gown with full-length sleeves that puffed at the shoulder, her shoulder-length dark hair was caught up under a matching pillbox hat and finished with a pearl necklace, white gloves and a clutch purse in the same fabric as the hat and gown (Fumio 2019). Rather than the large clip-on earrings of her Ministry wardrobe that were de rigueur in the late 1980s (Fumio 2009, 2019), Masako's outfit is completed with demure screw-back pearl earrings.

This yellow gown was revisited when Empress Masako stepped out on the balcony of Imperial Palace in Tokyo for the emperor and empress's first official public appearance on 5 May 2019 (see Plate vii). For this occasion, the men of the imperial family wore formal morning suits, while the princesses dressed in an array of pastels. Masako stands apart in a bright gold hat and gown (see Getty Images 2019). Royal Hats, a blog that provides coverage and commentary of the 'bold, beautiful and utterly bizarre world that is royal millinery' (Anon. 2019a: n.pag.), notes that this vibrant yellow was 'a colour we've not seen on her in recent memory' (Hat Queen 2019: n.pag.). Like the lemon yellow worn for the engagement photos, the balcony gown is teamed with a matching hat, white gloves and a strand of pearls. The hat on this occasion was a modest bumper brim style that Masako has favoured since the early 2000s.

This outfit is remarkable not only for its bright colour but for its apparent newness, as Masako is well known for re-wearing outfits – whether by choice or *Kunaicho* mandate. Royal watch sites are filled with collages of gowns giving the date and occasion they were worn (see Anon. 2013). Unlike the plain yellow 1993 gown, this new balcony gown was decorated with gold bugle beading on the hat band, collar and cuffs in a starburst, or rather, a sunray pattern. If we consider that 'all texts are indexical, in the sense that their meaning is not fully contained in them but completed in the setting of their reading' (Smith 1990: 197), this symbolically signifies the promise of her 1993 engagement. At the same time, it firmly links Masako, in her new role as empress, with the sun motif of Japan as a nation: a motif found in everything from the country's flag to the Japanese characters used to write 'Japan': 日本 ('sun + origin'). These two golden gowns celebrate Masako's initial entrée into the public sphere as an imperial bride and, in 2019, her triumphant return to public life as a new empress. Her new imperial ensembles bypass her former individual authority as embellished by her power suits at the Foreign Ministry and reinstate her imperial authority in a polished and well-established code of royal dress.

Formal afternoon wear: Negotiating kimono and western dress

Masako's yellow gowns are not just fitted suits, they are formal 'day' or 'afternoon dress' known in Japanese as a *rōbu montanto* (*robe montante*). While Japanese men follow the British hierarchy of dress: moving from jeans and t-shirts for leisure, to business or lounge suits for business day wear, morning suits for formal day wear, tuxedos for a cocktail or less formal evening wear, and tails or white tie for evening wear (see Hollander 1995), womenswear is far more complex, due to the sheer range of options and styles open to them. In Japan, this is further compli-cated after the hierarchy of kimono is appropriated into western-style formal dress, which introduces the following questions: If a formal *houmongi* ('visiting kimono') is worn as day wear, is it appropriate to wear the same garment for evening wear? Is changing an *eri* ('collar or false collar inserts'), *obi* sash and *zori* sandals for differ-ent coloured or more richly woven options enough or should a different style of kimono be worn altogether? Is it permissible to break restrictions on age or marital status in an effort to find an equivalent to western business, cocktail, and evening wear? (See for example Dalby 2001: 193–290.) Japanese women of position have demonstrated cultural workarounds rather than one-for-one equivalents – a strategy perfected by diplomatic wives in the early twentieth century. Sugihara Yukiko, the wife of Vice-consul Sugihara Chiune who helped over 6000 Jews flee Europe in 1940, noted the difference between the 'sparkling' heirloom jewellery of middle-aged European wives and her fine silk kimono (Sugihara 1995: 48; Levine 1996: 118). For Yukiko, what she lacked in diamonds was well compensated by the expensive silks and gold brocade of her ensembles.

These *robes montantes* were donned by Empress Masako, Empress Emerita Michiko and the Imperial princesses for the various Reiwa ceremonies, including the abdication ceremonies of the Heisei emperor, the ascension of the Reiwa emperor, and the various official greetings such as the 4 May 2019 appearance on the balcony of the Tokyo Imperial palace (Global News 2019). These gowns seem to be made principally from self-patterned jacquard fabrics with floral designs. The use of self-patterned jacquard silks, in 'polite' pastel colours that often appear in formal visiting *houmongi* kimono, sport similar floral motifs to those viewed in kimono bolts, makes the *robe montante* a kimono in all but cut. The *robe montante* is named for its collar. Here, the *montante* ('rising') refers to the high neckline of the gowns. *Robes montantes* are further characterized by their long sleeves and ankle- or floor-length hems.

These garments were set as formal western wear for women in a June 1886 decree (in order from most to least formal: the *manteau de cour, robe décolletée, robe mi-décolletée* and *robe montante*; Osakabe 2010: 168–70). These robes are distinguished by colour, collar and sleeve length. A year later, the Meiji empress issued a memorandum on the subject of women's clothing in Japan: 'She [the empress] believed that western clothes were in fact closer to the dress of women in ancient Japan than the kimonos currently worn and urged that they be adopted as the standard clothes of the reign' (Keene 2002: 404). Here, the Meiji empress, by dictating sartorial mores, cleverly places herself at the centre of the Meiji restoration. Here, she linked western dress to a pre-Sino (pre-Chinese) tradition, so that this modernization process could be legitimized as part of Japan's ancient tradition.

While the *manteau de cour* and *robe mi-décolletée* have fallen out of usage, the *robe décolletée* and *robe montante* have been retained as evening and afternoon dress in Japan as seen throughout the 2019 royal celebrations. At Emperor Emeritus Akihito's abdication ceremony, female members of the imperial family dressed in a spectrum from the empress emerita's silver and white, through Empress Masako's lace and cream, to the Crown princess and her daughter's pale green, pale blue, Prussian blue and into the jewel tones of the other princesses. In the *robe montante*, colour blocking is relieved by either decorative lace or applique or decorative draping and stitching, as well as matching hats, gloves and fans. These polite pastels, seen at the official greeting ceremonies on the first day of the Reiwa era, and again on the morning of the October enthronement ceremonies, further illustrate how striking Masako's balcony gown was not yellow, not lemon, but gold.

Imperial ensemble 2: A crown of bright stars

While royal day wear calls for high necklines, wrist-length gloves, hats and matching clutches, formal evening wear, known as the *robe décolletée*, exchanges these for décolletage, opera gloves, tasselled fans and diamond parures. Instead of pastel and jewel colours of the *robe montante* worn during the day, the *robe décolletée* is usually white silk and often worn with the gold and red sash of the Order of the Precious Crown that all Imperial princesses are admitted to upon coming of age at 20 years or upon marriage into the family. One of the most iconic images of the current Japanese emperor and empress is from their wedding parade on 9 June 1993. The couple are depicted smiling and waving from the back of an open-top car (Fumio 2019, see Plate viii). Both appear in a western dress with then Crown prince Naruhito wearing a white tie and the then newly titled Crown princess Masako in a white *robe décolletée* and matching bolero with a large, petal-like gold and white collar designed by Mori Hanae, the first Asian designer to be admitted to the haute couture association (Kawamura 2004). Upon marriage, Masako was given the floral emblem of the Japanese *hamanasu* rose, and both the petal collar and the jacquard pattern woven into the gown echoed her new symbol.

Twenty-six years later, it was this image that was sartorially invoked at both the gala banquet that followed the Enthronement ceremony on 22 October 2019 and the Enthronement parade that took place through the streets of Tokyo on 10 November 2019 (Global News 2019). The newly enthroned empress greeted her guests at the Enthronement banquet dressed in gold-tinged *robe décolletée* with a collar that featured petal-like flounces on one side and silk roses on the other – invoking not only the flower badge that she received upon her wedding but also her famous wedding gown, to indicate to the public that more promising times were ahead. A fortnight later, the Imperial couple were again driven through the streets in an open car (Ha 2019). Emperor Naruhito again wore white tie, but this time he wore the heavy chain of office and Order of the Chrysanthemum. For this ride, Empress Masako wore a petal-like *robe décolletée* that is so similar to the one designed by Mori Hanae in 1993 that it appears as the same garment (see Plate viii).

With the setting of this new car ride in mind – a triumphant parade and re-emergence post public withdrawal – this choice of attire – like the yellow suit – is indexical in that it calls back to one of Masako's most famous appearances. As the images of her wedding are arguably what Smith (1990: 195) would call 'public textual

69

images', these garments contain a public message of celebration and optimism of the royal wedding in 1993. This brings to mind Masako's former life, before her 'adjustment disorder' and signals her willingness to begin anew as Japan's empress.

All three of Masako's *robes décolletée* were crowned with imperial tiaras and matching necklaces or ropes of diamonds. As an empress, Masako has inherited the right to wear the Meiji tiara. The diamond scroll Meiji tiara was commissioned by the then Empress Haruko in the late 1880s, possibly around the time of the official edicts relating to formal western dress introduced above. The tiara is topped by diamond starbursts that can be removed depending on the wearer or occasion ('Tiara Timeline' 2015; Shimada 2020). The tiara has since been worn by every Japanese empress across the Taisho, Showa, Heisei and now Reiwa eras. This combination of white jewels (diamonds and pearls) on white metal (white gold or platinum) has been incorporated into headwear by all imperial empresses and princesses since the 1880s. Unlike many of the royal houses of Europe, including the British Royal family, where women must be married to wear tiaras (Hallemann 2018b), the women of the Japanese imperial family start are allowed to wear them either when they come of age at 20 years, or marry into the family. Note that these tiaras all belong to the Japanese state and are not inherited by individuals. By wearing them in public, the members of the Imperial Japanese Family are literally adorned with the wealth and beauty of the nation.

Imperial ensemble 3: Robes of silk and gold

If the most famous image of Empress Masako is from her wedding day, then the next contender is undoubtedly her marital *jyuu ni hitoe* (literally, '12 unlined silk robes'). This impressive image adorns Hill's book about Masako – that is, when they are not obscured by increasingly larger chrysanthemum blooms (2006). The reportage leading up to the May 2019 Reiwa ceremonies, in both English and Japanese, chose to focus on these robes (see Suzuki 2019). Japanese traditional clothing such as kimono indicates not only gender but also age, marital status, season, status, formality and occasion (Monden 2014: 8). The design of these robes dates back to the Heian period (784–1184) and was worn in imperial households up until the dress edicts of the 1880s: both a literal and physical link from the past to the future.

The colours of these outfits are strictly defined by rules laid out in the Heian period known as the *kuge* system. For his wedding robes as Crown prince, he wore a bright orange shade, but as emperor for the Enthronement ceremony, he wore a bronze/gold silk robe, a colour is limited to the reigning emperor of Japan. Part of the fabric is woven with gold thread meaning that when it catches the light, the wearer looks like they are wreathed in the sun's rays. The robe is also self-patterned with *kirin* ('Japanese or Chinese unicorns') and chrysanthemums (Anon. 2019d). These *kirin* (from Chinese *Qilin*) are fantastic animals: a sacred amalgam of wolf, snake and horse with a single horn encased in flesh, like dragons, they are linked to water and purity. Similarly, Masako wore green robes for her marriage (see Plate vix) but graduated to robes of shining whites and imperial purples as empress. This imperial purple was also worn by the imperial princesses whose robes darkened in colour according to their place in the order of precedence (Anon. 2019d) similar to the *robes montantes* discussed earlier.

As Smith argues, following strict rules with proficiency and precision is one of the ways women demonstrate agency as experts and highly skilled interpreters of the 'discourse of femininity' (1990: n.pag.). While tradition dictates every aspect of these formal outfits, there remains room for subtle deviation and personalization that enables the wearer to demonstrate both expertise and flair. Empress Masako's robes followed a similar colour scheme to those worn by previous Empress Michiko during her enthronement ceremonies in 1990 but the *mon* ('crest') differed. Masako's robes used mirrored cranes on the outermost layer, with chrysanthemums similar to those portrayed on her marital robes on the lower layers.

There is an irony here, as these traditional silk robes have become a centrepiece in the visual narrative of the Reiwa enthronement ceremonies. While these garments are often touted as dating from the tenth century, they are in fact a Meiji period interpretation – as dictated by the reforms of Empress Haruko, via the mid Edo period (Keene 2002: 404). Although the structure and colours comprising the garment remain largely unchanged, there are marked differences indicated by functionality and hairstyle. It is important to remember that at one point, these garments were daily wear that has since been codified. The weight of the layers of silk (not including undergarments, ranging from 5 to 20 kg) and the heavy wig were commented upon by women reporters who dressed up in similar outfits, not only during the prelude to the 2019 events but also to celebrate the 1993 wedding (see, e.g. Suzuki 2019; Anon. 2019d).

In the Heian period, women in this ceremony were to be mostly invisible, kept cloistered behind screens and sliding doors. If in public, the only part of a woman that should be visible was the trailing ends of her sleeves, hems and train: visible signs of her dainty elegance. The colour combinations of these trailing ends, as with modern kimono were dictated by taste, style, class, rank and decorum. Recently, Masako's robes were not only photographed but livestreamed on YouTube present a vast departure from tenth century mores and is more in keeping with the Meiji Empress's clothing edicts which 'where so important' represented the modernizing of Japan from the inside out (Hastings 1993: 678). Allowing herself to be visible,

Masako disrupts the traditional discourse by a 'striking opposition to idealistic discourse' (Smith 1990) while displaying her command of the necessary discourse dictated by royal femininity. Here, she appears both traditional and modern, feminine and bold.

An empress's wardrobe unlocked: Conclusion and further readings

This overview of the attire worn in Empress Masako's public appearances in the recent Reiwa coronation celebrations has analysed her garments from three specific moments in her life: her early-career wardrobe, her official engagement and wedding ensembles and her accession to the empress. By visually analysing this clothing and by drawing upon Japanese and English news reportage, we outline the potential meanings expressed in Masako's style and its relationship to tradition. We have argued that as a custodian of feminine tradition and modernity as princess and empress, Masako not only demonstrates both commands of these royal discourses but also subtly modifies her dress with flair with distinct linkages to her early career, engagement period and finally, life as a Japanese royal. Here, we offer that Masako's recent attire recalls the brighter and optimistic times of her earlier life and career before her period of 'adjustment disorder' which then is closed following her triumphant return as empress.

It is tempting to assume that the high collars and low brims favoured by the Masako are protective layers, designed to present a barrier between herself and the critical eyes of her detractors, but perhaps there is an easier connection to be made. Perhaps the styles Masako favoured as a private citizen were similarly layered and provided body-covering silhouettes so popular in the late 1980s and early 1990s fashions. As Joanne Entwhistle argues, this allows the consumption of work-related clothing as meaningful to one's career path, rather than a strictly fashionable exercise (1997: 322). While her royal attire is brighter and more feminine, it is evident that when accepting layers, this offers Masako a demonstration of command in what Smith (1990) calls 'the discourse of femininity' – to a nation-wide 'interpretive circle' – those in the media who scrutinize her fashions against traditional and modern ideals. Clearly, Masako operates within tight confines, and although she is certainly one of the most powerful women in Japan, this high profile does not afford her the luxury of overthrowing gender norms. Rather, we suggest that she exercises power by taking on the responsibility of representing the nation and through the sacrifice of her individuality for the greater cause of ensuring Japan's success.

These conclusions are based on research conducted through close reference to both Japanese and English press reportage and Twitter feeds. These media provide the data that Smith (1990: 121) observes as texts, relying on the 'reader's interpretative practices' to reinforce the idea that each viewer will find something new and interesting in the proffered reports and images, based on each individual's context, experience and training. However, other critics outline a method to visualize fashion in the public eye: as a site-specific installation. As art critic and historian Kim-Cohen suggests, 'one of the sites to which any work must be specific is the site of art history' (2016: 44).

Here, Seth Kim-Cohen (2016: 44) expands the established connection between the 'work' – be it an artwork or, in this case, a fashion ensemble – and delineates its relations to the rest of the world in which it both resides and is looked upon by others:

> It is incumbent upon the work [fashion] that it acknowledges its own relation to all the sites in which it engages: art history yes, but also, politics, economics, institutionality, race, gender, climate, violence and so on. Site specificity begs a transparency with regard to the work's [fashion's] relation to the various structures within which it operates.

The ensembles worn by Masako upon becoming a public figure as bride or princess-to-be, crown princess, empress-to-be and finally empress present not only the role of the kimono from the classical Heian period but also, through a continuance of the Meiji Empress's clothing edicts, an influence from modern western garb. The moments and ensembles that we have offered for consideration here are both legitimized by this long lineage but also hint at Masako's personal conversation with the viewing public. Further, there remain questions about the accuracy of worldwide media reportage and its capacity, both locally and internationally, to actually reflect the Japanese public's opinions as a nation. A more detailed deconstruction of locally held opinions about the Japanese royal family in general could underpin how effective Masako's public appearances have been in presenting herself to the nation and the world as a capable princess and empress.

For now, we choose to close the doors of this spectacular wardrobe but leave the key in its lock.

NOTE

1. Newspaper and televised news reportage scripts were sourced from media database, *Factiva* in a systematic review in October 2019, using key terms '小和田雅子' and 'Masako Owada', which yielded a return of 646 articles ranging in date from 1986 to 2019. All English translations provided in the chapter are from Emerald L. King.

REFERENCES

Anon. (2012), 'Za purinsesu; Masako hime monogatari', ('The Princess: The Tale of Princess Masako'), *Shunkan Bunshun*, 25 October, from Factiva database. Accessed 12 November 2019.

Anon. (2013), 'Oranda kokuou sokuishiki ni jyuunen mae no doresu wo chakuyousareta Masako sama no kukyou to kyouji' ('The pride and predicament of Masako wearing a ten year old dress to the enthronement of the Dutch King'), Kōshitsu mondai INDEX, http://imperialfamily-biasedmedia-report.jp/summary.html. Accessed 16 November 2019.

Anon. (2015), 'Tiara timeline: The Meiji Tiara', The Court Jeweller, 24 September, http://www.thecourtjeweller.com/2015/09/tiara-timeline-meiji-tiara.html. Accessed 17 November 2019.

Anon. (2018a), '[Heisei no shōgen] 5-nen 1 Gets'u' ('Hesei's Testimony: 5 years 1 month'), *Sankei Shimbun*, 20 June, from Factiva database. Accessed 12 November 2019.

Anon. (2018b), 'Masako-san no koto wa boku ga isshō, zenryoku de omamori shimasukara. Heisei no kotoba' ('I will protect Masako for the rest of my life. Heisei Words'), *Chunichi Newspaper*, 19 January, from Factiva database. Accessed 12 November 2019.

Anon. (2019a), 'About and comments', Royal Hats, https://royalhats.net/about/. Accessed November 2019.

Anon. (2019b), 'Heisei no kōshitsu o furikaeru/ shōchō no yakuwari taigen/ irei no tabi/ senbotsu-sha, hisai-chitsuneni yorisou/ kōzoku no kekkon/ shingō-machi puropōzu mo/ kōi keishō/ josei miyake no giron teichō' ('Looking back on the Imperial Family of Heisei / The Role of Symbols: Embodied / Journey of memorial service / War dead, stricken area Always be close / Marriage of royal family / Proposal for signal waiting / Inheritance of Imperial throne / Discussion of female palace weak'), *Miyazaki Daily News*, 2 April, from Factiva database. Accessed 12 November 2019.

Anon. (2019c), 'Masako sama no wakai koro no keirei sugiru shashin gazou! Kogoshii kagayaki yo yomigaere!' ('These images of young Empress Masako are too beautiful! Bring back that divine sparkle!'), Dricho.com, 2 May, https://dricho.com/20190419/. Accessed 25 November 2019.

Anon. (2019d), 'What Japan's royal women wear', *Sankei Shimbun*, 31 May, https://japan-forward.com/what-japans-royal-women-wear/amp/. Accessed 17 November 2019.

Anon. (2019e), 'Kiseki Heisei yuku 30-nen no kioku/ kōshitsu/ kōdō de shōchō ten'nō o taigen' ('Trajectory: memory of 30 years in the Heisei era / Imperial family / embody the emperor symbol by action'), *Nagasaki Shinbun*, 26 April.

Anon. (2020), 'Personal histories', The Imperial Household Agency, http://www.kunaicho.go.jp/eabout/history/history02.html. Accessed 19 January 2020.

Bardsley, Jan (1998), 'Japanese feminism, nationalism and the royal wedding of 1993', *Journal of Popular Culture*, 31:2, pp. 189–205.

Bhat, Upasana and Tae-jun Kang (2019), 'Empress Masako: The Japanese princess who struggles with royal life', BBC News: BBC Monitoring, 1 May, https://www.bbc.com/news/amp/world-asia-48118128. Accessed 12 May 2021.

Breen, John (2019), 'Abdication, succession and Japan's imperial future: An emperor's dilemma', *The Asia-Pacific Journal | Japan Focus*, 17:9, pp. 1–15, https://apjjf.org/-John-Breen/5281/article.pdf. Accessed 14 November 2019.

Cliffe, Sheila (2017), *The Social Life of Kimono: Japanese Fashion Past and Present*, London: Bloomsbury.

Dalby, Liza (2001), *Kimono: Fashioning Culture*, New York: Vintage.

Dees, Jan (2009), *Taisho Kimono: Speaking of Past and Present*, Milano: Skira.

Dode, Zvezdana (2012), 'Costume as text', in M. Harlow (ed.), *Dress and Identity*, Birmingham: University of Birmingham Press, pp. 7–18.

Entwhistle, Joanne (1997), 'Power dressing and the fashioning of the Career Woman', in M. Nava, I. MacRury, A. Blake and B. Richards (eds), *Buy this Book: Studies in Advertising and Consumption*, Routledge: London, pp. 211–322.

Entwistle, Joanne (2015), *The Fashioned Body: Fashion, Dress and Social Theory*, Cambridge, Oxford and Boston: Polity Press.

Ferguson, Niall (2011), *Civilization: The West and the Rest*, London: Penguin.

Fumio, Hirai (2019), 'A change of heart: The courtship of princess Masako', Nippon.Com, 8 March, https://www.nippon.com/en/news/fnn20190212001/a-change-of-heart-the-courtship-of-princess-masako.html. Accessed 16 November 2019.

Getty Images (2019), 'Emperor Naruhito makes first official public appearance since coronation', https://www.gettyimages.com.au/detail/news-photo/emperor-naruhito-of-japan-waves-to-members-of-the-public-as-news-photo/1141059429?. Accessed 1 November 2019.

Global News (2019), 'Japanese emperor Naruhito's coronation ceremony', https://www.youtube.com/watch?v=z_Xka42e9jE. Accessed 22 January 2019.

Ha, Kwiyeon (2019), 'Japan imperial couple rides through Tokyo in grand enthronement parade', *Reuters*, 10 November, https://www.reuters.com/article/us-japan-emperor-enthronement-parade/japan-imperial-couple-rides-through-tokyo-in-grand-enthronement-parade-idUSKBN1XK04C. Accessed 1 November 2019.

Hallemann, Caroline (2018a), 'The reason duchess Kate wears so many bright colours: She's taking fashion cues from the Queen', *Town & Country*, 16 January, https://www.townandcountrymag.com/society/tradition/news/a8027/kate-middleton-bright-colors/. Accessed 12 May 2021.

Hallemann, Caroline (2018b), 'Tiara etiquette: Everything you ever wanted to know about who can wear one – and who can't', *Town & Country*, 25 January, https://www.townandcountrymag.com/style/jewelry-and-watches/a15728465/tiara-etiquette-facts-explained/. Accessed 25 November 2019.

Hastings, Sally A. (1993), 'The empress' new clothes and Japanese women, 1868–1912', *The Historian*, 55:4, pp. 677–92.

Hat Queen (2019), 'Imperial royals appear on palace balcony', *Royal Hats*, 5 May, https://royal-hats.net/2019/05/05/imperial-royals-appear-on-palace-balcony/. Accessed 1 November 2019.

Howell, David L. (2009), 'The girl with the horse-dung haido', in J. Purtle and H.B. Thomsen (eds), *Looking Modern: East Asian Visual Culture from Treaty Ports to World War II*, Chicago: The Centre for the Art of East Asia, University of Chicago, pp. 203–19.

Isa, Masako and Eric Mark Kramer (2003), 'Adopting the caucasian "look": Reorganising the minority face', in E.M. Kramer (ed.), *The Emerging Monoculture: Assimilation and the 'Model Minority'*, Santa Barbara, California: Praeger, pp. 41–74.

Kanayama, Tomoko and Anne Cooper-Chen (2005), 'Hofstede's masculinity/femininity dimension and the pregnancy of princess Masako: An analysis of Japanese and international newspaper coverage', *Keio Communication Review*, 27, https://core.ac.uk/download/pdf/145784884.pdf. Accessed 24 November 2020.

Kato, Mariko (2019), 'Weight of Imperial world on Princess Masako: How can former Foreign Ministry star cope with royal straight jacket?', *The Japan Times*, 19 May, https://japantimes.co.jp/news/2009/05/19/reference/weight-of-imperial-world-on-princess-masako/#.XixVhFPZXqs. Accessed 1 December 2019.

Kawamura, Yuniya (2004), 'The Japanese revolution in Paris fashion', *Fashion Theory*, 8:2, pp. 195–223.

Keene, Donald (2002), *Emperor of Japan: Meiji and His World, 1852–1912*, New York: Columbia University Press.

Kim-Cohen, Seth (2016), *Against Ambience and Other Essays*, London and New York: Bloomsbury Academic.

King, E. and Rall, D.N. (2015), 'Re-imagining the Empire of Japan through Japanese schoolboy uniforms', *M/C Media Culture*, 18:6, http://journal.media-culture.org.au/index.php/mcjournal/article/viewArticle/1041. Accessed 24 September 2021.

Kunaicho.go.jp (2014), 'Exhibition in France *Kaiko: Sericulture of the Imperial Household, Ancient Textiles from the Shosoin Repository, and Exchanges of Silk between Japan and France*', https://www.kunaicho.go.jp/e-event/kaiko.html. Accessed 14 January 2020.

Levine, Hillel (1996), *In Search of Sugihara: The Elusive Japanese Diplomat Who Risked His Life to Rescue 10,000 Jews from the Holocaust*, New York: Free Press.

Matsunaga, Kazuyoshi (2019), *Opening Address at the 'Gender, Media and Japan's Imperial Succession' Symposium*, Melbourne, Victoria: Monash University.

Molloy, John (1975), *Dress for Success*, Peter H. Wyden: New York.

Monden, Masafumi (2014), *Japanese Fashion Cultures*, London: Bloomsbury.

Osakabe, Yoshinori (2010), 'Yōfuku sanpatsu dattō: Fuku-sei no Meiji ishin' ('*Clothes, Haircuts, and Swords: The Meiji Restoration of Clothing*'), Tokyo: Kodansha.

'Personal Histories' (2020), 'The Imperial Household Agency', http://www.kunaicho.go.jp/e-about/history/history02.html. Accessed 19 January 2020.

'Royal Wedding Jewels: Emperor Akihito and Empress Michiko' (2019), *The Court Jeweller*, 10 April, http://www.thecourtjeweller.com/2019/04/royal-wedding-jewels-emperor-akihito.html. Accessed 16 November 2019.

Ruoff, Kenneth J. (2001), *The People's Emperor: Democracy and the Japanese Monarchy, 1945–95*, Cambridge and London: Harvard University Press.

Sanger, David E. (1993), 'The Career and the Kimono', *The New York Times Magazine*, 30 May, https://www.nytimes.com/1993/05/30/magazine/the-career-and-the-kimono.html. Accessed 1 December 2019.

Sanz, Cynthia (1993), 'The princess bride', *People Magazine*, 21 June, https://people.com/archive/the-princess-bride-vol-39-no-24/. Accessed 15 December 2019.

Seaman, Amanda (1995), 'Modeling Masako: Commodities and the construction of a modern princess', *Chicago Anthropology Exchange*, 21, Spring, pp. 35–72.

Shimada, Ayaka (2020) '<Jistu ha kōshitu no tiara wa [...]> Meiji nijyuu nen kara uketuker-eru kagayaki no rekishi wo furikaeru' ('Actually, the imperial tiara is [...]" Looking back on the history of the radiance left to us in Meiji 20') FNN Prime, 1 January, https://sp.fnn.jp/posts/00049594HDK/20200101930_shakaibu_HDK. Accessed 24 January 2020.

Smith, Dorothy (1990), *Texts, Facts and Femininity: Exploring Relations of Ruling*, Oxon: Routledge.

sussexroyal.com (2020), 'Media', https://sussexroyal.com/media/. Accessed 26 January 2020.

Suzuki, Miwa (2019), 'Sceptres and silk: the kit and garb of Japan's enthronement', *The Jakarta Post*, 6 April, https://www.thejakartapost.com/amp/life/2019/04/05/sceptres-and-silk-the-kit-and-garb-of-japans-enthronement.html. Accessed 26 November 2019.

Tipton, Elise K. (2016), *Modern Japan: A Social and Political History*, 3rd ed., London: Routledge.

Tucker, Spencer C. (ed.) (2013), *A Global Chronology of Conflict: From the Ancient World to the Modern Middle East*, Santa Barbara: ABC-CLIO.

Sugihara, Yukiko (1995), *Visas for Life*, San Francisco: Edu-Comm Plus.

PLATE I: Seoul, South Korea on 12 November 2010. Attending members of the world's economic forum for the top 20 world economies (G20) and invited guests wave as they pose together for the 'family photo' following the plenary sessions at the G20 Summit. Three women are present of twenty members: Argentina's President Cristina Kirchner, Australia's Prime Minister Julia Gillard and Germany's Chancellor Angela Merkel. Photo: Tim Sloan/AFP via Getty Images.

PLATE II: Australia, Former Prime Minister Julia Gillard with her official portrait painted by Vincent Fantauzzo unveiled at Parliament House in Canberra on 24 October 2018. Photo: Alex Ellinghausen/Fairfax Photos/Nine Publications.

PLATE III: Berlin, Germany, 9 November 2009. Germany's Chancellor Angela Merkel meets with United States's Secretary of State Hillary Clinton during celebrations marking the 20th anniversary of the fall of the Berlin Wall and reunification of Germany. Photo: Sean Gallup/Getty Images.

PLATE IV: Canberra, Australian Capital Territory, 26 November 2018. Liberal MP Julie Bishop posing with the red satin block heels at Parliament House. Photo: Alex Ellinghausen/Nine Publications.

PLATE V: Berlin, Germany, 17 April 2018. German Chancellor Angela Merkel greets New Zealand's heavily pregnant Prime Minister Jacinda Ardern with military honours in the forecourt of the Federal Chancellery. Photo: Wolfgang Kumm/dpa /picture alliance via Getty Images.

PLATE VI: Christchurch, New Zealand, Mosque Shooting, 22 March 2019. New Zealand Prime Minister Jacinda Ardern walks past the crowd at the Al Noor Mosque at a national call to prayer. Photo: Jason South/Nine Publications.

PLATE VII: Tokyo, Japan, 23 December 2010. Japanese Crown Princess Masako greets the public at the Imperial Palace on Emperor Akihito's 77th birthday. Photo: Tatsuyuki TAYAMA/ Gamma-Rapho via Getty Images.

PLATE VIII: Tokyo, Japan, 10 November 2019. Emperor Naruhito and Empress Masako wave from their car during the imperial parade for enthronement of Emperor Naruhito. They paraded in a convertible sedan along a 4.6-km route from the Imperial Palace to their residence in the Akasaka Estate to mark the enthronement. Photo: Takashi Aoyama/Getty Images.

PLATE IX: Tokyo, Japan, 22 October 2019. Japanese Empress Masako leaves the ceremony hall after Emperor Naruhito proclaimed his enthronement at the Imperial Palace on 1 May 2019 after his father Emperor Emeritus Akihito abdicated on 30 April 2019. Photo: Kimimasa Mayama/Pool/Getty Images.

PLATE X: Canberra, Australia, 4 May 2016. Canberra Reacts to the 2016 Federal Budget Release. Bronwyn Bishop gives her valedictory speech in the House of Representatives at Parliament House to offer the Federal Budget to the Parliament. Photo: Stefan Postles/Getty Images.

PLATE XI: Australia, 30 March 1998, Cartoon of Cheryl Kernot, 'Is that a policy in your pocket or are you glad to see me?' lampooning her cover photo for the Australian Women's Weekly magazine on 13 February. Illustration: Peter Nicholson, The Australian newspaper, 30 March 1998. The caption reads: 'Kernot asking Labor leader, Kim Beasley, for 'policy guidance' in the lead up to the 1998 Federal Election'.

PLATE XII: Las Vegas, Nevada, USA, 14 October 2015. Hillary Clinton, former US secretary of State and 2016 Democratic presidential candidate, speaks at Hillary for America Nevada Rally, Springs Preserve Amphitheater. Photo: Joseph Sohm/Shutterstock.

PLATE XIII: Washington DC, USA, 9 May 2009. Michelle Obama at White House Correspondents' Association Dinner held at the Washington Hilton Hotel. Photo: Reuters.

PLATE XIV: Perth, Western Australia, 28 October 2011. The Queen Attends CHOGM - Day 1 (Commonwealth Heads of Government Meeting). From left to right, Bangladesh Prime Minister Sheikh Hasina, Queen Elizabeth II, Australian Prime Minister Julia Gillard, Trinidad and Tobago Prime Minister Kamla Persad-Bissessar pose for the official female heads of state photo. Photo: Mike Bowers-CHOGM/via Getty Images.

PLATE XV: Larkarna, Sindh, Pakistan, 1 January 1986. Benazir Bhutto poses for a photograph in her family's residence in Larkarna. Behind her is a picture of her father Zulfikar Ali Bhutto, former President of Pakistan. She has recently returned to Pakistan to marry Asif al Zardari, and as the head of the Pakistan People's Party (PPP), proclaiming she would bring democracy to this largely Islamic country. Photo: Peter Charlesworth/LightRocket via Getty Images.

PLATE XVI: Sindh, Pakistan, 1 January 1986. Benazir Bhutto works the crowd at a rally. She is the leader of the Pakistan People's Party (PPP), proclaiming she would bring democracy to this largely Islamic country. Photo: Peter Charlesworth/LightRocket via Getty Images.

PLATE XVII: Harbour City, Tsim Sha Tsui, Hong Kong, 4 September 2012. Chief Secretary Carrie Lam Cheng Yuet-ngor talks to the press after officiating the Community Chest Dress Casual Day 20th Anniversary in Harbour City, Hong Kong shopping centre. Photo: Jonathan Wong/South China Morning Post via Getty Images.

PLATE XVIII: Taipei, Taiwan, 11 January 2020. Taiwan's President Tsai Ing-wen waves to supporters outside her campaign headquarters, declaring victory in Taiwan's election on 11 January as votes were being counted after an election battle dominated by the democratic island's fraught relationship with China. Photo: Sam Yeh/AFP via Getty Images.

PLATE XIX: London, England, UK, 13 July 2016. New Prime Minister Theresa May makes a speech outside 10 Downing Street, London, after meeting Queen Elizabeth II and accepting her invitation to become prime minister and form a new government. PA Images/Alamy Stock Photo.

PLATE XX: London, England, UK. Leopard print Household department of big BIBA. ©The Design Council Slide Collection.

PLATE XXI: Jakarta, Indonesia, 28 March 2019. Indonesia Fashion Week 2019 – Day 2. A model showcases designs on the runway during the Althafunissa Syar'i by Karina show. Photo: Robertus Pudyanto/Getty Images.

PLATE XXII: Jakarta, Indonesia, 23 October 2012. Muslim girls outside Retribution Museum in Jakarta. Photo: Adam Jones, PhD. Own work. https://commons.wikimedia.org/wiki/File:Muslim_Girls_-_Outside_Retribution_Museum_-_Jakarta_-_Indonesia.jpg

PLATE XXIII: Hong Kong, 6 September 2020. Protesters react after police fired tear gas during a rally against a controversial extradition law proposal outside the government headquarters. Photo: Stratos Brilakis/Shutterstock.

PLATE XXIV: London, England, UK, 12 December 2020. Protesters stage a demonstration in Leicester Square, London. Protesters called for solidarity with Hong Kong citizens opposing Chinese government. Photo: Ilyas Tayfun Salci/Shutterstock.

PART II

MAKING POLITICS
THROUGH FASHION

4

Women Politicians, Fashion and the Media in Australia: Enid Lyons to Julia Gillard

Amanda Laugesen

Introduction

In May 1953, Dame Enid Muriel Lyons, Australia's first woman to be elected to the lower house of federal parliament, left Sydney for Britain with her daughter Janice. Dame Enid was heading abroad to attend the coronation of Queen Elizabeth II. Australian newspapers provided extensive descriptions of what Lyons would wear on the day: a gown of ivory Italian silk with silver hand embroidery, with a rose satin mantle lined in pearl grey. The mantle was embroidered with the badge of the Order of the British Empire: Dame Enid was one of only two Dames Grand Cross of the Order of the British Empire in Australia at the time. The collar of the Order was worn over the mantle and attached to it was the pale blue star of the Dame Grand Cross, inscribed with 'For God and Empire' (Anon. 1953: 12).

Dame Enid Lyons was no longer a working politician at the time she attended the coronation – she had retired before the 1951 federal election – but Dame Enid was one of Australia's most prominent representatives at this important international event. Media attention on Dame Enid's wardrobe was nothing new, as she had long been the focus of commentary about what she wore. But this outfit, detailed so carefully by the press, seemed to be an expression of Australia's national identity in the 1950s, at least insofar as it was articulated by the conservative government of Robert Menzies. Australia was still in many ways 'British to its bootstraps', and Dame Enid's outfit spoke of this important loyalty to Britain and to empire.

Fast forward to 2011, and Australia finally has its first female prime minister, Julia Gillard (Leader of the Australian Labor Party [ALP] 2010–13). (Note that the ALP changed the spelling to 'Labor' a few years after Australian Federation in the 1901 although both Labour and Labor can be used except in official party materials.)

Gillard has been invited to the Royal Wedding of Kate Middleton and Prince William, and she is under media pressure to get her outfit 'right' for such an important occasion. She ultimately selects a silver-cream jacket by Perth designer Aurelio Costarella and a knee-length Anthea Crawford navy skirt. She matches this with a Carla Zampatti-designed navy camisole and Alan Pinkus navy shoes and handbag (Hudson 2011: 13). All of these items were purchased by Gillard from Myer, Australia's pre-eminent department store founded in 1900 (Anon. 2010), and from another Australian store that she frequently patronized, David Jones. Julia Gillard's fashion had been subject to much criticism through her time as a prime minister, some of it positively vicious. In fact, an attack on Julia's 'big arse' was broadcast by the Australian Broadcasting Corporation (ABC) voiced by so-called 'feminist' provocateur Germaine Greer with a series of sneering comments on her appearance (2012: n.pag.).

However, when Prime Minister Julia Gillard represented Australia on the international stage at Westminster Abbey in 2011, her donning of attire from 'Aussie' designers and fashion purchased at familiar Australian stores where the public also shopped, garnered media approval. Like Enid Lyons before her Julia Gillard had, in this instance 'done Australia proud' by expressing Australian values and its place within the world's view of fashion.

This chapter covers several key figures and periods in our history: Dame Enid Lyons, the first member of the House of Representatives in Australia; the decade of the 1990s in Australia and the 'celebrity' treatment of women politicians; and Julia Gillard, first female prime minister from 2010 to 2013.

Australian women politicians and the fashion dilemma

Politics has long been constructed as a masculine sphere, with women considered to be a 'deviation' from the 'norm'. It seems evident that women politicians are generally subjected to closer scrutiny and are more harshly judged than men, especially when it comes to their appearance and their fashion choices. Almost two decades ago Karen Ross noted that in Australia there is a parliamentary 'unwritten dress code' that condemns women who dressed either too conservatively or too colourfully: so sartorial presentation should signal their conformity to parliamentary conventions (2002: 193). Women outside the norms, or who are overly aggressive in their style are often attacked (Van Acker 2003: 116). Carol Johnson (2015: 293) observes that female political leaders are particularly condemned for excess ambition. Hall and Donaghue (2013: 633) argue that ambitiousness displayed by female politicians is often regarded as undermining their femininity and 'relatability'. Women in politics have also been condemned if they seek to 'call out' such treatment, especially if they label it as sexist. Women who confront sexism in the public sphere, as Donaghue writes, are often labelled as 'complainers' and 'troublemakers' (2015: 164).

In a series of interviews with women politicians in the 1990s, Anne Henderson's interviewees attested to the constant pressure to curate their clothing for each and every public appearance (1999). Chris Gallus, a state politician in the 1990s, commented that when she stood for preselection, '[e]verybody wanted to tell me how to dress and how to do my hair. I had to wear bright colours' (Henderson 1999: 90). Joanna Gash, a federal member of parliament, commented: 'You have to dress up and sometimes dress down. I have a permanent wardrobe wherever I go. And it can require three to four changes a day. Men can wear the same suit' (Henderson 1999: 124). Similarly, Mary Easson, another federal member of parliament, commented on how she would need to prepare her clothes, bags and shoes for the week ahead, observing how important it was to wear something 'suitable' for every event and function she attended (Henderson 1999: 125). Marie Ficarra, a member of the New South Wales parliament, also commented that 'people are more judgmental of women if they are sloppy' (Henderson 1999: 128).

Enid Lyons: First Australian member of parliament and mother

Dame Enid Lyons came to office in the 1940 federal election, as the first female member of the House of Representatives, elected alongside the first female Senator, Dorothy Tangney. Dame Enid Lyons was born in 1887 in Tasmania and married the much older Joseph Lyons at the age of 17 in 1935. By the age of 36, she had twelve children and her husband was serving as Australia's prime minister. Joseph Lyons died in 1939, and in 1943, Enid ran for federal parliament as a member of the United Australia Party and then the Liberal Party. She was a member of parliament until 1951 and also served as a minister.

Lyons had a large family, and as a prime ministerial wife, there was already an established interest in her on the part of the press and the public as a mother. Cathy Jenkins' journalistic study of newspaper reports of Enid Lyons' career in politics notes that the focus remained on her in the context of family. While there was certainly an interest in her fashion, the overall bias of the coverage was her depiction as a mother (Jenkins 2003: 196). Indeed, the newspapers of the day identified Enid Lyons closely with her role as mother to a large brood. For example, when Lyons' victory in the federal election of 1943 was announced in the *Sydney Morning Herald*, the journalist noted that she had heard the news while ironing, and preparing five of her children for their return to boarding school (Anon. 1943: 4).

Scholars have noted that Lyons exemplified her role in parliament that reflected her experiences as wife and mother (Henderson 2008: 292); this also fitted with the conservative politics she represented as a member of the UAP/Liberal Party. Of course, she would 'naturally' be interested in issues to do with the family and women (Jenkins 2003: 186). Van Acker (2003: 118) has noted that both Lyons and Dorothy Tangney were constructed in the media within a framework of motherhood. This framing of Lyons was not only the product of political pressure and the media, as Lyons herself acknowledged and understood the importance of presenting herself as a nurturer of others. It was essential, she believed for women in parliament to not be threatening if they wished to expand their political careers. Lyons (1972: 2) wrote in her memoir that she represented a 'risky political experiment', and so her 'femininity would be crucial. I must do nothing either to emphasise it or deny it. Above all, I must never allow it to become a subject for ridicule'.

Lyons clearly claimed the right for women to participate in politics and to serve in parliament. But she also claimed women's essential difference. In discussing how women should behave in parliament (or in any 'man's world'), she wrote:

> In a man's world, there must be no assumption of masculine characteristics, no aggressiveness, no crudity of speech or behaviour, and at the same time no expectation of special privileges nor any suggestion of overconfidence. To appear to any way unfeminine would be fatal, I knew, to acceptance by my fellow workers.
>
> (1972: 5)

Lyons did acknowledge that dress was important for a woman within this 'man's world' of parliament and it was natural for an Australian of the day to look to England. Lady Astor was the first woman to sit in the British Parliament and she chose a quasi-uniform of black suit and white blouse as 'the ideal costume for her role'. While Lyons felt she was 'not built for tailored clothes, and the summer climate of Canberra called for something cooler and more comfortable than the stiffly severe suits of a quarter century ago', she decided that a 'simply-cut black dress with detachable white neck-piece [...] would admirably serve my purpose' (1972: 5–6). She later wrote in her memoir that

> for as long as I stayed in Parliament my working wardrobe consisted of two black dresses and a variety of lace and muslin jabots. A selection of these was always with me, and I could change them in a moment as freshness or occasion demanded.
>
> (Lyons 1972: 6)

Lyons had strong views on the value of dress for a woman, something she openly advocated to the public. She advised in 1951 that wearing good clothes in the

FIGURE 4.1: The Hon. Dame Enid Lyons Member for Darwin (Tasmania) UAP; LIB, 1943–51. https://upload.wikimedia.org/wikipedia/commons/1/16/Enid_Lyons_1940s.jpg. Accessed 14 October 2021.

Adelaide *Advertiser*, a sign of 'developing a greater consciousness of […] dignity as a human being'. 'Nothing external to ourselves', she continued, 'so influences our conduct and deportment as our clothes'. 'A woman knowing herself shabby or even unfashionable', argued Lyons to her public, 'is self-conscious and unhappy' (Lyons 1951: 2).

Lyons was awarded approval for her appearance by her parliamentary colleagues – Billy Hughes famously called her 'like a bird of paradise among carrion crows' (Lyons 1972: 7) – as well as in the media (see Figure 4.1). Her fashion choices provided photos and commentary in the press, especially her hats, which, Lyons notes in her memoir, 'made the headlines in nearly every paper in Australia' (1972: 150). But coverage did not always reveal the reason for some of her fashion choices – for example, her wearing of strings of pearls around her neck was used to disguise goitre surgery (Jenkins 2003: 194). Here, Dame Enid Lyons used her black dress as a means of asserting her restrained identity in parliament. Lyons also had strong beliefs about the importance of dress as a sign of character, engaging with issues of clothing and dress throughout and beyond her political career. During the Second World War, Lyons engaged in 'austerity dressing', remodelling her wardrobe so that she did not have to buy new clothes. In a 1944 interview, she told the interviewer that she was wearing a suit that was eight years old, and further planned to wear a velvet dress to the farewell dinner party for

Governor-General that had eight patches on the bodice (!). During wartime, she had proudly 'scrimmaged four new frocks out of some real antiques' and said that for all Australian women, '[t]here is very little in the possible line that gets tossed into the ragbag these days' (Seager 1944: 9).

Lyons also intervened several times in parliament about issues with clothing for ordinary Australians. She became embroiled in discussions about the cost of living for migrants just after the end of the war. The Department of Information had put out a booklet 'Australian and Your Future' for prospective migrants, but the prices quoted for everyday expenses were not realistic, at least for dressing the way the 'average Australian family' did. Lyons led the debate in parliament to challenge the figures proffered in the booklet (Anon. 1946b: 7). In parliament, she challenged the Minister for Immigration, Arthur Calwell, by asking him if he 'ever went shopping' (Anon. 1946a: 5). And in 1949, Lyons spoke in parliament, condemning the manufacturers of shoddy goods as 'traitors to Australia', after she had met a woman in Brisbane who received only '"six hours" wear out of a pair of shoes before they began to disintegrate' (Anon. 1949: 4).

In summary, Lyons' career was boosted by her strong identification, in both the parliament and in public reports, as a wife and mother and the media of the day perpetuated this image. Her strongly held belief was that the path to a successful political career included the cultivation of a distinctive femininity to ensure men would continue to welcome women into Australian public life. Lyons' fashion – and her interventions in questions of clothing relevant to the Australian public – was essential to her career, and how her career was viewed by media and public perceptions. In her memoir Lyons wrote about how she had taken on the role of the 'mother figure' in Australian public life, while reflecting that this role ultimately held some drawbacks (Lyons 1972: 167). She had often been consulted to comment as an 'expert' on issues regarding Australian families, but the statements she made on political matters that she considered held more weight and importance were left unrecorded by the press (Lyons 1972: 167).

Women politicians in the 1990s: Fashion and celebrity politics

The number of women in the Australian parliament remained low until the 1980s when they began to rise. The decade of the 1990s proved to be extremely important for how women politicians were represented and depicted in the media; it was a decade that saw women rising to positions of considerable power and influence in both federal and state parliaments. First, women had fought for increased social and political power through the second wave of feminism of the 1970s and 1980s (see Magarey 1996). By the 1980s women gained increased opportunities across the professions, and successful campaigns were waged to change, for example, discriminatory language in government and the media (Laugesen 2019).

Unfortunately, the mid-1990s saw conservative John Howard (Liberal Party leader 1996–2007) in office as prime minister who fomented a backlash towards women's leadership. It was impossible to push women out of the workforce, but consider the Liberal Party Treasurer Peter Costello's 'baby bonus', 'where he encouraged Australian women to have more babies, "one for mum, one for dad and one for the country"' (Hall 2007: n.pag.). In one stroke, Costello brought into question the status of women as workers rather than reproductive mothers and carers, with an undertone to increasing 'white' Australian births rather than increasing the immigration quota. Statements in the National Archives release of Australian Cabinet Papers from 2000 recorded these parliamentary concerns over falling birth rates due to 'financial pressures' on families and 'egalitarian attitudes among women' (Wright 2021: 13).

As the Australian media landscape diversified with multiplying commercial television channels this funnelled the content towards an international obsession with celebrity, raising interest in the British royals and the Kardashians in the United States. During this sensationalist trend in television, women politicians faced a crisis of 'celebrity' but were judged against TV's broadcasts of soap opera, 'infotainment' and reality TV stars in the public's eyes. As Julia Baird reflects, the 1990s were 'a shocking decade for women in politics. One after the other, they were hyped then trashed, glorified then muddied' (2010: 2).

The following sections consider three Australian women politicians of the 1990s and track their careers through views about their dress, including Bronwyn Bishop, Cheryl Kernot and Natasha Stott Despoja. They were not the only Australian female politicians to gain 'celebrity' status during the 1990s – others include Ros Kelly, Pauline Hanson and Amanda Vanstone – but they exemplify the different ways in which women leaders employed fashion to assert their public presence as well as their political identity. These examples show how each politician's appearance was variously manipulated through the media and resulting public perceptions.

Bronwyn Bishop

Bronwyn Bishop entered the Senate in 1987 and shifted to the House of Representatives in 1994 becoming the longest serving female member of the Liberal Party (Anon. 2021). She held ministerial positions in the John Howard government. Bishop has been described as the first female political celebrity in Australia (Baird 2004: 26). Since the 1970s, Baird argues, the conservative Australian media had been seeking an Australian 'Margaret Thatcher' (27). In fact, Bishop consciously modelled herself on Thatcher in both politics and style (Baird 2004: 34). One contemporary interview described Bishop's fashion changes to emulate that of Thatcher, observing that Bishop 'abandon[ed] her former wardrobe of glitzy frou frou and junk jewellery in favour of Thatcher-style pared-down business chic' (Jones 1994: 29).

Further, Bishop was extremely ambitious, and several descriptions of her reported negatively on this where she was dubbed 'Menzies in a frock' (Baird 2004: 37). One journalist wrote that for Bishop,

> [a]ny expressions of emotion that might muddy the picture of strength and unwaver-
> ing resolve have been edited out of her repertoire. Hence we are left with the static
> image of the wrap-around smile, or the glowering look of the inquisitor.
>
> (Jones 1994: 29)

Bishop's appearance was widely commented on by the press, reflecting this image of her as a ruthless and ambitious political animal. Journalist Peter Bowers dubbed Bishop 'the White Sharkess', with her 'blonde swept-back hair giv[ing] her a flash-ing, predatory presence' (1990: 36). Her beehive hairstyle was particularly distinc-tive and became the signature feature used by cartoonists and journalists alike (see Plate x). In 1993, journalist Peter Smark (1993: 17) commented that 'John Hewson without the GST is like Bronwyn Bishop without the hair and shoulder-pads'. As Bishop's career began to decline by the end of the decade, she was criticized for having a 'concrete hairstyle' that didn't change – one commentator even suggested that this only served to communicate that her views similarly were unchanging and stuck in the past (Anon. 1998: 22).

Bishop's career in politics continued, as she served in parliament until 2016 and has become a television commentator. But the 1990s was the decade when she had been touted as possible candidate for the Liberal Party prime ministership. Many things conspired to thwart her ambitions, including a number of political missteps, but her hard image, underpinned by her Thatcher-like persona, ultimately did little to increase public sympathy for her. An unfortunately timed and extremely expensive helicopter ride signalled a rousing finale to her political career (Donald and Henderson 2015). She perhaps did not aspire to be liked, but towards the end, her style was embraced by neither media nor public.

Cheryl Kernot

Cheryl Kernot's political career was off to a good start as she was popular as a former leader of the Australian Democrats turned Labor Party hopeful. Kernot entered the Senate in 1990 and was a leader of the Australian Democrats from

1993; she switched to the Labor Party in 1997, ran for the lower house and served as a member of parliament from 1998 to 2001. However, Kernot's parliamentary career proved to be particularly tumultuous. Although popular as the leader of the Democrats, Kernot's switch to Labor Party was subject to much criticism in the press. She was accused of not only betrayal but also condemned for her selfish ambition (Baird 2004: 168). Her move to Labor was also viewed as influenced by her affair with Labor Party Minister Gareth Evans, which led to much sexual innuendo in the press (Baird 2004: 170). When Kernot first entered politics, she was noted for her signature fashion style that included wearing bright colours, big earrings and lots of natural fibres. Kernot noted her own preference for a more casual style of dress, such as long skirts and loose trousers made from materials such as linen and cotton (O'Reilly 1998: 159). One male journalist, Brian Toohey commented that she projected a 'comforting image as Big Sister' (1998: 19).

In 1998, Kernot's career would become unstuck by a single fashion blunder when she chose to wear and be photographed in an outfit that definitely contradicted her previous 'big sister' image. Kernot appeared in a photoshoot for the most popular Australian women's magazine, the *Australian's Woman's Weekly*, in a scarlet 'bordello dress' and feather boa (see Plate xi). Kernot was instantly ridiculed and criticized for the 'glamour' shots – although she claimed that she had not been warned about which shot they were going to use – as she had worn several dresses during the shoot (Kernot 2002: 111). As *Australian* reporter Shelley Gare (1998: 2) commented: 'It's the scarletness, the frou-frouness of the frock that has most whistling through her teeth, especially after the scrutiny Kernot's private life has borne'. A former Labor adviser, Carmel McCauley excoriated Kernot for allowing herself to be 'photographed like that, like a sex kitten' (quoted in Gare 1998: 2). Further, a professional image consultant, Jenny Hanson, weighed in on the discussion to declare that the outfit 'says tart' and that Kernot appeared 'more than a little silly. I think she lost a lot of respect' (quoted in Anon. 1998: 22).

Various other politicians weighed in with their opinions about the photoshoot, but not all were negative. It is no surprise that parliamentary males seemed much less appalled by the image than their female counterparts. Kim Beazley, then ALP leader (1996–2001; 2005–06), commented that he thought Kernot looked 'very nice', and a male member of Kernot's electorate also said it was a 'nice photo', arguing that it was 'about time we got a bit of glamour into parliament' (quoted in Gare 1998: 2). This unfortunate cover photo was promptly lampooned by the noted cartoonist Peter Nicholson in the national newspaper *The Australian*, accompanied by her speech bubble, 'Is that a policy in your pocket or are you glad to see me?' (see Plate xi). The caption underneath reads: 'Kernot asking Labor leader, Kim Beasley, for "policy guidance" in the lead up to the 1998 Federal Election', and above Nicholson's signature the tagline appears, 'with apologies to Mae West' (Nicholson 1998: n.pag.). A spokesperson for the Office of the Status of Women commented that public interest in the issue was 'dreadful', and dismissed the whole thing as insignificant to women's political careers (Anon. 1998: 22).

It gets worse for Cheryl Kernot, as rather than seen as a victim of the media, she was actually accused of bringing the negative press on herself by 'trying her luck' as a media celebrity. Journalist Brian Toohey then criticized her for 'cater[ing] to the media's willingness to turn her life into a soap opera as she repeatedly discusses how she handles the stress of her latest personal crisis' (1998: 19). Further, many media commentators saw her as someone who tried to manipulate the press and then complained when they turned against her. But the whole controversy damaged her career and arguably, her life, irreparably. In her 2002 memoir, Kernot reflected that '[c]elebrity can have a big downside, not just for movie stars, but for politicians as well' (75). Celebrity had, she reflected almost ruined her marriage and her life (Kernot 2002: 146). Clearly, the media excoriated her for a single poor fashion choice – wearing a loud red dress for a women's magazine fashion shoot – that became a red flag to a bull, rather than a minor 'wardrobe malfunction' to be easily laughed off, thus alienating her from the both Australian- and the Labor-voting public.

Natasha Stott Despoja

By contrast, Democrat Natasha Stott Despoja, who was only 26 years when she was elected to the Senate in 1995, was able to successfully portray herself as a celebrity image. Her fashion and style were much in the media because of both her youth and her 'youthful' fashion choices, such as her wearing of Doc Martens boots were regarded as a symbol of her 'Gen X' status. As Baird (2004: 139) notes, descriptors such as 'hip', 'groovy', 'chic' and 'cutting edge' were all used to describe her. Baird (2004: 141) argues that Despoja did much to cultivate her own celebrity image, for example, posing in an Armani dress for the Australian popular women's magazine *Cleo*. Despoja willingly embraced her celebrity status and chose not to moderate her behaviour even when it was viewed as 'sexual'. She replied that she was just being human, and also that it is a feminist act to make her own choices in crafting her political identity, which meant wearing whatever she fancied (Baird 2004: 142). The subtext read that men wear what they like in Parliament and out. These outfits ranged from the modest tracksuits worn during John Howard's morning power walks to the much later Prime Minister Tony Abbott flaunting an extremely scanty swimming costume – the so called 'budgie smugglers' in Australian slang – at surf-lifesaving events. Afterwards, an irate female journalist commented that the Australian public really 'did not need [to] see quite as much of its prime minister' (Anderson 2016: 4).

Stott Despoja was much more successful than Kernot's attempt to harness the power of celebrity. But the question remains: did it benefit her political career? It certainly gave her press attention. But Baird (2004: 142) argues that her media attention and celebrity status ultimately did diminish her career, because she was viewed to lack genuine political intent. The fallout began when Stott Despoja started to receive patronizing and snide commentary by the media (Baird 2004: 151, 152). Jenny Hanson, the same image consultant who commented on Cheryl Kernot's red dress, also regarded Stott Despoja's outfits as 'inappropriate' within the workplace of parliament and Ms. Despoja would not be taken seriously, Hanson argued, unless she toned down 'the sensuality or overt sexual look' (Anon. 1998: 22). After a medical problem in 2006, Stott Despoja chose not to re-contest her election as an Australian Democrat and stepped down on 30 June 2008, an action that precipitated the demise of the Party (AAP 2006).

The 1990s thus can be read as a decade that saw much media criticism of women politicians by critizing their personalities and politics through their attire. The 'celebrity image' they hoped would project confidence morphed into something to be used against them. For Bishop, the Thatcher style did little to cultivate likability and made her look both staid and silly in changing times; Kernot was undone when she tried to 'play' with fashion and media-driven public perceptions of her backfired, and Despoja's image as a Gen X-er was regarded as insubstantial when it came to her policies.

Near the end of the decade, a Liberal Senator, Helen Coonan, wrote an op-ed in the *Sydney Morning Herald* about the unequal treatment of women politicians. While acknowledging that women politicians are sometimes 'amenable to overtures from the media that they dress up, assume poses and provide a bit of colour and movement to distinguish themselves from the grey-suited mass of the parliamentary ranks', she argued that

> media scrutiny which focuses on women politicians as merely decorative pieces or objects of ridicule does profound damage to the cause of women in public life. Such images ruthlessly reinforce the stereotype that women politicians are not to be taken seriously.
>
> (1998: 19)

Coonan continued,

> so long as we are more notable for our outfits and comparative glamour than for the quality of our contribution to debate, we only demean ourselves and diminish our credibility. The cult of celebrity that has been created around certain women politicians distorts the purpose for which we are elected.
>
> (1998: 19)

Julia Gillard: Australia's first female prime minister

When Julia Gillard assumed the prime ministership of Australia on 24 June 2010, after she successfully challenged Prime Minister Kevin Rudd (Leader 2007–09; briefly 2013) for the leadership of the Labor Party (Leader 2010–13). As the first woman to hold the office in Australia, Gillard faced an unprecedented amount of media scrutiny. From the very start, she incited controversy as the national press labelled her a traitor to her party following her desertion of Prime Minister Kevin Rudd. Consequently, discussions about her physical body became a site for 'open slather' – Australian slang for 'free-for-all' – by the Australian press.

Gillard herself stated that she had little interest in fashion (Grattan 2010: 13). When she was appointed opposition spokeswoman for population and immigration in 2001, she recalled a phone call from a former political aide who mentioned Cheryl Kernot's feather boa fiasco and warned her to think twice before accepting any proffered 'photo shoots'. Gillard response was clear that such outfits lay outside her connection to her work (Baird 2010: 2). In the end, it made no difference, as Gillard observed after becoming prime minister that she received '[e]ndless commentary about hair and make-up and clothes [...] I don't really worry about any of that'. She said that she did 'not want to be judged on how she looked', 'I seek to be judged by what I do' (Kearney 2010: 22).

Gillard's image before becoming prime minister could best be described as 'dull'. She tended to stick to suits in colours such as beige, and she wore her hair in a not-particularly flattering style. Her choices were frequently labelled 'asexual' and 'androgynous' (Jansens 2019: 212). Initial commentary on her style makeover as prime minister – for example, adopting a 'sleek' new hairstyle was described as 'modern' and 'less masculine' (Truman 2010: 7) and the wearing of brighter colours (Jansens 2019: 212) – was not all negative. She received a great deal of 'advice' from stylists who were interviewed by the media. One encouraged her to go for 'colour, colour, and more colour' (quoted in Van Den Berg 2010: 7). Another commented that the prime minister 'should opt for a clean, tailored look and steer clear of florals' (quoted in Carruthers 2010: 53). The same stylist also noted that she was 'pretty sure [Gillard's] a David Jones shopper' – suggesting her patronage of a slightly down-market department store was a bit ordinary – and that her look needed to 'be more crisp and streamlined – more beautifully tailored pants suits' (quoted in Carruthers 2010: 53).

Sadly, her memoirs recall the 'over the top' reactions by the press towards a buttoned-up beige trench coat she wore on her first full day in the job (Gillard 2014: 25). After media criticism for wearing beige, she subsequently came under fire for a colourful coat, which the press quickly dubbed the 'technicolour scream-coat'. One consultant interviewed by the *Daily Telegraph* complained that Gillard's 'clothes are distracting from the message' and declared that the jacket 'honestly looked like a cheap motel bedspread'. The same consultant added that Gillard should dress 'as if she is saying "This is how we run the country"', a message she apparently was not communicating when she wore such outfits. The article continued with a list of 'fashion "dos and don't's" for Julia', instructing her on such fashion matters as losing the big collars and cuffs, ditching trousers for skirt suits, picking pin stripes over patterns, avoiding wearing bright white, choosing autumnal colours and 'for casual occasions, try a classic wrap dress' (Toohey 2010: 3).

As the first female prime minister of Australia, Julia Gillard lacked a role model for her fashion, noting afterwards:

> Undoubtedly a male leader who does not meet a certain standard will be marked down. But that standard is such an obvious one: of regular weight, a well-tailored suit, neat hair, television-friendly glasses, trimmed eyebrows. Being the first female prime minister, I had to navigate what that standard was for a woman.
>
> (Gillard 2016: n.pag.)

Her failure to 'navigate this standard' came early in her leadership when Julia Gillard visited the state of Queensland, which had been devastated by unprecedented flooding from December 2010 to January 2011. Queensland's economy was mainly based on farming and mining, all of which sustained enormous losses and interruptions, and the capital city of Brisbane along with the greater Southeast of the state felt infrastructural damage. For a first in Queensland's history, an entire town was evacuated, and the regional losses included 35 confirmed human casualties, alongside an estimated 400,000 farm animals perished, with untold losses to wildlife (see van den Honert and McAneney 2011; Queensland Flood Commission of Inquiry 2012). As prime minister of Australia, Julia Gillard flew promptly to Brisbane to address both Queenslanders and the nation during this calamity.

As expected, the event was reported heavily via media when Gillard fronted a press conference alongside Queensland Premier Anna Bligh. Afterwards, some Australian journalists criticized Gillard's business-like attire as opposed to Bligh's more casual style. This played out in news reports by way of contrast between how Bligh and Gillard looked, with an emphasis on Gillard's inappropriateness for the occasion.[1] In *The Sydney Morning Herald* a journalist opined that Gillard 'struggles to strike the right note [...] for women politicians, it is always a fine balance between showing emotion and being perceived as too emotional. Gillard has perhaps erred towards being too cool' (Davies 2011b: 4). As evidence, the piece described Gillard being 'perfectly coiffed in a dark suit, nodding', unlike Bligh, who 'fronted the media in a utilitarian white shirt, hair looking like she had been working all night' (Davies 2011b: 4). It quoted a Queensland historian who said that Gillard 'has seemed wooden and not caring'; he conceded that she may care but 'doesn't appear to' (Davies 2011b: 4). *The Age* published a version of the piece (Davies 2011a: 4) with the same commentary on her appearance. A piece in *The Herald Sun* said that one of Gillard's mistakes was 'appearing in a black mourning suit' on her return from Queensland to Canberra (O'Brien 2011: n.pag.). Its headline – 'Anna Bligh outperforms Julia Gillard in the greatest leadership test of all' – summed up the tenor of reportage that used dress as evidence of the women's respective qualities as leaders. Journalists subsequently commended Bligh's leadership, especially celebrating her delivery of an impassioned speech where she identified proudly as a Queenslander, people known for their innate resilience (Williamson 2012). This favourable image of Bligh also demonstrated empathy as she visibly aligned herself with the people who had experienced the devastation.

The tabloids then considered whether Gillard should be given a special clothing allowance so that she could avoid such fashion faux pas. In 2010, Georgina Safe, writing for the right-leaning *The Australian* newspaper, which was owned then by NewsCorp and dubbed 'the Murdoch press' criticized not only the 'bedspread jacket', but also Gillard's wearing of a white suit jacket deemed to be 'unflattering' in how it flared and further, a suit with shiny striped fabric and piping that looked 'like a pair of pyjamas' (2010: 5).

Attacks on Gillard's fashion were not as extreme as the misogynist attacks she was subject to from the Liberal opposition and right-wing media commentators. As Johnson (2015: 304) has noted, Gillard was demonized throughout her time as prime minister with slogans such as 'ditch the witch'. Radio shock jock Alan Jones called for her to be put in a chaff bag and dumped at sea (Sawer 2013: 112). Finally, Jones went too far when he suggested that Julia Gillard's father 'died of shame' after viewing her so-called 'lies' in the Australian Parliament (Rourke 2012: n.pag.). The press went further when interrogating her partnership with unmarried partner, Timothy Mathieson, and his career as a professional hairdresser, suggesting his source of income challenged his manhood. And it followed that Gillard herself was likewise 'unnatural' by not marrying him and having a family. A careful comparison of Gillard's and Prime Minister Malcolm Turnbull's treatment – Turnbull similarly deposed a sitting prime minister of his own party to gain the leadership – reveals starkly just how different their treatment was by the media (Williams 2017). Even when Julia Gillard received positive remarks, there remained negative references to her gender, personal life, sexuality (Williams 2017: 561) and even her broad 'Aussie' accent (Hudson 2011). The emphasis on Gillard's fashion outlined the broader sexist discourse behind the media's constant commentary.

Where do things stand now?

Conclusion

Bethany Phillips-Peddlesden when discussing the masculine image of Australian Prime Minister Gough Whitlam concludes that 'we need to pay critical attention to the historically specific, and therefore contingent and mutable, enactments of masculinity and femininity on which Australian political leadership is based' (2019: 278). Fashion in women's leadership plays a critical role in shaping the performance of gender in the public sphere when filtered through public and media commentary. The media have played a critical role in framing how women politicians are viewed even as they seek to craft their own public image.

Gillard took office at a time when 'ostensibly the Australian sphere of parliament remain[ed] an environment infused with hegemonic masculinity' (Crawford and Pini 2010: 100). The media's critical evaluation of what Gillard wore, along with her hairstyles comprised a gendered reporting of her political performance (Joseph 2015; Williams 2017). However, she was hardly alone. As indicated by Vanessa Friedman writing in the *New York Times* Critic's Notebook (2017: 1–3) media attention to gender, politics and fashion intensified from 2010 to 2015, influenced by Michelle Obama alongside the stratospheric rise of fashion and its dictates expressed in social media (see Findlay 2012), where posters on social media 'literally dress [themselves] into view' (p. 201). In Australia, this scrutiny by the media intensified coinciding with and immediately following Gillard's prime ministership and also other women with leadership roles at the national level: Julie Bishop, who occupied various positions during this period, including Minister for Foreign Affairs (2013–18; Deputy Leader of the Liberal Party 2007–18) and Quentin Bryce, the first female Governor-General of Australia (2008–14) (Jansens 2019). The irony is not lost: as women rose to prominent positions in the antipodes, so their attire was brought to the forefront by the media.

While there is not the same frenzied focus on fashion as in the 1990s or when Julia Gillard was prime minister, women politicians still pay careful attention to what they wear. Sober colours and tailored fashions predominate for most women politicians on both sides of politics. Most probably try to sail under the radar when it comes to fashion, rather than calling attention to it (Gillard and Okono-Iweala 2020). Foreign Minister Marise Payne (formerly defence minister) has managed to avoid much commentary on her fashion choices – she sticks largely to darker colours and suit jackets and dark trousers – but she is also a low-profile politician who does little to cultivate a 'celebrity' image. Thus, she avoided being targeted for displaying ambitions as either leader or celebrity. But her predecessor as foreign minister Julie Bishop by contrast was well known for her interest in fashion, her presence on the social circuit and her preference for extremely high heels (see Plate iv). She was even known during her time as foreign minister for her 'fashion diplomacy', wearing Australian designers abroad so as to promote them on the world stage (Singer 2019: 17).

While some female politicians successfully make strategic use of fashion to draw public attention to themselves and to make public statements, this should never eclipse judging them on their on their merits and their skills. Unfortunately, today's constant media attention presents a double-edged sword for women who just want to get on with the job and succeed on their own merits. Writing over twenty years ago, the observation that '[b]eing allowed the mistakes and having the privileges of men is the key' to women's parity in the world of politics (Henderson 1999: 260). Clearly, women politicians in Australia have yet to reach this point.

NOTE

1. This section on Gillard's response to the flooding in Brisbane was authored by Denise N. Rall with additional references to Gillard's fashion, gender and responses to calamity while in office authored by Rosemary Williamson. The authors gratefully acknowledge her contributions.

REFERENCES

Anderson, Fleur (2016), 'The old bag o' fruit maketh the man: Comment', *The Australian Financial Review*, 9 April, p. 4.

Anon. (1943), 'Dame Enid Lyons wins Darwin', *Sydney Morning Herald*, 14 September.

Anon. (1946a), 'Paradise lost!', Examiner (Launceston), 31 July.

Anon. (1946b), 'Women contest Minister's clothing price list', *Advertiser* (Adelaide), 1 August.

Anon. (1949), 'Makers of shoddy goods "traitors"', *Mercury* (Hobart), 27 May.

Anon. (1953), 'Dame Enid's wardrobe for coronation', *Advocate* (Burnie, Tas.), 13 May.

Anon. (1998), 'Attired and emotional', *Sunday Telegraph*, 29 March.

Anon. (2010), 'Myer's place in history', 19 August, https://www.bendigoadvertiser.com.au/story/710520/myers-place-in-history/. Accessed 1 June 2021.

Anon. (2021), 'Hon Bronwyn Bishop MP – Former Member', Parliament of Australia, https://www.aph.gov.au/Senators_and_Members/Parliamentarian?MPID=SE4. Accessed 14 March 2021.

Australian Associated Press (AAP) (2006), 'Stott Despoja to quit politics', 23 October, https://www.smh.com.au/national/stott-despoja-to-quit-politics-20061023-gdonmu.html. Accessed 30 March 2021.

Baird, Julia (2004), *Media Tarts: How the Australian Press Frames Female Politicians*, Carlton North: Scribe.

Baird, Julia (2010), 'Lessons from sister who fell on the way', *Sydney Morning Herald*, 25 June.

Bowers, Peter (1990), 'The art of running last', *Sydney Morning Herald*, 3 March.

Carruthers, Fiona (2010), 'Gillard faces a grilling from the fashion police', *Australian Financial Review*, 12 July.

Coonan, Helen (1998), 'Time for a good look in the mirror', *Sydney Morning Herald*, 25 November.

Crawford, Mary and Pini, Barbara (2010), 'The Australian Parliament: A gendered organisation', *Parliamentary Affairs*, 64:1, pp. 82–105.

Davies, Anne (2011a), 'Bligh a white light beside the cool, coiffed Gillard', *The Age*, 13 January, p. 4.

Davies, Anne (2011b), 'Captain Bligh steers the ship in face of adversity', *The Sydney Morning Herald*, 13 January, p. 4.

Donaghue, Ngaire (2015), 'Who gets played by the "gender card"? A critical discourse analysis of coverage of Prime Minister Julia Gillard's sexism and misogyny speech in the Australian print media', *Australian Feminist Studies*, 30:84, pp. 161–78.

Donald, Peta and Henderson, Anna (2015), 'Bronwyn Bishop spends $5,000 on 80 km charter helicopter flight from Melbourne to Geelong', Australian Broadcasting Corporation (ABC), 15 July, https://www.abc.net.au/news/2015-07-15/bronwyn-bishop-spends-5000-dollars-80km-charter-flight/6622134. Accessed 22 April 2020.

Findlay, Rosie (2012), 'At one remove from reality: Style bloggers and outfit posts', *Australasian Journal of Popular Culture*, 1:2, pp. 197–208.

Friedman, Vanessa (2017), 'How clothes defined the First Lady', *Sunday Styles, The New York Times*, 18 January, pp. 1, 3.

Gare, Shelley (1998), 'Political covergirls find if the dress fits…', *The Australian*, 25 March.

Gillard, Julia (2014), *My Story*, North Sydney: Knopf.

Gillard, Julia and Nogozi Okono-Iweala (2020), 'The stand-out lessons from eight lives and eight hypotheses', *Women and Leadership: Real Lives, Real Lessons*, Penguin Random House Australia: Vintage, pp. 274–301.

Grattan, Michelle (2010), 'The special glow of power', *The Age*, 2 July.

Greer, Germaine (2012), '"Julia, you've got a big arse; so just get on with it!", "Mutilation and the Media Frenzy" broadcast, Q&A', *ABC Television*, 27 August, https://www.abc.net.au/qanda/mutilation-and-the-media-generation/10660564. Accessed 20 April 2020.

Hall, Ashley (2007), 'Costello takes credit for baby boom', broadcast on ABC's PM program, 27 June, https://www.abc.net.au/pm/content/2007/s1963979.htm Accessed 21 April 2020.

Hall, Lauren. J. and Ngaire Donaghue (2013), '"Nice girls don't carry knives": Constructions of ambition in media coverage of Australia's first female prime minister', *British Journal of Social Psychology*, 52:4, pp. 631–47.

Henderson, Anne (1999), *Getting Even: Women MPs on Life, Power and Politics*, Pymble, NSW: Harper Collins.

Henderson, Anne (2008), *Enid Lyons: Leading Lady to a Nation*, Sydney: Pluto Press.

Jansens, Freya (2019), 'Suit of power: Fashion, politics and hegemonic masculinity in Australia', *Australian Journal of Political Science*, 54:2, pp. 202–18.

Jenkins, Cathy (2003), 'A mother in cabinet: Dame Enid Lyons and the press', *Australian Journalism Review*, 25:1, pp. 181–96.

Johnson, Carol (2015), 'Playing the gender card: The uses and abuses of gender in Australian politics', *Politics and Gender*, 11, pp. 291–319.

Jones, Andrea (1994), 'Signs of life behind the mask', *Sun Herald*, 27 March.

Joseph, Sue (2015), 'Australia's first female prime minister and gender politics: Long-form counterpoints', *Journalism Practice*, 9:2, pp. 250–64.

Hudson, Phillip (2011), 'Aussie from her head to her toes', *Herald-Sun*, 30 April.

Kearney, Simon (2010), 'It's not about looks, says Julia', *Sunday Mail*, 12 December.

Kernot, Cheryl (2002), *Speaking for Myself Again: Four Years with Labor and Beyond Sydney*, Sydney: Harper Collins Australia.

Laugesen, Amanda (2019), 'Changing "man made language": Sexist language and feminist linguistic activism in Australia', in M. Arrow and A. Woollacott (eds), *Everyday Revolutions: Remaking Gender, Sexuality and Culture in 1970s Australia*, Canberra: ANU Press, pp. 241–60.

Lyons, Dame Enid (1951), 'The importance of clothes', *Advertiser* (Adelaide), 12 September.

Lyons, Dame Enid (1972), *Among the Carrion Crows*, Adelaide: Rigby.

Nicholson, Peter (1998), 'Kernot asking Labor leader, Kim Beasley, for 'policy guidance' in the lead up to the 1998 Federal Election', *The Australian*, 30 March.

O'Brien, Susie (2011), 'Anna Bligh outperforms Julia Gillard in the greatest leadership test of all', *The Herald Sun*, 14 January, https://www.heraldsun.com.au/news/opinion/anna-bligh-outperforms-julia-gillard-in-the-greatest-leadership-test-of-all/news-story/1e1bf24ff047a98d892df5b84d1dea80?sv=4bb75e9f68d8a0c7e556845c411b24f8. Accessed 6 February 2020.

O'Reilly, David (1998), *Cheryl Kernot: The Woman Most Likely*, Milsons Point: Random House.

Phillips-Peddlesden, Bethany (2019), '"A race of intelligent super-giants": The Whitlams, gendered bodies and political authority in modern Australia', in M. Arrow and A. Woollacott (eds), *Everyday Revolutions: Remaking Gender, Sexuality and Culture in 1970s Australia*, Canberra: ANU Press, pp. 261–78.

Queensland Floods Commission of Inquiry – Final Report 2012, 16 March, http://www.floodcommission.qld.gov.au/. Accessed 14 February 2020.

Ross, Karen (2002), 'Women's place in "male" space: Gender and effect in parliamentary contexts', *Parliamentary Affairs*, 55, pp. 189–201.

Rourke, Alison (2012) 'Alan Jones apologises for latest Julia Gillard tirade', *The Guardian*, 1 October, https://www.theguardian.com/world/2012/oct/01/alan-jones-apology-julia-gillard. Accessed 14 April 2020.

Safe, Georgina (2010), 'Julia moving her wardrobe forward', *The Australian*, 27 July.

Sawer, Marion (2013), 'Misogyny and misrepresentation: Women in Australian parliaments', *Political Science*, 65:1, pp. 105–17.

Seager, Helen (1944), 'Dame Enid Lyons tells of some crises in her public career', *Argus* (Melbourne), 18 July.

Singer, Melissa (2019), 'No grey zone for black and white judge Bishop', *The Age*, 2 November.

Smark, Peter (1993), 'It's time to bury Ming, and mercilessly', *Sydney Morning Herald*, 17 March.

Toohey, Brian (1998), 'Kernot soap won't wash', *Australian Financial Review*, 24 March.

Toohey, Paul (2010), 'Does a technicolour screamcoat prove our PM needs an allowance?', *Daily Telegraph*, 6 July.

Truman, Peter (2010), 'Corporate cut very chic', *Gold Coast Bulletin*, 25 June.

Van Acker, Elizabeth (2003), 'Media representations of women politicians in Australia and New Zealand: High expectations, hostility or stardom', *Policy and Society*, 22:1, pp. 116–36.

Van Den Berg, Lucie (2010), 'Why reds are turning heads', *Herald-Sun*, 26 June.

Van den Honert, Robin C and John McAneney (2011), 'The 2011 Brisbane floods: Causes, impacts and implications', *Water*, 3:4, pp. 1149–73.

Williams, Blair (2017), 'A gendered media analysis of the prime ministerial ascension of Gillard and Turnbull: He's "taken back the reins" and "she's a backstabbing murderer"', *Australian Journal of Political Science*, 52:4, pp. 550–64.

Williamson, Rosemary (2012), 'Breeding them tough north of the border: Resilience and heroism as rhetorical responses to the 2011 Queensland floods', *Social Alternatives*, 31:3, pp. 33–38.

Wright, Shane (2021), 'Low fertility sparked budget fear, brought on baby bonus', *The Sydney Morning Herald*, Cabinet Papers, 23 January, p. 13.

5

'Dressing Up' Two Democratic First Ladies: Fashion as Political Performance in America

Denise N. Rall,

Jo Coghlan,

Lisa J. Hackett and Annita Boyd

As stated by the Smithsonian Institute during an exhibition entitled 'First Ladies' fashions, 'clothing […] illustrate[s] the personal style of a First Lady […][and] the official style of a presidential administration' (Anon. 2016a: n.pag.). An American First Lady, argues Anderson, 'influences conceptions of American womanhood' and by 'virtue of their husband's elections[,] First Ladies become *sites* for the symbolic negotiation of female identity' (2004: 18, original emphasis). Clearly, all First Ladies hold a place of symbolic significance in American political culture. First, she represents the emblematic separation of women between the public and private spheres; second, her marriage affords her the unique status as a direct political influence on the American President. In American culture, First Ladies have functioned as 'symbols of traditional white middle to upper class femininity in America' (Anderson 2004: 18).

Both Hillary (Diane Rodham) Clinton (1947–present) and Michelle (LaVaughn Robinson) Obama (1964–present) adopted a style of dress that situated their identities as women in power during their tenure as First Ladies. As a result, Hillary (as First Lady from 1993–2001) adopted an eclectic look that challenged the conventions of the Republican women who preceded her. Less concerned with the domesticity of the White House, her style signalled her independence, individuality and agency. As both a feminist and a lawyer, Hillary's style expressed that she was an active political participant not only in American society but also in the inner workings of the Clinton Administration. When asked during the 1992 presidential campaign about her roles as a lawyer and likely First Lady, Hillary replied that she intended to have an 'independent life and to make a difference', a direct departure from the 'traditional role' played by previous First Ladies (Clinton cited in Anderson 2004: 17). However, Hillary Clinton was not immune to the more feminine style apparently required for a political wife. As early as the late 1970s, she had already transformed her appearance in terms of being a wife of a Southern Governor who refused to wear make-up and kept her maiden name (Anderson and Sheeler 2005: 26).

Michelle Obama similarly adopted fashions to situate her role in American society. However, in her case, not only gender but also race and class played a role in shaping her performance (Guerrero 2011). The socio-political conventions of an American First Lady were previously white, and so a racial re-negotiation was required to contextualize the place of Michelle Obama in American political life (Williams 2009). Perhaps in response to the novelty of a Black First Lady, Michelle expressed her ethnic background early in the Obama administration by returning the First Lady narrative back to the more normative confines of family and domesticity (Dillaway and Paré 2008). To do this, she presented a middle-class casualness by wearing mass retail items from popular chain stores and the use of emerging American designers for her formal political appearances.

Michelle Obama's tenure as First Lady had further constraints: she inherited the legacy of the United States' changed political landscape following the attacks of September 11, 2001. The 'Buy American' and the 'Support the Troops' logos on badges, bumper stickers and in shop windows dominated many retail venues (see Bell 2002). As a result, Michelle was constrained to adopt an American-based style, rather than look towards European designers and, when she did, it was to purpose. Her bona fide American values were put on show during her revelation to television host Jay Leno where she was wearing a J. Crew sweater, saying, 'Ladies we know J. Crew. You can get some good stuff online' (Clifford 2008: n.pag.). This simple statement, Friedman argues, started 'a new approach to the story of dress and power' for American political figures (2017: 1). As the style critic for the *New York Times*, Friedman comments:

> Mrs. Obama's dress choices were often labeled 'sartorial diplomacy' and 'democratic', and they were that; she made something of an art out of pairing designers with countries during state dinners or trips [...] but above all, her wardrobe was representative of the country her husband wanted to lead. It was about the melting pot and the establishment; the 1 per cent and the accessible. There was something in her closet for everyone, yet she was beholden to no designer.
>
> (2017: 3)

When 'dressing up' for their positions as American First Ladies, both Hillary and Michelle struggled with issues of individual identity, agency and power that were re-negotiated through their choices in fashion (Barnard 2014).

The role of the American First Lady

While the role of the US President is outlined in Article II of the Constitution, there is no mention of the First Lady. The First Lady is a spouse (and to date only women have taken up this role). She is not elected, has no official title, no statutory responsibilities and earns no salary. She holds the position solely by virtue of her marriage to the President during his tenure in office (Seals Nevergold and Brooks-Bertram 2009; Winfield 1997a). Until 1870, the wives of American Presidents were referred to as 'Mrs President'. However, the suffix 'Mrs' did not properly distinguish a First Lady from the influx of industrial wage-earning working wives who were likewise titled as 'Mrs', and so the prestigious status of a White House wife was dignified with the term of 'Lady' (Welter 1975), the nomenclature borrowed from the English aristocracy. Historically, First Ladies became symbolically significant in American society only after their marriages (Seals Nevergold and Brooks-Bertram 2009). As such, the First Lady is valued in America's social imagination as the emotional supporter of her husband, and the carer and protector of their (if any) children (Stacey 1994); the American public are resistant to a First Lady being publically involved in anything more than ceremony (Oles-Acevedo 2012: 35). This, argues Gardetto, 'contributes to women's subordination by supporting the idea that women's proper place is in the home' (1997: 226) – even if this home is the White House. The national spotlight on the First Lady as the White House homemaker does not negate her influence, but her behaviour is carefully monitored. She can try to shape policy, but only in a very subtle and dignified way (Anderson and Baxendale 1992).

Until recently, public expectations have continued to focus on the First Lady's ability to act as 'a single universally accepted ideal for US womanhood' (Campbell 1996: 191), denoting each First Lady as a site of an authentic American woman (Anderson 2005). Each First Lady serves as a 'metaphor for her generation of women' and ontologically as an authentic modern American woman (White 2011: 11), arguably a symbolic construct that has never existed (Campbell 1998: 15). Yet, each First Lady has also become a negotiated 'site' for American womanhood, representing either the virtues of the family, or the Nation, or even the values of their 'husband's administration' (Friedman 2017: 3). Outside of her family role, the public persona of the First Lady has long depended on a façade of the gracious hostess, as she takes on the primary guardianship of the White House, its appearance and its functions: its renovations, gardens and surroundings, and its entertainments for visiting Heads of State and others (Truman 1996).

Since the twentieth century, the First Lady's role has been viewed through photos, news reports and gossip columns about her engagements during both her domestic and public duties. For both Hillary and Michelle, this social commentary on their individual personalities was reflected in their choice of clothing, and as a result, was constrained (or not) within the bounds of a normative and appropriately dressed body (Entwistle 2000: 338). The dominance of these visual images defines their functionality as both 'ordinary' domestic women and political personages (Baker and Chozick 2014). Referencing Judith Butler, dress affords the ability to communicate a political point of view and/or allows the wearer to take on an authority (not previously granted) in the outside world (1988: 521, cited in Findlay 2012: 203).

Here, it is argued that in both their dress and their actions, Hillary Clinton and Michelle Obama rewrote the rules that delimited the contested 'site' of the idealized American First Lady. As a result, the public image of what a First Lady should be, or could become, migrated from the previous gentility of an upper class, white, family-oriented and politically marginalized woman to a new breed of American First Lady who could be more professionally qualified, equality-based, racially diverse and feminist in orientation. The first section of the discussion considers how American First Ladies either project or reject an idealization of American womanhood. The second section explores the tensions of domestic responsibilities and the roles of a career in First Ladies. The third section explores how Michelle Obama re-negotiated her role as the first African American First Lady in the White House. We conclude with a discussion of the legacy of fashion and how it influences social and political identities of women in positions of power.

American First Ladies' gender performance and identity

First Ladies are seen as widely scrutinized objects, carrying their femaleness on the national stage as a symbolic burden (Watson 2003). Her titled role as First Lady requires each of these women to normatively perform gender, a process directly linked to notions of body, appearance and dress. She must conform to the notion of the 'ideal women' (Kahl 2009: 316). To rebel against gender norms would bring her into conflict with American popular culture, wherein physical appearance is paramount, so that the myth of female beauty is continually perpetuated (Tate 2012: 234; Wolf 1991). This Beauty Queen standard, argues Anderson, is 'used tacitly in media narratives to prove political women's supposed authenticity as women':

> When political women resist traditional beauty standards, it's easier to stereotype them as radical feminists, making them seem threatening to some voters. Because the Beauty Queen knows how to adhere to society's rules for appearance, it follows that she will not use public power improperly. However, a woman who challenges conventions of appearance is signalling her intention to undo other traditional standards.
>
> (2008: n.pag.)

It can be argued that both Hillary and Michelle enlarged the public's view of the role of First Ladies, while remaining subject to gender performance, especially women's pre-assigned roles as supportive wives and mothers. Women, as First Ladies are not free to perform their own gender because to do so risks social and political sanctions (White 2015: 319). The embedded nature of gender performance is conformity. This, argues White, 'masks the contradiction and volatile nature' (2015: 318) of gender performance because to resist performing appropriately as female results in social punishment.

Clothing plays a role here as garments 'have an ability to *pick up* subjects, to mould and shape them both physically and socially, to constitute subjects through their power as material memories' (Jones and Stallybrass 2000: 2–3, original emphasis). While cultures and clothing change, dress remains as a situated bodily practice socially embedded and considered 'fundamental to the microsocial order' (Entwistle 2000: 325). Sociologically, the dressed body posits the existence of social and political categories and reinforces and sustains views about identities (Douglas 1979). Clothing, far from being a choice or freedom, exists as a socially and commercially regulated practice (Klein 2000; Ferguson [2011] 2012). What this means is that the body becomes 'heavily mediated by culture' and becomes a 'symbol of its cultural location' (Entwistle 2000: 327). As Jennifer Craik has observed, the dressed body is a 'communicative device that speaks to observers and demands a response and a connection' (2014: 5). Hence, clothing acts as a visible envelope of the self and serves as a metaphor for identity (Davis 1992). Finkelstein agrees, arguing that how we dress is a sign of identity and, hence, how we dress is seen as 'symbolic of the individual's status and morality' (1991: 128). For Entwistle, this means that the dressed body is a 'presentation' (2000: 325) imbued with discursive meanings and as such the dressed body is a key site for interrogating gender performance and its articulation of an 'idealised identity of womanhood' (2000: 327–28). An analysis of Hillary's and Michelle's fashion reveals that the dressed bodies of both women were embedded with significant meaning about their own identity and, as women in power, they sought to restructure the 'ideal' American woman.

The career issue for Hillary Clinton

Both Hillary Clinton and Michelle Obama came into the role of First Lady as working professionals rather than wives and mothers. However, they arrived at the White House during very different political landscapes (pre- and post-9/11), and each faced her own set of challenges regarding her identity as female and her agency in the role of First Lady. While both First Ladies chose clothing to situate them authentically within American fashion trends, Hillary's garments were judged as quite reactive to the norm. To locate her sense of fashion, it is important to consider her previous incarnations during the Clintons' long political careers.

Her decision to keep her maiden name during William Jefferson 'Bill' Clinton's 1980 race for the Governor of Arkansas was blamed for her husband's defeat, and later, when she adopted the surname Clinton, she was criticized for capitulating (Jamieson 1995: 23). However, Hillary had already begun the transformation from Hillary Rodham to that of Hillary Clinton (later, Hillary Rodham Clinton). As the First Lady of Arkansas, Hillary chose outfits from local designer Barbara Jean, a set of partners who opened an emporium in West Little Rock in 1972 (Anon. 2009: 43). She also changed her hairstyle frequently and stopped wearing glasses.

The First Iraq War was already underway when Bill Clinton came into office in January 1993. This initial 'War on Terror' was a time of divisive American politics. Early in the first Clinton administration (1993–97), the media could not easily define Hillary, 'except for noting violations of standard behaviour for a First Lady' (Winfield 1997b: 250). Hillary chose an eclectic style of multi-coloured, mixed textures in her clothing and ostentatious jewellery and accessories that marked her as 'bold', employing the Dominican-born designer Oscar de la Renta (1932–2014) for his vibrant palette. Shortly before his death, Hillary Clinton presented him with the Carnegie Hall's Medal of Excellence and joked, 'this man has been working for more than 20 years to turn me into a fashion icon, despite [my] best efforts' (Hyland 2014: n.pag.). Her style was based on her choice to have an 'independent life and to make a difference' (Clinton cited in Anderson 2004: 17).

In 1992, Hillary's feminism was used to position her as an 'unruly woman', an 'intimidating feminist' and a 'nagging wife' (Anderson 2008: n.pag.). Her appearance as a well-educated, career-orientated and independent woman was used against her to label her a 'radical feminist, greedy attorney [...] and co-president' (Oles-Acevedo 2012: 34). The 'co-president' barb had actually originated with Bill Clinton, who quipped during the 1992 presidential election that the Clinton presidency would deliver a 'buy one, get one free' deal, which was fulfilled when Hillary Clinton was appointed by her husband to lead health care reform (Public Broadcasting Service [PBS] 2016: n.pag.). The American press, bolstered by the power of the American Medical Society and medical insurance companies, viewed Hillary's takeover on health care reform as offensive (PBS 2016).

Furthermore, her expertise conflicted with 'authentic' American womanhood, particularly in her signature garb: the pantsuit. Somehow, the Hillary pantsuit became the most ridiculed outfit ever worn by a First Lady (Campbell 1998). Extreme right-wing talk radio hosts and a fashion show co-host, Tim Gunn, insisted that her pantsuits meant that although she was not a lesbian, she dressed like one (Krupnick 2011). Later, an article in *Slate* summarized that her 'sense of style has been criticized for as long as she has been on the national scene' along with 'the "rumours" of secret lesbianism, supposedly evidenced by her pantsuits and her (actually not always full-throated) support of gay rights' (Anon. 2016b: n.pag.). In a final nod to the infamous Hillary pantsuit, Bill Clinton was reported to wear 'a fetching pantsuit' to accompany Hillary's nomination for US President at the 2016 Democratic National Convention (Avins 2016: n.pag.).

As the former First Lady of Arkansas and the American First Lady, and a mother and a lawyer, Hillary Clinton did not 'live in a world of either-or, however, but of a both-and' (Jamieson 1995: 22). She became a surrogate for that which was incompatible: an educated woman and a mother. She also embodied the figure of a powerful unelected woman: the first First Lady to have an office in the White House and, further, a defined role in American public policy. The public reaction, and especially that of the right-wing press, was unfavourable (Campbell 1998). Hillary Clinton (particularly in the first eighteen months of Bill Clinton's presidency) did not give lifestyle interviews or comment on her social activities. Only when it became apparent that she had an 'image problem' did she revert to the 'safety net' or 'protective shield' afforded by appearing in women's magazines and talking about women's issues and framing herself as a traditional wife, mother and national hostess (Winfield 1997b: 251; Bystrom et al. 1999). Early in the first Clinton administration, the media could not easily define her 'except for noting violations of standard behaviour for a First Lady' (Winfield 1997b: 250). What resonated in the national mood was that Americans chose to 'fear women with power' and to 'admire women with the status of victims' (Parry-Giles 2000: 221).

The notion of 'being feminine' means 'adopting a personal or self-disclosing tone', and yet Hillary Clinton's commanding tone was viewed as strident (Campbell 1998: 6). In her later incarnation as a presidential candidate, her clothing remained an issue (see Plate xii). For Jamieson, this presents the double-bind that public women have to negotiate: 'The negotiation is figuring out how to walk a fine line between being regarded as too feminine [...] or too tough'

(1995: 121). In the binds of woman-mother-wife-lawyer and policy-maker, Hillary Clinton was probably the 'most maligned' of all First Ladies (Beasley 2005: xi). This trend of public condemnation for the fashion choices of a female political figure was echoed by Germaine Greer's diatribe against Julia Gillard's 'suitcoats', during her service as the first female prime minister of Australia from 2010 to 2013 (Greer 2012).

Hillary Clinton's professionalism reacted against previous conservative administrations and challenged the preconceived role of a proper American First Lady. Further complexity in the role of an American First Lady arrived with the election of Barack Obama (Barack Hussein Obama II) on 4 November 2008.

The first African American First Lady: The race body

Far from the idealized 'post-racial' politics that were heralded with the election of President Obama, 'if anything, race and racial attitudes have become more salient during the Obama presidency' (Knuckey and Kim 2016: 382). Michelle Obama, the first African American First Lady (2009–17), embodied a complex terrain of racial divisiveness that has tainted American politics since the American Civil War (1861–65). A generation younger than Hillary Clinton, Michelle Obama was similarly educated as a lawyer, with an independent career that mostly went unnoticed, for two reasons. First, the American public was more comfortable with career women sixteen years after Hillary Clinton served as First Lady (McGinley and Boyd 2009: 722). Next, as the first African American First Lady, her race inscribed her body and her working-class background challenged the historical narratives of previous American First Ladies in a very different way. As quoted in Anderson, Michelle Obama challenged the ideal of the First Lady as embodying 'traditional *white* middle-to-upper class femininity' (2004: 18, original emphasis). For both of the Obamas, race was the defining issue of their tenure in office (Marable and Clarke 2009; Winfield 1997a).

From the previous ideals postulated as essential to a First Lady, Michelle Obama's body, more so than any other First Lady, was framed as atypical. As an African American woman, Michelle does not embody the physical norm of a genteel First Lady (Dworkin 2003). As Shirley Tate explains,

> the white body continues to be the somatic norm, even if it is no longer judicially or constitutionally supported, because the racial contract demarcates and reserves space for its first-class citizens. Michelle [Obama] causes severe disorientation because, as a member of the abject outside that is America's racialised internal colony, she is now inside the First Lady space. As a body out of place Michelle Obama shows

us how Anglo-whiteness is being sustained as the proper location of the First Lady even though the American dream insists 'anyone can get there'.

(2012: 232–33)

Michelle's 'bodily hexis', that is, her location in the White House as wife of the American President enabled her to belong. However, once in the White House her body 'disturbs the traditional imagining of her position and will always encounter the questioning, categorising gaze of whiteness, the question of "what is she doing here?"' denigrated her appearance in society's view (Tate 2012: 233).

As a result, Michelle Obama's body parts also came under scrutiny. She has been described as having an 'uncommon figure for an American First Lady', characterized by a 'long, lean, athletic frame' and her 'buff biceps', which were often revealed by the sleeveless dresses that she favoured (see Plate xiii). Particularly, the commentary on her arms erupted in popular articles entitled 'Sleevegate', 'The right to bare arms' and 'The upper body stimulus plan', suggesting that 'a little more [clothing] coverage is appropriate' (see Fuller [2009] 2011: n.pag.). During the height of this public 'controversy', McAllister argues that the

bodily standards by which [Michelle] Obama is being measured are clearly gendered, but they are also classed, animated by anxiety over the sight of muscular arms (fit for menial labour, but unfit for display in polite company) on the figure of the First Lady.

(2009: 312)

Therefore, African American women in the political sphere have become 'effaced or distorted' (James 2009: 2). The feminist bell hooks notes that 'racist stereotypes of the strong, superhuman Black woman are operative myths in the minds of many white women' (1984: 24).

As First Lady, Michelle Obama was required to perform a 'transracial, upper middle class and heterosexual identity' or risk 'censure' (Tate 2012: 235). Her innate fashion sense, along with guidance from aide Meredith Koop (Friedman 2017: 3), assisted her to project a dignified appearance as a First Lady through her attire, make-up, hair styling and demeanour. It is notable that Michelle Obama eschewed the unfeminine Hillary Clinton pantsuit. When interrogated by a reporter, she replied, 'You know, I'm not that into labels [...] I wouldn't identify as feminist' (cited in White 2011: 13–14). Instead, Michelle Obama's image signifies elements of 'post-feminism' as she is 'portrayed as a strong woman who can be interested in ostensible frivolities (as a penchant for fashion is understood to be un-, anti-, or post-feminist) and yet not be dismissed as frivolous' (Joseph 2011: 60). Her clothing choices, both ready-to-wear off-the-rack and high-end fashion, show her style as 'outside' the feminist framework, opening up the discussion of fashion to 'embrace the outside' post-feminist stance (Joseph 2011: 61).

Perhaps responding to her unprecedented status as the first African American First Lady, Michelle (with young daughters) first limited herself to the more 'acceptable' frameworks of family and domesticity (Dillaway and Paré 2008). Her clothing reflected a low-key attitude towards the formality once expected of a First Lady. Michelle dressed in off-the-shelf department store fashion from Target, Macy's, Neiman Marcus, J. Crew and Tracey Reese. Two examples of this include Michelle Obama's 2008 appearance on *The Ellen DeGeneres Show* (2003–present) wearing a J. Crew floral dress, and her 2011 appearance on the *The Tonight Show with Jay Leno* (1992–2009) wearing a $34.95 H&M polka-dot dress. This coded Michelle Obama as an everyday woman, normatively performing the pragmatic and utilitarian roles associated with American middle-class womanhood (Joseph 2011: 71–72). This style of dress alleviated the conflicts of taking up a feminist standpoint to maintain the professional profile of a career woman as experienced by Hillary Clinton.

However, Michelle did not reject high-end fashion and she regularly wore designs from Vera Wang and Ralph Lauren. Her most lauded fashion selections came from previously unknown 'hyphenated American' designers such as Jason Wu (Chinese-Canadian) and Cuban heritage-American Narciso Rodriguez (Tate 2012: 231; Brown 2012: 248). Michelle Obama, via her clothing, not only coded herself as a utilitarian everyday woman often wearing off-the-shelf cardigans, she also wore the sleeves rolled up to express a 'can-do' attitude. She also blended mass-produced fashion with high-end fashion, as evident in American *Vogue*, where she coupled an off-the-rack J. Crew sweater with a formal full-length Michael Kors ball skirt in a photograph titled 'American Ideal' (Anon. 2013).

In order, then, to function as an appropriate First Lady, Michelle's race had to be reclassified, which was accomplished through her astute sense of style. The result was that her Blackness was 'beautified, intellectualized and domesticated' into a 'new configuration of patriotism and what it means to be an American' (Madison 2009: 324). Through her dressed body, she 'embodied a new symbol of (post)black womanhood' (Madison 2009: 324).

The legacy of fashion

The legacy of fashion lies in its enduring sense of meaning, not only for those who consume, wear and discard it but also regarding how clothing reveals one's identity and one's embedded sense of self to others. That said, fashion also presents a case study for how post-modernity addresses the worldwide fascination for instant consumerism. As Rocamora and Smelik have established:

fashion [exists] as both material culture and symbolic system (Karamura 2005) [...] as a commercial industry [...] a socio-cultural force bound up with the dynamics of modernity and post-modernity; and an intangible system of signification [...] [which] coalesce through practices of production, consumption, distribution and representation.

(2015: 2)

For American First Ladies, dress becomes scrutinized by the public and social media users as a political statement about the role, positioning and appropriateness of their attire in a dynamic landscape of American national identity and economic status in the world. The dressed-and-displayed body of the American First Lady is continually reviewed in the media during events that reflect on international diplomacy and more 'private' confessional moments projected during appearances on broadcast television and circulated via social media.

Conclusion

In conclusion, Hillary Clinton and Michelle Obama came to the White House in conflicted eras in American history. Both women appeared determined to re-shape the idealization that the First Lady is a white, upper-middle class and domesticated woman, in the process opening the door to further diversity in their ability to realize their personal career objectives, family values and moral principles. At times, their ability to act as dressed-and-displayed bodies within a dynamic political landscape and contrary to expectations was fraught with difficulty.

First, Hillary Clinton's role of First Lady confounded expectations by coming to the White House as a professional woman who did not choose to give up her career and adopted the male-gendered pantsuit as her working attire. Hillary chose a style that challenged the conventions of the Republican women who preceded her. Rather than expressing her domesticity within the White House, her style signalled her independence, individuality and agency. As both a feminist and a lawyer, Hillary's clothing expressed her active political participation in the inner-workings of the Clinton Administration. This is not a trivial concern; it is possible that Hillary Clinton's fashion style, as portrayed in 'shock jock' radio and television commentary, influenced her loss of the American 2016 Presidential election.

Subsequently, Michelle Obama confounded all expectations of an appropriate First Lady by the unmistakable fact of her colour. As American First Ladies were all previously white, Michelle was required to negotiate her racial heritage within American political life. Early in the Obama administration, Michelle expressed her ethnic background aligned to the more normative idea of family and domesticity. She presented a middle-class casualness to fashion by wearing mass retail items from popular chain stores and selected clothing from emerging American designers for her formal political appearances. Further, as an African American, Michelle Obama will always represent a watershed in American presidential history; her tenure will always denote First Ladies 'before' and 'after' her arrival in the White House (Spillers 2009: 308). Both her exuberant uptake of glamourous fashion and her commitment to the values of middle America through wearing off-the-rack garments reflected not only the values of her husband's presidency, but her own commitment to a wider scope of dress for women in politics. As Friedman, style critic for the *New York Times*, recently summed up:

> The twin conditions of the historical nature of this presidency and the fact it occurred alongside the rise of social media, which turned every public second into a sharable, comment-worth moment, combined to create a new reality where every appearance mattered. Not everyone listened to all of the speeches or read the analysis or considered the context. But everyone paused for a moment to *assess the visual* [...] If you know everyone is going to see what you wear and judge it, then what you wear becomes fraught with meaning. Certainly Mrs. Obama's significance as a contemporary role model goes far beyond her image, but no one understood the role of fashion, and the potential uses of that, better than the First Lady.
>
> (2017: 3, original emphasis)

These two American First Ladies offer another way forward. Their style served personal goals of self-definition and also expressed the importance of agency for women of political importance to 'dress up' to take on prominent positions in leadership, rather than to serve previous conservative ideologies about what is 'appropriate' in fashion for women in power.

REFERENCES

Anderson, Alice and Baxendale, Hadley (1992), *Behind Every Successful President: The Hidden Power and Influence of America's First Ladies*, New York: David A. Boehm Productions.

Anderson, Karrin Vasby (2004), 'The First Lady: A site of "American womanhood"', in M. Wertheimer (ed.), *Leading Ladies of the White House: Communication Strategies of Notable Twentieth-Century First Ladies*, London: Rowman & Littlefield, pp. 17–30.

Anderson, Karrin Vasby (2008), 'Framing gender: Pioneers, beauty queens and unruly women', *Communication Currents*, 3:5, https://www.natcom.org/CommCurrentsArticle.aspx?id=1083. Accessed 25 June 2016.

Anderson, Karrin Vasby and Sheeler, Kristina Horn (2005), *Governing Codes: Gender, Metaphor and Political Identity*, Lanham: Lexington Books.

Anon. (2009), 'Barbara/Jean Ltd', *Inviting Arkansas*, July, p. 43.

Anon. (2013), 'American ideal: Michelle Obama', *Vogue*, April, http://www.vogue.com/slide show/759100/michelle-obama-april-2013-photos/#2. Accessed 31 March 2017.

Anon. (2016a), 'First Ladies' fashions', National Museum of American History, The Smithsonian Institute, http://americanhistory.si.edu/first-ladies/first-ladies-fashions. Accessed 27 June 2016.

Anon. (2016b), 'Hillary Clinton isn't a lesbian – but she dresses like one', *Slate*, 15 January, http://www.slate.com/blogs/outward/2016/01/15/decoding_hillary_clinton_s_style_choices. html. Accessed 27 June 2016.

Avins, Jenni (2016), 'Hillary Clinton's husband wore a fetching pantsuit to honor her nomination for US president', 27 July, https://qz.com/743526/hillary-clintons-husband-wore-a-fetching-pantsuit-to-honor-her-nomination-for-us-president. Accessed 31 March 2016.

Baker, Peter and Chozick, Amy (2014), 'Hillary Clinton's history as a First Lady: Powerful but not always deft', *New York Times*, 5 December, https://www.nytimes.com/2014/12/06/us/poli tics/hillary-clintons-history-as-first-lady-powerful-but-not-always-deft.html?_r=0. Accessed 27 March 2017.

Barnard, Malcolm (2014), *Fashion Theory: An Introduction*, London: Routledge.

Beasley, Maurine (2005), *First Ladies and The Press: The Unfinished Partnership of the Media Age*, Evanston: Northwestern University Press.

Bell, Diane (2002), 'Good and evil: At home and abroad', in S. Hawthorne and B. Winter (eds), *September 11, 2001: Feminist Perspectives*, Melbourne: Spinifex Press, pp. 432–49.

Brown, Caroline (2012), 'Marketing Michelle: Mommy politics and post-feminism in the age of Obama', *Comparative American Studies*, 10:2&3, pp. 239–54.

Butler, Judith (1988), 'Performative acts and gender constitution: An essay in phenomenology and feminist theory', *Theatre Journal*, 40:4, pp. 519–31.

Bystrom, Dianne, McKinnon, Lori and Chaney, Carole (1999), 'First ladies and the fourth estate: Media coverage of Hillary Clinton and Elizabeth Dole in the 1996 presidential campaign', in L.L. Kaid and D. Bystorm (eds), *The Electronic Election: Perspectives on the 1996 Campaign Communication*, Mahwah: Lawrence Erlbaum Associates, pp. 81–96.

Campbell, Karlyn Kohrs (1996), 'The rhetorical presidency: A two person career', in M.J. Medhurst (ed.), *Beyond the Rhetorical Presidency*, College Station: Texas A & M University Press, pp. 179–95.

Campbell, Karlyn Kohrs (1998), 'The discursive performance of femininity: Hating Hillary', *Rhetoric & Public Affairs*, 1:1, pp. 1–19.

Clifford, Stephanie (2008), 'J. Crew benefits as Mrs. Obama wears the brand', 16 November, *The New York Times*, https://www.nytimes.com/2008/11/17/business/media/17crew.html Accessed 31 March 2021.

Craik, Jennifer (2014), 'Contextualising fashion and war within popular culture', in D.N. Rall (ed.), *Fashion and War in Popular Culture*, Bristol: Intellect, pp. 5–8.

Davis, Fred (1992), *Fashion, Culture and Identity*, Chicago: University of Chicago Press.

Dillaway, Heather and Paré, Elizabeth (2008), 'Locating mothers: How cultural debates about stay-at-home versus working mothers define women and home', *Journal of Family Issues*, 29:4, pp. 437–64.

Douglas, Mary (1979), *Implicit Meanings: Essays in Anthropology*, London: Routledge.

Dworkin, Shari (2003), '"Holding back": Negotiating a glass ceiling on women's muscular strength', in R. Weitz (ed.), *The Politics of Women's Bodies: Sexuality, Appearance and Behavior*, New York: Oxford University Press, pp. 219–39.

Entwistle, Joanne (2000), 'Fashion and the fleshy body: Dress as embodied practice', *Fashion Theory*, 4:3, pp. 323–48.

Ferguson, Niall ([2011] 2012), *Civilization: The West and the Rest*, London: Penguin Books.

Findlay, Rosie (2012), 'At one remove from reality: Style bloggers and outfit posts', *Australasian Journal of Popular Culture*, 1:2, pp. 197–208.

Finkelstein, Joanne (1991), *The Fashioned Self*, Hoboken: Wiley.

Friedman, Vanessa (2017), 'How clothes defined the First Lady', Sunday Styles, *The New York Times*, 18 January, pp. 1, 3.

Frontline (2016), 'The [Clinton] campaign', *Frontline*, USA: PBS, 24 October, http://www.pbs.org/wgbh/pages/frontline/shows/clinton/chapters/1.html. Accessed 25 June 2016.

Fuller, Bonnie ([2009] 2011), 'Michelle Obama's Sleevegate: Why can't America handle her bare arms?', 25 May, http://www.huffingtonpost.com/bonnie-fuller/michelle-obamas-sleevegat_b_171172.html. Accessed 17 May 2018.

Gardetto, Darlaine (1997), 'Hillary Rodham Clinton, symbolic gender politics, and The New York Times: January–November 1992', *Political Communication*, 14, pp. 225–40.

Greer, Germaine (2012), '"Julia, you've got a big arse; so just get on with it!", "Mutilation and the Media Frenzy" broadcast, Q&A', *ABC Television*, 27 August, http://www.abc.net.au/tv/qanda/txt/s3570412.htm. Accessed 29 April 2018.

Guerrero, Lisa (2011), '(M)Other-in-Chief: Michelle Obama and the ideal of Republican womanhood', in R. Gill and C. Scharff (eds), *New Femininities*, London: Palgrave Macmillan, pp. 68–82.

hooks, bell (1984), *Feminist Theory: From Margin to Center*, Boston: South End Press.

Hyland, Véronique (2014), 'Oscar de la Renta loved powerful women', 20 October, http://nymag.com/thecut/2014/09/oscar-de-la-renta-loved-powerful-women.html. Accessed 31 March 2017.

James, Joy (2009), 'Resting in the gardens, battling in the deserts: Black women's activism', *The Black Scholar*, 38:4, pp. 2–7.

Jamieson, Kathleen Hall (1995), *Beyond the Double Bind: Women and Leadership*, New York: Oxford University Press.

Jones, Ann Rosalind and Stallybrass, Peter (2000), *Renaissance Clothing and the Materials of Memory*, Cambridge: Cambridge University Press.

Joseph, Ralina (2011), 'Hope is finally making a comeback: First Lady reframed', *Communication and Critical/Cultural Studies*, 4, pp. 56–77.

Kahl, Mary (2009), 'First Lady Michelle Obama: Advocate for strong families', *Communication and Critical/Cultural Studies*, 6:3, pp. 316–20.

Karamura, Yuniya (2005), *Fashion-ology: An Introduction to Fashion Studies*, London: Berg.

Klein, Naomi (2000), *No Logo*, London: Flamingo.

Knuckey, Jonathan and Kim, Myunghee (2016), 'Evaluations of Michelle Obama as First Lady: The role of racial resentment', *Presidential Studies Quarterly*, 46:2, pp. 365–86.

Krupnick, Ellie (2011), 'Tim Gunn: Hillary Clinton is confused about her gender', 27 July, https://www.huffpost.com/entry/tim-gunn-hillary-clinton-_n_911456. Accessed 21 March 2021.

Madison, Sonyini (2009), 'Crazy patriotism and angry (post)black women', *Communication and Critical/Cultural Studies*, 6:3, pp. 321–26.

Marable, Manning and Clarke, Kristen (eds) (2009), *Barack Obama and African American Empowerment: The Rise of Black America's New Leadership*, New York: Palgrave Macmillan.

McAllister, Joan (2009), 'Trash in the White House: Michelle Obama, post-racism and pre-class politics of domestic style', *Communication and Critical/Cultural Studies*, 6:3, pp. 311–15.

McGinley, Ann and Boyd, William (2009), 'Hillary Clinton, Sarah Palin and Michelle Obama: Performing gender, race and class on the campaign trail', *Denver University Law Review*, 86, pp. 709–25.

Oles-Acevedo, Denise (2012), 'Fixing the Hillary factor: Examining the trajectory of Hillary Clinton's image repair from political bumbler to political powerhouse', *American Communication Journal*, 14:1, pp. 33–46.

Parry-Giles, Shawn (2000), 'Mediating Hillary Rodham Clinton: Television news practices and image-making in the postmodern age', *Critical Studies in Media Communication*, 17:2, pp. 205–25.

Rocamora, Agnes and Smelik, Anneke (eds) (2015), *Thinking through Fashion: A Guide to Key Theorists*, London: I.B. Tauris.

Seals Nevergold, Barbara and Brooks-Bertram, Peggy (2009), *Go Tell Michelle: African American Women Write to the New First Lady*, Albany: State University of New York Press.

Spillers, Hortense (2009), 'Views of the east wing: On Michelle Obama', *Communication and Critical/Culture Studies*, 6:3, pp. 307–10.

Stacey, Judith (1994), 'Scents, scholars and stigma: The revisionist campaign for family values', *Social Text*, 40, pp. 51–75.

Tate, Shirley (2012), 'Michelle Obama's arms: Race, respectability and class privilege', *Comparative American Studies*, 10:2&3, pp. 226–38.

The Ellen DeGeneres Show (2003–present), (USA: CBS).

The Tonight Show with Jay Leno (1992–2009), (USA: NBC/NBC Universal Television Studio/Universal Media Studios /Universal Television).

Truman, Margaret (1996), *First Ladies: An Intimate Portrait of White House Wives*, New York: Ballantine.

Watson, Robert (2003), 'Toward the study of the First Lady: The state of scholarship', *Presidential Studies Quarterly*, 33:2, pp. 423–41.

Welter, Rush (1975), *The Mind of America, 1820–60*, New York: Columbia University Press.

White, Khadijah (2011), 'Michelle Obama: Redefining the (White) House house-wife', *Journal of Feminist Theory and Culture*, 10:1, pp. 1–19.

Williams, Verna L. (2009), 'The First (black) Lady', *Denver University Law Review*, 86, pp. 833–50.

Winfield, Betty (1997a), 'The First Lady, political power and the media: Who elected her anyway?', in P. Norris (ed.), *Women, Media and Politics*, New York: Oxford University, pp. 168–80.

Winfield, Betty (1997b), 'The making of an image: Hillary Rodham Clinton and American journalists', *Political Communication*, 14:2, pp. 241–53.

Wolf, Naomi (1991), *The Beauty Myth: How Images of Beauty are Used against Women*, New York: Random House.

6

Codes of Power: Transforming the Dress and Appearance of Female Asian Politicians

Jennifer Craik and Anne Peirson-Smith

Introduction

Women in politics have always faced public scrutiny in manners of their dress, and it seems evident that the rise of female politicians in Asia offers special challenges. Currently, political fashions are dominated by the norm of male leaders through a westernized two-piece or three-piece business suit completed with conservative collared, button-down shirt and a long neck tie, popularized in the American 'dress for success' (Molloy 1974) movement of the mid-1970s and 1980s and adopted around the world. The suit, and especially the suit coat or jacket connotes masculinity, authority, discipline, convention and formality associated with the ideals of democratic political systems (Craik 2008; Hollander [1994] 2016). This standard 'uniform' has become spread around the world, where donning 'the suit' conveys an acceptance of western political ideology in countries that straddle the sartorial conventions between East and West.

Historically, costume has signified how political power is attained, maintained and remembered. Uniforms that stem from the military and other agencies involved in the management of authority are the most obvious and universal example (see Rall 2014). Military regimes of states epitomize how uniforms construct power to the point where the uniform itself becomes a visible sign – a shorthand – for the efficiency and presence of the grip on power, including intimidation and ruthless retribution, as Zygmunt Bauman quotes Elias Canetti's reference to 'murderous uniforms':

> At some point in our century it became common knowledge that men [*sic*] in uniforms are to be feared most. Uniforms were the insignia of the servants of the State, that source of all power, and above all the coercive power aided and abetted

by the absolving-from-inhumanity-power; wearing uniforms men became that power in action; wearing jackboots, they trample, and trample on behest and in the name of the State.

(1997: 81)

In non-military regimes, strategic forms of dressing for power equally represent and exert authority, 'the flight hostess [in her dress] too reflects a path up to power, up through a permanent hierarchy' (Black 2014: 94). Globally, the act of dressing for power is central to political control. These codes of dress are well known and internalized by the subject citizens who recognize the display of power in their heads of state and how they signify political authority (Tseëlon 2018).

Since the majority of heads of state have been and remain male, the fundamental dress code for male politicians is based on the suit. Hats were once mandatory but are now rare, although headpieces are worn in some states and during certain occasions (see McDowell 1992). Note that these male garments also constitute most dress codes for female politicians and heads of state, although jackets are mostly worn with skirts, and fabrics are generally (but not always) more colourful and varied. A display of colour in female politicians was catalogued in the 'Pantone Merkel' colour chart of 100 jackets worn by Angela Merkel (Chancellor of Germany 2005–21) photographed by Dutch designer Noortje (van Eekelen 2018).

Nonetheless, as female leaders adopt the suit, they reflect the symbolic status of masculine power.

As the number of female Asian politicians increases, their choice of dress remains the object of intense media coverage and speculation. Like female politicians elsewhere, they are judged repeatedly by what they wear rather than what they do. It is noted that Asian cultures often retain patriarchal structures and beliefs, as well as strong cultural tropes that deter the uptake of western governmental systems (Lee 2017). For Asian female leaders, new dress codes are required to balance their authority as global political leaders that includes a media that blends femininity and cultural identity alongside professionalism. Since the 1960s, the rise in Asian female politicians necessitated that they constrain their clothing to first convince the public of their credibility as leaders, and secondly to display decorum when constructing a public image that reclaims female social power in order to define their own political identity in this male-dominated political space.

The background and context of female politicians in Asia

In Asia, how politicians dress reflects the East–West divide almost always within the broader context of global postcolonialism. Male politicians' attire assumes the normalized stereotypes of western masculinity and leadership as it is performed in the public sphere, while women's roles in Asia were often limited to the micro-politics of running their families:

> in politics, [women] are also supposed to do double duty – that of a wife, mother, and politician [...] if a female politician is a mother, she is often asked how she will take care of her children [...] In this scenario, a woman must appear as the caring mother yet strong enough to lead the nation.
>
> (Sanghvi and Hodges 2015: 1686–87)

As a result, female Asian politicians are located within the context of national and cultural traditions that often frames them in a maternal, supportive or nurturing way (Lee 2017). As the number of female politicians continues to rise so does their dress come into public scrutiny. Outfits must portray and convey a balance of a professional woman alongside a figure that the citizenry can identify as 'a good mother' as well as a public figure who 'projects charisma' (Wijekoon 2015: 63).

While traditions in political dress vary throughout Asian countries, many women have increasingly adopted a version of the business suit, with business-style buttoned jacket, neat skirt, feminine formal shirt and low-heeled shoes. This outfit may be varied with trousers, a feminine necktie, statement jewellery and a coifed hairdo. For special ceremonial occasions, women may wear customary dress, presenting a colourful spectacle similar to their more numerous male counterparts in the group photos taken during the annual Asia-Pacific Economic Cooperation (APEC) meetings, which were founded in 1989. During these forums, the Asian and Oceanic heads of state pose in their colourful reproductions of a traditional garment of the host country (Roces and Edwards 2007a: 36; Roces and Edwards 2007b: 1, 3). This moment of 'fancy dress' prompts a bit of ridicule in the press, especially at the uncomfortable body language of the various leaders when the 'exotic' non-western cultures encounter the 'civilized' west. This staged photo is designed to acknowledge the Pacific's unique cultural identities, presenting face-to-face 'trans-national and trans-cultural' exchanges, even elevating 'symbols of dispossessed minority populations to signifiers of national status' (Roces and Edwards 2007b: 4–5). The few female leaders attending or hosting the APEC meetings are outliers in this posed performance, and stand out in their minority representation and 'otherness' in the Asia-Pacific political space.

Consequently, it is vital to consider how dress codes are changing both the look and connotations of female politicians in Asia through selected examples of recent and contemporary female politicians. The following analysis highlights how the management of appearance by Asian female politicians is multivalent and mutable – as women leaders must represent and reflect the structural changes in various Asian governments, their politics, economy, religion and culture. Here, the structural constraints of a traditional culture and society encounter the global pressures of the broader international political sphere, making it even more diffi-cult for Asian female politicians to negotiate their rightful status in the political landscape. Consequently, interpretations of female political dress and appearance are open to a variety of contested codes of power as they are portrayed through the media and judged by public opinion.

The background and context of female politicians in Asia

It is a truism that Asian societies conform to patriarchal authority, feudal struc-tures, traditional strictures and Confucian ideals (Huntington 1996) that serve to subordinate women across time, space and place. However, from the second half of the twentieth century into the first two decades of the twenty-first century, there have been a significant number of highly visible female politicians at the helm of national governments in the region. Significantly, these female leaders often emerged from women's movements and involvement at grassroot level in local political initiatives (Skard 2015). This ascendancy appears against the odds, given the low status and diminished respect accorded to women in general and their relegation to roles within the private sphere. As Skard (2015: 122) observed:

> Women participated in national social movements and struggled for peace, democ-racy and better living conditions [...] However, traditional beliefs about the role of women (emphasizing their responsibility for the private sphere), opposition against female politicians, voters' lack of trust, fear of mental and physical violence, and lack of self- confidence, in addition to poverty and illiteracy, prevented many women from engaging in political activities.

Note that Asian female politicians are often located in countries that emerged from colonial rule, as in India, Sri Lanka, colonial Burma (modern-day Myan-mar),[1] Hong Kong, the Philippines and Pakistan. Here, male-dominated colonial regimes often subjugated indigenous women further by sexual enslavement or objectified them in orientalist fantasies such as the 'Suzy Wong' syndrome (Clark 1999). Yet, other accounts of the role of women in colonial enclaves such as the former Burma shows increased access to education and employment, especially for middle-class women (Ikeya 2008).

In the early 2000s, Myanmar faced conflict as young women demonstrated through their 'bodily practices' their rights to wear western-influenced clothing and hairstyles, such as sheer gauze blouses and 'crested' hairstyles. This caused panic

118

in the media and the public as immorality, to the extent that some were harassed by Buddhist monks who tried to cut off flimsy silk blouses with hooks and scissors (Ikeya 2008: 1278). Further, anti-colonial critics and revolutionaries challenged this modernization as evidence of poor taste, ignorance and low-level consumerism – as the young women became 'ensnared' by imperialist western capitalism (see Ferguson 2011). The 'problem of what to wear' (Tarlo 1991) for Asian women, and by extension female politicians is exacerbated as western clothing signified colonial rule and the perceived betrayal of rising nationalist loyalties that set up a 'local versus western' dualistic logic (Tarlo 1996). Ironically, male politicians could don the western suit as a show of power against the colonizers, but this option was difficult for women (Tseëlon 2018). Again, the cultural framework positioned the modern, powerful, cosmopolitan male versus the local, subservient and ethnic female (Lee 2017).

However, in colonial Burma and likewise in the emerging People's Republic of China women adopted modern dress with masculine overtones signalling their social mobility and political awakening (Finanne 1996). Chie Ikeya suggests this culminated in,

> a crisis in masculinity, resulting largely from the political, social, and economic displacement of indigenous men, and second, shifts in understandings of gender roles and relations, namely the newfound social mobility and cultural authority of educated and urban working women [...] fashion, as the epitome of change and mutability, symbolized these disruptions in existing notions of masculinity and femininity and the effects of these developments on relations between the sexes.
>
> (2008: 1281)

Clearly, the disputation between male and female attire and appearance was problematic for the emerging independent nation states in Asia. But it is noted that the 'Mao' jacket and trousers became a ubiquitous symbol of the revolution as well as a non-gendered uniform under his rule (see Lim 2019). In other locales, dress extended beyond the construction of nationhood towards a means of protecting customary practice from the past and present incursions of the West. As the historian Niall Ferguson outlines, the Orient had become subject to a 'long history of sartorial westernization' and he states, 'this is about more than clothes. It is about embracing an *entire popular culture* that extends through music and movies [...] to soft drinks and fast food' (2011: 197, emphasis added). Clearly, the clothed body becomes the site of a culturally important object where masculinity versus femininity and East versus West both play a deciding role when articulating Asian national politics.

How dress signifies power

As above, men's clothing reflects their own efficacy and power through the adoption of an authoritative uniform, most often based on the western business suit. However, the appearance and dress of women, even in ancient times (Olson 2002) have become objects of speculation and attention. For example, Lady Curzon, as the Vicerine of India (1899–1905), like other women displaced in British and/or European colonies faced the challenge of dressing to reflect imperial authority, alongside her embracement of current European fashions. Unusually, she also employed local textiles and artisans in her costumes whose talents were largely spurned by the European fashion industry (Thomas 2007). These fraught choices between colony and colonizer have persisted into contemporary times as women have entered politics as candidates, representatives and leaders.

As the entry of Asian women into the political bear pit follows a series of diverse impacts, colonization, subsequent decolonization, rising opportunities for girls and women to gain educational qualifications and employment alongside the widening 'monoculture' (Shiva cited in Klein 1990: 130) created through globalization (Edwards L. 2007; Edwards P. 2007). However, the available dress codes for Asian female politicians have often lagged behind other cultural changes and stylistic trends (Parkin 2002; Sanghvi and Hodges 2015).

In earlier decades, female politicians largely stuck to conservative business attire, with skirts rather than pants. Youri Oh contrasted the wardrobe of Margaret Thatcher with Hillary Clinton, arguing that Thatcher chose conservative yet fashionable business suits paired with a skirt as a carefully calculated 'armour against critique' despite her devotion to fashion, especially of high-heeled shoes (2019: 376–77). Women who choose business suits can face backlash by the media faced by both Helen Clark of New Zealand (see Chapter 2), and Hillary Clinton's pantsuits were ridiculed during her tenure as First Lady of the United States (see Chapter 5). Overall, by the 2000s, trousers and informal but stylish outfits were commonplace amongst European female politicians as they increasingly abandoned more conservative dress codes (Flicker 2013).

Recently, the wardrobe of female politicians in Asia has expanded to include more colourful fabrics, informal outfits and generally more mainstream fashion in garment's cuts and styles, while avoiding looks that could be read as unprofessional or distracting. Usually this meant opting for 'a dress' rather than 'the suit' until the 2010s. In Korea, the 'present female politicians fashion has globally standardised as "the suit", which represents masculinity and western imperialism in global politics' (Oh 2019: 374). But some have also retained the customary *hanbok*, (Korean Ministry of Culture, Sports and Tourism of the Republic of Korea 2018) which consists of a very short jacket princess-style jacket (*jeogori*), very loose pants (*baji*) and a

FIGURE 6.1: Traditional Korean Woman's Hanbok, illustration by Maxine Vee, used by permission of the artist with acknowledgement of her artwork. Source: https://maxinevee.com/. Instagram: https://www.instagram.com/artofmaxinevee/. Twitter: https://twitter.com/maxinevee. Accessed 5 November 2021.

full-flowing long overskirt (*chima*), established during the Goguryeo Kingdom (37 BCE–668 CE), and it remains culturally appropriate for women in politics to wear during ceremonial and international occasions (Oh 2019: 379–81) (see Figure 6.1).

The Chinese *qipao* 'meaning banner gown' or *cheongsam* (also *cheong sam*) 'meaning long dress in Cantonese' (Mears 2010: 548) comprises a long, close-fitting dress that is side-fastened with 'frogs' or pankou knots with a stand-up small 'Mandarin' collar can also be worn in a shortened version as a blouse. The long, tight and therefore 'seductive' dress became a signature look for a temptress appearing in both Hollywood and Asian movies (Mears 2010: 548). While portrayed as ethnic Chinese attire, the *cheong sam* did not appear until the 1920s in Shanghai, and has been politicized both positively and negatively as the garment choice for Chinese female politicians (Clark 1999) as 'a single vestimentary sign of nation' (Finnane 1996: 125), therefore beyond mainstream fashion or everyday life in China. However, it was adopted by Carrie Lam early in her career as the administrator and later, Chief Executive of Hong Kong (see Plate xvii). Another example is the *kebaya* worn in the Straits of Indonesia and Malaysia although there is considerable discussion as to its origins (Seri 2004). This garment, purportedly derived from the Arabic word *kaba* meaning 'clothing' was introduced to Indonesia via Portuguese traders between the fifteenth and sixteenth centuries. This garment includes a more transparent or gauzy long-sleeved blouse with an embroidered lapel but no collar, and a slimline long skirt or wrapped skirt or *sarong* often in a traditional batik pattern. These two forms of traditional eastern or 'foreign' dress are suggested to display cultural exoticism or 'otherness', but potentially threatening to those outside the borders (Leshkowich and Jones 2003). Today, Asian male politicians rarely wear traditional garb while in office, whereas women are still subject to additional cultural demands for their formal attire (see Chapter 3).

The politics of dynasties

Many Asian female politicians have become leaders of parties and/or nations on the strength of their position in familial political dynasties, often after the overthrow, death or assassination of a male relative (see Table 6.1). Their elite social status propels them to lead, albeit with misgivings among conservative elements of a state. But their figure can also retain the taint of association with prior political transgressions, such as corruption, scandals and convictions or even death by assassination or execution. These successions may benefit female politicians from dominance by males through their status acquired from powerful familial and social legacies. That said, in the countries like the Philippines, Malaysia and Indonesia this 'dynastic reputation' and lingering associated abuses burdens a female leader with political fallout that often delimits their moral authority (Derichs et al. 2006; Wijekoon 2015; Ikeya 2008). A large number of Asian female politicians, especially party leaders and heads of state, arise from the ranks of elite political dynasties (Derichs and Thompson) (see Table 6.1). In these cases, their birthright or family association enables their candidature for political office and signifies strong national allegiance, cultural identity and social success.

Two notable examples from the Philippines include Corazon Aquino (President from 1986 to June 1992), who displaced Ferdinand Marcos after 20 years in office, and Gloria Macapagal Arroyo (President from 2001–10). These two Philippina Presidents challenged the male incumbents and their corrupt regimes by utilizing people power (Thompson 2002). They also chose to embrace modern styles as the vehicle to communicate with their people. Aquino's couturier, Auggie Cordero is credited with engineering her transformation from housewife to national leader. The designer Cordero utilized Aquino's Chanel-inspired wardrobe to embrace simple practical silhouettes and block colours that she often re-wore to signal her frugal commitment to austerity. Her attire stands in sharp contrast to deposed First Lady Imelda Marcos famed for her thousands of shoes and clothing collections. Marcos also relied on the Philippine national dress using home-grown textiles

TABLE 6.1: Female Heads of State in Asia 1960 to present.

Name	Country	Dates in Power	Years	Dress	Dynasty	In Office By	Assassinations
Sirimavo Bandaranika	Sri Lanka	1960–65; 1970–77; 1994–2000	15	Traditional	Yes	Husband assassinated	No Husband was
Indira Gandhi	India	1966–77; 1980–84	15	Traditional	Yes	Succeeded	Yes Father and son were
Corazon Aquino	Philippines	1986–92	6	Modern	Yes	Husband assassinated Corruption allegations	No Husband was
Benazir Bhutto	Pakistan	1988–90; 1993–96	5	Traditional (previously modern)	Yes	Father executed Corruption allegations	Yes Brother was
Chandrika Kumaranatunga	Sri Lanka	1994–2005	1	Traditional	Yes	Elected	No Father was
Sheikh Hasina	Bangladesh	1966–2001; 2009–present	16	Traditional	Yes	Elected	N/A
Gloria Macapagal-Arroya	Philippines	2001–10	9	Modern/Hybrid	Yes	Elected Corruption allegations	No Father was

(Continued)

TABLE 6.1: Female Heads of State in Asia 1960 to present. (*Continued*)

Name	Country	Dates in Power	Years	Dress	Dynasty	In Office By	Assassinations
Megawati Sukarnoputri	Indonesia	2001–04	3	Modern	Yes	Succeeded predecessor Corruption allegations	No Father was
Pratibha Patil	India	2007–11	4	Traditional	No	Elected	No
Roza Otunbayeva	Kyrgyzstan	2010–11	1	Modern	No	Succeeded predecessor	No
Yingluck Shinawatra	Thailand	2011–14	3	Modern	Yes	Elected	No Brother was
Park Geun Hye	South Korea	2013–17	4	Modern	Yes	Elected	No Father was
Carrie Lam	Hong Kong	2017–present	3	Modern/ Hybrid	No	Appointed	N/A
Tsai Ing-wen	Taiwan	2016–present	4	Modern	No	Elected	N/A
Aung San Suu Kyi	Myanmar	2016–2021	4	Traditional	Yes	Elected Corruption allegations	N/A
Halimah Yacob	Singapore	2017–present	3	Traditional	No	Elected	N/A
Dang Thi Ngoc Thinh	Vietnam	2018 (interim)		Traditional	No	Succeeded predecessor	No

Adapted from: Szczepanski, Kaillie (2019), 'Female heads of state in Asia', *ThoughtCo*, 12 August, https://www.thoughtco.com/female-heads-of-state-in-asia-19,5688. Accessed 9 June 2020. Note that Halimah Yacob is the president, not the prime minister of Singapore.

(*panuelo*) resplendent with the traditional winged 'butterfly sleeves' (*terno*) 'in her attempt to equate herself with the body politic' in the 1970s (Roces 2004: 8).

While some female leaders strove to update their image, the continued performance of the housewife role could command their people's respect. In Malaysian politics, Wan Azizah Wan Ismail (Aziah) adopted the dutiful role 'appropriately veiled' ideal Muslim wife, by personifying Malay Islamic values (Derichs et al. 2006: 260). She also headed the reform movement against a political system that jailed her husband Anwar Ibrahim for immorality which she tried to neutralize by her proper Muslim attire and demeanour (for further discussion of appropriate Muslim attire, see Chapter 8).

In his analysis of the rise and fall of the female South and Southeast Asian politicians, legal scholar Lavanga Wijekoon has identified several key factors shaping the representation and reception of female leaders. First, the historic patriarchal perceptions of women focus on the control, subordination and exclusion of women from the public sphere, denying them entry into the political arena. Secondly, the cult of motherhood, namely the overriding pressures for women in these cultures to have children signifies a caring, moral and incorruptible virtues of womanhood. A related theme connects the public's sympathy with widowed and parentless women as victims, who often present a self-effacing and modest image amidst their desolation and loss.

Wijekoon's third factor outlines the complications of an Asian culture's responses to colonialism. Towards the middle 1900s, British, American, Australian and New Zealand women began to demand equal rights (see Chapter 1). These foreign concepts promoted the emancipation of women and often grudging began to acknowledge their place in public life, and articulated the necessity for educational opportunities. However, Wijekoon concludes that while this movement may have contributed to the rise of female leadership in Asia, these concepts 'have also contributed to the women's difficulties in consolidating their authority while in power' as is 'evident in the prevalence of both military uprisings against and political infighting within their respective regimes' (2005: 69).

The adoption of so-called power dressing in Asian female politicians remains more conservative than their western counterparts, with many opting mostly for dresses or business suits with a skirt (Derichs et al. 2006; Oh 2019) or on special occasions a modified customary dress, and a limited display of contemporary fashions (see Szczepanski 2019; Wijekoon 2005). Further discussion of nation-based fashion and its role in international diplomacy are offered elsewhere (see the Introduction to this volume). Note that the current 'First Lady' of China (PRC) Peng Liyuan, during her overseas visits chooses to champion fashion by domestic designers such as Ma Kei, whose garments promote the state's environmental ethics and thereby publicize China's strong national creativity (Li 2016).

The semiotics of garment choices and styling

The question here is that when Asian female politicians appropriate the male business suit, does this begin to neutralize the focus on their appearance and clothing to highlight their real purpose, that is, to influence policies? Such an optimistic view overlooks the prevalence of social media commentary and its influence on public opinion of political leaders, in Asia and around the world. So, how to communicate power – through fashion – becomes a perilous exercise. As stated, women leaders in Asia have the option to wear native or ethnic dress and textiles at ceremonial, high-profile occasions or during economic forums to symbolize national pride and their unique power of 'otherness'. They can choose to reject modern style and its western-centric baggage, but still must negotiate between the East–West divide by utilizing modified tailoring, silhouettes, colours or fabrics, as when wearing the Chinese *cheongsam* or Korean *hanbok* at state banquets or during media conferences (such as at the APEC forums). The traditional fashions expressed in Asian ceremonial dress still provide an important way to display eastern sensibilities to the wider world. For example, the 2011 photo taken at the Commonwealth Heads of Government Meeting (CHOGM) in Perth, Australia shows the range of dress style among four women leaders: Sheikh Hasina of Bangladesh in traditional dress, Queen Elizabeth II in her signature hat matched to a ladylike tailored suit, Julia Gillard, prime minister of Australia, in a relaxed blousy jacket tied with a draped bow and black skirt and Kamla Persad-Bissessar, the sixth prime minister of Trinidad and Tobago (May 2010–September 2015) in a longer, straight-lined dress and thus less revealing of body shape, but brightly coloured (see Plate xiv).

As above, Asian female politicians often opt for well-tailored and professional dresses. Structured trousers are also increasingly worn in a range of colours. In terms of fabrics, a greater choice of type, hues and patterns (from plaids to abstract art), are also used (see Wijekoon 2005). A much wider choice of embellishments and accessories have become popularized throughout Asia, but rarely towards the extreme or the avant-garde as seen in high fashion (Parminter 2003). Overall, Asian female politicians are physically smaller, with body structures that enable them to wear clothes well, but generally care is taken to limit the visibility of the body (cleavage, legs, arms) by design features such as modest necklines. The 'protection' offered by larger profiles through exaggerated shoulders and a longer suit coat on a smaller-framed Asian woman is discussed elsewhere (see Chapter 3). In contrast, ethnic styles are often exoticized as more sensual. Commentary by French feminist Hélène Cixous introduced the notion of women and their need for 'sheltering' inside their clothing (1994: 97). The body shape of a female leader remains under scrutiny since women are judged in a mediated, celebrity culture where perfect bodies are associated with discipline and control (Hackett and Rall 2018). This very restrained look does deliver an authoritative presentation of self as either a matriarch or 'Chief Executive Officer' of a nation (Goffman 1959). While dress codes have perhaps relaxed in recent years with a greater range of fashion codes including greater informality, hybridity and individualization of outfits, the requirement to convey respectability, authority and credibility remains crucial. The following examples illustrate the contours and limits of how four Asian female leaders have negotiated dress codes.

Four Asian case studies: Pakistan, Bangladesh, Hong Kong and Taiwan

This brief summary of four prominent Asian female politicians describes some common aspects of how Asian women leaders dress for their role. In Pakistan, Benazir Bhutto (1953–2007), who was assissintated while she was in office, served two terms as prime minister (see Table 6.1). In Bangladesh, Sheikh Hasina Wazed, usually titled Sheikh Hasina has served two terms as prime minister and currently retains her position. These two politicians represent dress codes in two comparable states in the Indian sub-continent. In the Chinese sphere of influence, Carrie Lam, or Carrie Lam Cheng Yuet-ngor, has been Hong Kong's current Chief Executive since 2017. In Taiwan, Tsai Ing-wen has served as President in the Republic of China (commonly known as Taiwan) since May 2016, re-elected in 2020. In terms of politics and ideologies, these pairs present opposite approaches to dress and politics. In East Asia, Bhutto and Hasina have preferred customary dress, while Lam and Tsai have adopted very similar forms of contemporary modern dress but with differences in the formality of their modified business attire.

Benazir Bhutto and Sheikh Hasina

Bhutto and Hasina both stem from politically elite families and dynasties (see Table 6.1), but while Bhutto was high profile and commanded massive media and public attention, Hasina (sometimes spelled Hasini) has slid under the radar of public attention outside of Bangladesh. Bhutto became the first female to become Pakistan's prime minister after a semi-independent life. As a young girl, she studied at Radcliffe College, followed by Harvard University (1969–73) in the United States, and later studied at Lady Margaret's College at Oxford University in the United Kingdom from 1973 to 1977 (Anon. 2018). Her return to Pakistan following the suspected assassination of her father, Premier Asif Ali Zardari, transformed her appearance from collegiate 'party girl' and socialite to a demure, but very attractive prime minister in traditional garments. In her official campaign portrait, she sits without a veil but also indicates her allegiance to her father's politics by including his portrait in the photo (see Plate xv). Later in her public appearances and while overseas she adopts a loosely wrapped veil (see Plate xvi).

Prior to her shocking assassination in 2007 at the age of 54 years, her commitment to modernizing Pakistan, especially to elevate the position and rights of women was noted globally, although scholars suggest that she achieved little of her agenda while in office (Fleschenberg 2013). In Bangladesh, Hasina has been accused of electoral rigging, has enacted measures to suppress freedom of speech and has also faced graft and corruption accusations, and even was imprisoned for almost a year (Momen 2008). Currently, she remains a controversial figure but still firmly in power, as she is figured alongside women politicians in the CHOGM in 2011 (see Plate xiv).

Broadly speaking, Bhutto and Hasina display the traditional or customary side of the Asian dress code spectrum, although Bhutto created her own contemporary customary look by modifying and streamlining traditional garments. When she lived in the United States, Oxford and Europe her photos display a preference for t-shirts and jeans and at parties, designer clothing. On return to her political duties, Bhutto adopted the 'national dress' of Pakistan, or the *shalwar kameez*. This costume includes trousers held up by an elastic waistband, which can be very wide, or tapered for a more modern look. A long tunic, or the *kameez* is worn over the trousers, where the side seams are left open below the waistline for ease of movement, and later the tunic included a western-style inset sleeve. Bhutto wore, but also altered these traditional garments for comfort and a more streamlined European look. After her initial campaign photo, Bhutto employed the traditional Muslim shawl, a white *dupatta* that she artfully draped over her head to campaign for the prime ministership. She continued to don some western-style clothing while abroad meeting world leaders, but retained the shawl demonstrating her strategic mix-and-match of clothing genres (Manzoor 2019).

Hasina, on the other hand, has persisted wearing customary dress in the form of the sari, called *sharis* in Bangladesh, that includes layers of elaborate draping. Hasina now has an extensive collection of saris in her wardrobe. These outfits are composed of many colours and embellishments, featuring extensive and elaborate embroidery and often gold beaded. Both Bhutto and Hasina's dress while serving in political office became a 'quasi-uniform' that conveyed their modesty and conservatism in line with prevailing ideologies of these dominantly Muslim sub-continent nations (Gelman Taylor 2007).

Carrie Lam and Tsai Ing-wen

By contrast, Carrie Lam and Tsai Ing-wen's dress illustrates their very different leadership trajectories. Lam was elected in the fraught Hong Kong election in 2017 by chosen representatives or sympathizers of mainland China (PRC). She has been called a puppet of Beijing who has seemingly been prepared to endorse the winding back of Hong Kong's autonomy and independence enshrined in the Basic Law (see Chapter 9). This has been extremely unacceptable to Hong Kong's populace who are watching their 'one country two systems' government vanish when Hong Kong became part of China in 1989. Lam was opposed to the 'Umbrella' opposition movement in 2014 and subsequently appointed as Chief Executive in 2017. In terms of dress codes, Lam has often proclaimed a lack of interest in fashion that assists her conservative or anti-western stance (see Lo 2017). Lam was publicly known to reject stylists and customarily purchased her own clothes. Early in her career, she wore either a pastel-hued tailored suit with toned silk neck scarf or even a traditional *cheong sam* in gentle silk fabrics such as 'pale pink, green or white' as reported in the media (Ko 2019: n.pag.) (see Plate xvii).

Lam's anti-protest pronouncements continued during Hong Kong's 2019–20 period of social unrest triggered by the threat of increasing control by the Chinese mainland (PRC). Further, as the street protest movement intensified in numbers between June and December 2019, Lam modified her political wardrobe from suits to donning pale-coloured *cheong sams* in traditional self-patterned white silk at press conferences. This change in dress echoed her earlier 'love' of the traditional *qipao* worn during her inauguration in Beijing two years before (Cheung 2017) and perhaps signified the purity of her intent and her present commitment to Beijing's party line. As the protests intensified her garments became more severe, often wearing dark single-breasted navy skirt suits with a white button-up blouse (Ko 2019). Even her sharp short haircut seemed to reflect her sombre mood and seemed to take a more power-suited, or masculine approach when denouncing the protest movement to the world's journalists (see Chapter 9).

The first female Taiwanese President, Tsai Ing-wen, was elected in 2016 and re-elected with a landslide on 2020 due to her steadfast advocacy for the difference and independence from the so-called Republic of China, Taiwan's official name. She was dubbed the 'Angela Merkel of Asia' for her strategic, methodological, competent and technological approach to national politics (Hass 2020: n.pag.). Tsai is highly educated in Taiwan, the United States and the United Kingdom, she has been an uncompromising thorn in the side of Beijing by advocating progressive policies such as support for the Indigenous peoples, same-sex marriage (Lee 2019) and maintaining relations with allies. With her signature jaw-length hairstyle dubbed the 'Little Tsai' bob, Tsai consistently opts for a variety of monotone tailored pantsuits and jackets, even when attending state banquets. The American media praised her strength in her cover photograph in *TIME*'s Asia edition magazine, as photographer Adam Ferguson reports, 'with Tsai I was hoping to capture an expression that was serious, contemplative and strong–all emotions that I believed epitomized her current political aspirations' (Laurent 2015: n.pag.). Her re-assuring intellectual look includes a subtle femininity that is embedded in the details, such as her pale make-up or waist-cinched jackets. While also wearing modified business suits, her dress code became much more informal and on her electoral victory on 11 January 2020, she wears a black zipped-up 'hoodie' with a raised open hand and her supporters in zip-up jackets are cheering in the background (Nachman and Drun 2020) (see Plate xviii).

These two regional Chinese leaders illustrate significant trends in dress codes for female Asian politicians that communicate through their divergent styles their political intentions. Tsai's choice of garments and her policies reflect a closer connection with many, especially the younger Taiwanese citizens through her contemporary attitudes and clothing. Tsai's image stands in opposition to Lam's who signalled her response to the growing political crisis amid the 2019–20 protests in her 'uniform' of conservative dark-coloured business suits.

Concluding Remarks

Adoption of a specific dress code while in office is a vital component of how female political leaders create their political personae in order to gain and maintain power as well as promote their countries' national interests in the international public sphere.

Like all women in political leadership, they must succeed in negotiating gender and femininity in a normatively masculine domain. Their choice of clothing becomes a strategic calculation that originates from and relies on the type of political regime they manage and the cultural mores enshrined within. These two pairs of case studies contrast leaders who chose traditional or customary dress codes with leaders who preferred to craft a more modern, or even informal style through outfits closer to the fashion zeitgeist of the citizens they represent and the global fashion industry.

Scholars of 'oriental' fashion history note that from the mid-1900s, the East strove to achieve the superior global power of the United Kingdom and Europe, also adopting their fashions (Pyun and Wong 2018; Ferguson 2011). While the era of outright imitation is clearly over, the 'mono-multiculturalism' of American (western) fashion values still reigns (Shiva cited in Klein 2000: 130). Therefore, every Asian female political leader must balance their image between traditional clothing alongside western and contemporary fashion. They often 'self-orientalize' by wearing the customary dress but can introduce a modern twist with different colours or fabrics. This expression of self supports an individual agency in their clothing that resists patriarchal expectations or neo-colonial appropriation by rejecting cinema-based stereotypical Asian female imagery (Jones and Leshkowich 2003). Their attire then signals their position of authority, whilst grounding it within a unique cultural base articulated on the wider global political stage (see Plate xiv). Above all, they chose to employ their fashion to reflect the authority and power of leadership through a 'disciplinary power' (Tynan 2015: 185), while still retaining a more feminine aura. It is concluded here that Asian female politicians can become empowered by occupying a contested space through a subtle sartorial power play that includes references to tropes such as the mother figure, housewife and head girl at school in the process of housekeeping the nation, both real and imagined (Lee 2017).

The dress choices of contemporary female politicians have expanded considerably as well as their strategic goals in attaining, and retaining their positions in their countries' national political landscape. To do so, it is necessary for them to calculate the message they wish to convey with an awareness of how their attire will be received and recorded visually by the press and especially through the social media. New dress codes for women Asian politicians hinge on three main themes: traditional or customary outfits, power dressing in western 'business' clothes or more contemporary fashion-forward styles. These clothing codes are often mixed and matched for the occasion, such as the necessity to indicate a strong national presence. In some cases, as with Carrie Lam's dress during the HK protests, this reflected a less stable political situation. Asian female leaders, much more than their normatively constructed male counterparts must communicate both power and authority through a sartorial camouflage and a nuanced reading of dress codes that represent competence, charisma, confidence and credibility in the Asian political sphere.

NOTE

1. To prevent confusion, colonial Burma will still be referred to as Burma, while the modern country is called Myanmar.

REFERENCES

Anon. (2018), 'Remembering the style icon Benazir Bhutto on her 66th birth anniversary', *The Express Tribune*, 27 December, https://tribune.com.pk/story/1875625/4-style-icon-benazir-bhutto/. Accessed 9 June 2020.

Bauman, Zygmunt (1997), *Postmodernity and Its Discontents*, Cambridge: Polity Press.

Black, Prudence (2014), 'The discipline of appearance: Military style and Australian flight hostess uniforms 1930–1934', in D. N. Rall (ed.), *Fashion and War in Popular Culture*, Bristol: Intellect, pp. 91–105.

Cheung, Elizabeth (2017), 'A qipao collector: Hong Kong's new leader Carrie Lam on her love for traditional Chinese dress', *South China Morning Post*, 2 July, https://www.scmp.com/news/hong-kong/politics/article/2100922/qipao-collector-hong-kongs-new-leader-carrie-lam-her-love. Accessed 29 June 2020.

Cixious, Hélène (1994), 'Sonia Rykiel in translation', in S. Benstock and S. Ferriss (eds), *On Fashion*, Brunswick: Rutgers University Press.

Clark, Hazel (1999), 'The cheung sam: Issues of fashion and cultural identity', in V. Steele and J. Major (eds), *China Chic: East Meets West*, New Haven: Yale University Press, pp. 55–166.

Craik, Jennifer (2008), *Uniforms and Men's Fashion: Tailoring Masculinity to Fit*, New York: Fairchild Books.

Derichs, Claudia, Fleschenberg, Andrea and Hüstebeck, Momoya (2006), 'Gendering moral capital: Morality as a political asset and strategy of top female politicians in Asia', *Critical Asian Studies*, 38:3, pp. 245–70.

Derichs, Claudia and Thompson, Mark R. (eds) (2013), *Dynasties and Female Political Leaders in Asia: Gender, Power and Pedigree*, Münster: LIT Verlag.

Edwards, Louise (2007), 'Dressing for power: Scholars' robes, school uniforms and military attire in China', in M. Roces and L. Edwards (eds), *The Politics of Dress in Asia and the Americas*, Eastbourne: Sussex Academic Press, pp. 42–64.

Edwards, Penny (2007), '"Dressed in a little brief authority": Clothing the body politic in Burma', in M. Roces and L. Edwards (eds), *The Politics of Dress in Asia and the Americas*, Eastbourne: Sussex Academic Press, pp. 121–38.

Ferguson, Niall (2011), *Civilization: The West and the Rest*, London: Penguin.

Finnane, Antonia (1996), 'What should Chinese women wear?: A national problem', *Modern China*, 22:2, pp. 99–131.

Fleschenberg, Andrea (2013), 'Benazir Bhutto: Her people's sister? A contextual analysis of female Islamic Governance', in C. Derichs and M.R. Thompson (eds), *Dynasties and Female Political Leaders in Asia: Gender, Power and Pedigree*, Münster: LIT Verlag, pp. 63–113.

Flicker, Eva (2013), 'Fashionable (dis-)order in politics: Gender, power and the dilemma of the suit', *International Journal of Media & Cultural Politics*, 9:2, pp. 183–201.

Gelman Taylor, Jean (2007), 'Identity, nation and Islam: a dialogue about men's and women's dress in Indonesia', in M. Roces and L. Edwards (eds), *The Politics of Dress in Asia and the Americas*, Eastbourne: Sussex Academic Press, pp. 101–20.

Goffman, Erving (1959), *The Presentation of Self*, New York: Doubleday Dell Publishing.

Hackett, Lisa J. and Rall, Denise N. (2018), 'The size of the problem with the problem of sizing: How clothing measurement systems have misrepresented women's bodies, from the 1920s to today', *Clothing Cultures*, 5, pp. 263–83.

Hass, Ryan (2020), 'Taiwan's Tsai Ing-wen enters second term with a strong political mandate but no room for complacency', *The Brookings Institute*, 13 May, https://www.brookings.edu/blog/order-from-chaos/2020/05/13/taiwans-tsai-ing-wen-enters-second-term-with-a-strong-political-mandate-but-no-room-for-complacency/. Accessed 29 June 2020.

Hollander, Anne ([1994] 2016), *Sex and Suits: The Evolution of Modern Dress*, London: Bloomsbury Publishing.

Ikeya, Chie (2008), 'The modern Burmese woman and the politics of fashion in colonial Burma', *Journal of Asian Studies*, 67:4, pp. 1277–1308.

Jones, Carla and Leshkowich, Ann Marie (2003), 'Introduction: The globalization of Asian fashion or re-orientalising Asia?', in S. Niessen, A. M. Leshkowich and C. Jones (eds), *Re-Orienting Fashion: The Globalisation of Asian Dress*, London: Berg, pp. 1–48.

Klein, Naomi (2000), *No Logo: No Space, No Choice, No Jobs*, London: Flamingo.

Ko, Christina (2019), 'Why Carrie Lam's fashion choices may say more than she does', *South China Morning Post*, 27 August, https://www.scmp.com/lifestyle/fashion-beauty/article/3024339/why-carrie-lams-fashion-choices-may-say-more-she-does. Accessed 30 June 2020.

Korean Ministry of Culture, Sports and Tourism of the Republic of Korea (2018), '"Hanbok" literally means "Korean clothing"', Korean Culture and Information Service, http://www.mcst.go.kr/english/. Accessed 6 June 2021.

Laurent, Olivier (2015), 'Behind TIME's Cover With Tai'an's Tsai Ing-Wen', *TIME* [Asia edition], 22 June, https://time.com/3930616/taiwan-cover-tsai-ing-wen/. Accessed 29 June 2020.

Lee, Yean-Ju (2017), 'Multiple dimensions of gender role attitudes: Diverse patterns among four East Asian Societies', in M-C. Tsai and W-C. Chen (eds), *Family, Work and Wellbeing in Asia*, Singapore: Springer, pp. 67–88.

Lee, Yimou (2019), 'Love wins: In first for Asia, Taiwan says yes to same sex marriage', *The Sydney Morning Herald*, 17 May, https://www.smh.com.au/world/asia/love-wins-in-first-for-asia-taiwan-says-yes-toseksme-sex-marriage-20190517-p51okh.html. Accessed 29 June 2020.

Leshkowich, Ann Marie and Carla Jones (2003), 'What happens when Asian chic becomes chic in Asia?', *Fashion Theory*, 7:3&4, pp. 281–300.

Li, Xinghua (2016), 'The "useless" sustainability discourse of eco-Fashion and the Utilitarian Fantasy', in T.R. Peterson, H.L. Bergeå and A.M. Feldpausch-Parker (eds), *Routledge Studies in Environmental Communication and Media*, London: Routledge, pp. 106–40.

Lim, J. L. (2019), 'Wang'Guangmei's crimes of fashion: The politics of dress in China's cultural revolution', *Fashion and Politics*, D. Bartlett (ed.), London: Yale University Press, pp. 73–85.

Lo, Sonny Shiu-Hing (2017), *Asia Pacific Journal of Public Administration*, Special Issue: On the Second Decade of the Hong Kong Special Administrative Region of China: 'Factionalism and Chinese-style democracy: the 2017 Hong Kong Chief Executive election', 39:2, pp. 100–19.

Manzoor, Abiya (2019), 'Remembering iconic fashion moments of the late Benazir Bhutto!', *Niche*, 27 December, https://niche.com.pk/remembering-iconic-fashion-moments-of-the-late-benazir-bhutto/. Accessed 9 June 2020.

McDowell, Colin (1992), *Hats: Status, Style and Glamour*, New York: Rizzoli International.

Mears, Patricia (2010), 'Orientalism', in V. Steele, (ed.), *The Berg Companion to Fashion*, Oxford: Berg, pp. 546–49.

Molloy, John T. (1974), *Dress for Success*, New York: Warner Books.

Momen, Mehnaaz (2008), 'Bangladesh in 2008: Déjà Vu Again or a Return to Democracy?', *Asian Survey*, 49:1, pp. 66–73, http://online.ucpress.edu/as/article-pdf/49/1/66/76747/as_2009_49_1_66.pdf. Accessed 30 June 2020.

Nachman, Lev and Jessica Drun (2020), 'Tsai Ing-wen 2.0: Tsai's first term had its successes and failures, yet she still won a historic re-election victory. What can she deliver in her second term?', *The Diplomat*, 1 May, https://thediplomat.com/2020/04/tsai-ing-wen-2-0/. Accessed 30 June 2020.

Oh, Youri (2019), 'Fashion in politics: what makes Korean female politicians wear "the suit" not "a dress"', *International Journal of Fashion, Design, Technology and Education*, 12:3, pp. 374–84.

Olson, Kelly (2002) 'Matrona and whore: The clothing of women in Roman antiquity', *Fashion Theory*, 6:4, pp. 387–420.

Parkin, Wendy (ed.) (2002), *Fashioning the Body Politic: Dress, Gender, Citizenship*, Oxford: Berg.

Parminter, Bhachu (2003), 'Designing diasporic markets: Asian fashion entrepreneurs in London', in S. Niessen, A. M. Leshkowich and C. Jones (eds), *Re-Orientating Fashion: The Globalisation of Asian Dress*, London: Berg.

Pyun, Kyunghee and Wong, Aida Yuen (2018) (eds), *Fashion, Identity, and Power in Modern Asia*, Cham: Springer.

Rall, Denise N. (2014) (ed.), *Fashion and War in Popular Culture*, Bristol: Intellect.

Roces, Mina (2004), 'Women, citizenship and the politics of dress in twentieth-century Philippines', *THEME: Women and Politics in Asia*, p. 8.

Roces, Mina and Edwards, Louise (2007a) (eds), *The Politics of Dress in Asia and the Americas*, Eastbourne: Sussex Academic Press.

Roces, Mina and Edwards, Louise (2007b), 'Trans-national flows and the politics of dress in Asia and the Americas', in M. Roces and L. Edwards (eds), *The Politics of Dress in Asia and the Americas*, Eastbourne: Sussex Academic Press, pp. 1–18.

Sanghvi, Minita and Hodges, Nancy (2015), 'Marketing the female politician: an exploration of gender and appearance', *Journal of Marketing and Management*, 31:15&16, pp. 1676–94.

Seri, Datin (2004), *Nonya Kebaya: A Century of Straits Chinese Clothing*, Singapore: Tuttle Publishing.

Skard, Torild (2015), *Women of Power: Half a Century of Female Presidents and Prime Ministers Worldwide*, Bristol: Policy Press.

Szczepanski, Kaillie (2019), 'Female heads of state in Asia', *ThoughtCo*, 12 August, https://www.thoughtco.com/female-heads-of-state-in-asia-195688. Accessed 9 June 2020.

Tarlo, Emma (1991), 'The problem of what to wear: The politics of khadi in late colonial India', *South Asia Research*, 11:2, pp. 134–57.

Tarlo, Emma (1996), *Clothing Matters, Dress and Identity in India*, London: Hurst & Company.

Thomas, Nancy (2007), 'Embodying imperial spectacle: Dressing Lady Curzon, Vicerine of India, 1989–1905', *Cultural Geographies*, 14, pp. 369–400.

Thompson, Mark R. (2002), 'Female leadership of democratic transitions in Asia', *Pacific Affairs*, 75:4, pp. 535–55.

Tseëlon, Efrat (2018), 'Fashion tales: How we make up stories that construct brands, nations and gender', *Critical Studies in Fashion & Beauty*, 9:1, pp. 3–33.

Tynan, Jane (2015), 'Michel Foucault: Fashioning the body politic', in A. Rocamora and A. Smelik (eds), *Thinking through Fashion: A Guide to Key Theorists*, London: I.B. Tauris, pp. 184–99.

van Eekelen, Noortje (2018), http://www.noortjevaneekelen.nl/, website no longer available.

Wijekoon, Lavanga (2005), 'Why do South and Southeast Asians vote for female heads of state?', *Res Publica*, pp. 57–72.

PART III

WOMEN AND DRESS: SOCIAL MEDIA, POLITICS AND RESISTANCE

7

Leopard in Kitten Heels: The Politics of Theresa May's Sartorial Choices

Rachel Evans

Fashion is a site where politicized embodiment emerges in response to various local, national and global influences, and where power is both formative and transformative.

(Shinko 2016: 45)

How does it matter what clothes a politician wears? What do the sartorial choices they make mean? Why did Jeremy Corbyn's sandals make him unfit to lead a country? Mark Twain's sardonic observation that 'naked people have little or no influence in society', states the long-held western view that clothes are essential to civilization (cited in Shapiro n.d.: 843). Once the preserve of royalty, the role of projecting a visual statement of the body politic has devolved to democratically elected bodies such as the House of Commons (Behnke 2016). Clothes became markers of political beliefs and could literally mean life or death in turbulent times such as the English and French Revolutions (Parkins 2002). While in everyday life clothes are no longer so acutely important, for today's politicians they are an important method of asserting and maintaining authority and a means of widening their appeal to the voting public.

All professionals have choices about the clothes and accessories they wear and there are a variety of pressures that come into play in balancing those choices. For heads of state, these include issues of projecting national identity, religious considerations, supporting national designers and adhering to dress codes. By exploring Theresa May's sartorial choices as prime minister and in particular her choice of shoes, this chapter seeks to investigate the politics of dress in projecting a visual image of a British leader and in her day-to-day job within the House of Commons.

The discussion first examines the role of ideology and dress in European political life after the English Civil War (1642–51) and most importantly the French

Revolution of 1789. The work of Behnke (2016) and Parkins (2002) presents many implications for female politicians. Second, the contemporary political concern over national identity arises, and how Theresa May's outfit on 13 July 2016 addressed this issue. The third section attends in detail to May's choice of kitten heels and leopard print for the feet of a British prime minister and then, drawing on the work of Vinthagen and Johansson, considers the possibility of her choice of shoes as a form of 'everyday resistance'.

The ideology of political dress

As expounded by Behnke and Parkins, alongside the rise of elected governments in Europe ran the change in male clothing known as 'The Great Male Renunciation' (Flügel 1930: 110) that saw a polarization in male and female clothing in terms of visual extravagance. This moment also encompassed a mapping of eighteenth-century French concerns over the political activities of sexually licentious women, embodied by the French Queen Marie Antoinette, onto women in general and established a suspicion of women who wish to enter politics. The polarization of sartorial codes means that it is the role of a ruler's female consort rather than the ruler himself to display appropriate elegance and/or extravagance in their clothing. An exemplary example of this in western politics is Michelle Obama's wardrobe during her terms as First Lady of the United States (see Chapter 5). Accepting that in the majority of situations leadership has either been exclusively male or is still understood as a masculine preserve, then female politicians find themselves in a double bind. Following Behnke's discussion of the symbolic form of Michelle Obama's clothing choices as First Lady, it can be seen that western female heads of state carry the burden of representing the nation sartorially (Behnke 2016). In Britain, the adoption of more modest masculinity can be traced back to the reign of Charles II after the Restoration of 1688. To distance himself from dangerous associations with the French court, Charles II introduced a distinctly English form of dress known as the 'vest' that has transformed into the three-piece suit of male dress of today (Cumming et al. 2010: 218). To show his disdain for this innovation Louis XIV had his servants all dressed in the new vest. This modest masculinity, and the consequent political legitimacy, aligned the display of luxury with femininity and so reinforced the exclusion of women from politics (Parkins 2002).

Women in politics face far more commentary on their sartorial dress than their male counterparts and each female politician has to develop her own response to this scrutiny. Theresa May's contemporary, the German chancellor, Angela Merkel, resolutely refuses to discuss her clothes and has adopted a uniform of jacket and trousers with little variation. In contrast, May answers questions on her clothing choices, asked for a year's subscription to *Vogue* as her luxury item when she was interviewed on Desert Island Discs (Young 2014). She commented at the Women of the World Conference in 2015: 'I like clothes and I like shoes. One of the challenges for women in the workplace is to be ourselves, and I say you can be clever and like clothes. You can have a career and like clothes' (Conti 2016: n.pag.).

Within the western tradition of the primacy of self-expression, the dominant clothing system is understood as fitting to the body. The feminist ideological stance that women are entitled to wear what they want also plays into the range of fashion for female politicians to wear (Marzel and Stiebel 2014) (see Chapter 4).

However, their personal expression must always be balanced against the need to not appear too feminine, to not be morally lax and to not become an over-dressed figure, that is, a 'Marie Antoinette'. This is a dividing line that can be transgressed all too easily and without warning creating a backlash of commentary. Theresa May's leather trousers worn for *The Sunday Times Magazine* interview and photo-shoot (Mills 2016) shortly after becoming prime minister were a step too far for her British audience. For May the visible luxuriousness of her £995 trousers, made from a material that is associated with fetishism (Bolton 2004), moved too close to the extravagance of 'Marie Antoinette', and therefore out of touch with the populace. This outfit departed too much from from the plain-tailored silhouette that represents 'public virtue' through 'modest masculinity' (Parkins 2002).

National identity in dress

The contemporary importance of dress as a statement of political beliefs, famously mobilized by Gandhi's adoption of a *dhoti* ('a loincloth worn by Hindu males') (trans. Cumming et al. 2010: 65) is more easily seen in the dress choices of politicians from former colonial nations than in countries that dress in the western tradition (see Chapter 6). However, colonial dress can give us clues as to Theresa May's clothing choices. Two examples are the former Pakistani president Benazir Bhutto, a contemporary of May's at Oxford and Aung San Suu Kyi, the former head of state of Myanmar. Both have chosen to wear clothes that reflect a concept of ethnic national costume, and so reject the wearing of western dress that signified the 'modernization/civilization' of their countries in colonial periods. The subject of 'traditional', 'heritage' and 'modern' dress is the subject of considerable scholarship recently (see Jansen 2016). In particular, the choice of traditional clothing allows women to avoid the pitfall of inappropriate sexuality if adopting western-style clothing (Ross 2008). These dress choices align both leaders with their constituents and help to reinforce their image as approachable (wo)man of the people (see Chapter 6).

So for a British prime minister the task in dressing is to represent both the western ideal of individuality and also indicate membership of a larger British society (Root 2002). But what constitutes British national dress? British national dress lies firmly within the western clothing tradition of male tailoring with its close links to military uniform and sporting attire. In *The Englishness of English Dress*, Breward et al. (2002) identify tailoring as a key aspect of English dress, building as it does on the long tradition of Savile Row and Jermyn Street businesses. Whilst the English clientele of land-owning aristocracy and gentry have declined, these businesses now draw on their long history and connections to British royalty to sell their wares to Middle Eastern customers who can afford the £3500 pound unit price in multiples of ten (Gerard 2009).

Aileen Ribero (2002) identifies tradition and 'a deep-seated concern with the past' as fundamental to understandings of Englishness, demonstrated by Breward et al. (2002) through a *Country Life* spread from 1996. This layout includes, within its all-male examples, Jermyn Street shirts, Guardsmen's Uniforms, Clark's Desert Boot, a Land Rover and cricket players. (*Country Life* 2017: n.pag.). Further, their 'Gentleman's Test' includes on their list of 39 things that a gentleman should have on hand, to '[p]ossesses at least one well-made dark suit, one tweed suit and a dinner jacket' at number 7 and 'Sandals? No. Never' at Number 34 (*Country Life* 2017: n.pag.).

Within the Houses of Parliament, the importance of the past in defining Englishness is reinforced by the daily visual displays of tradition and the understanding, by many of the members of parliament, of 'the importance of tradition' to their carrying out of twenty-first-century politics (BBC: n.pag.). Hobsbawm and Ranger explore the rebuilding of the Houses of Parliament in the Gothic style in both the nineteenth century and also following the Second World War as an exemplar of invented tradition designed to establish continuity with the past ([1983] 2017). This emphasis on tradition means that the field of British politics promotes a clothing-society culture rather than the dominant fashion-society culture of western dress (Marzel and Stiebel 2014). This clothing-culture reinforces the adoption of puritanical clothing codes already supported by the understanding of the political body as male. Clothing-culture is also reinforced by the value placed in the United Kingdom on putting party before personality, despite the rising dominance of personality politics.

British distrust of personality, an aspect in play when comments arise about Britain's Westminster style of democracy, means that too much interest in fashion, in personal appearance or luxury, that is, 'fashion', is not acceptable for British politicians, particularly prime ministers. For female members of parliament this expectation of unchanging approaches to dress impacts at two levels in the British political system: the constituency selection committees and on the floor of the House of Commons.

Despite a century of equal opportunities legislation, the proportion of female members of parliament still does not reflect the British population. At the election in 2017, women accounted for 208 out of 650 elected members of parliament representing 32 per cent of the total. This was against a level of approximately 51 per cent in the general population in 2016 (Statista 2016: n.pag.). In the 1970s and 1980s, Silvia Rodgers examined the situation of women members of parliament in the 1990s; only nineteen female members of parliament out of a total of 635 seats (1993). As Rodgers points out this is not due to male members of parliament, who as the majority in the House of Commons have passed this equal opportunities legislation. In her research, she identified that the problem of selection for female candidates arose as they were chosen by committees who still expected male candidates and masculine forms of dress. As exemplified by comments to one candidate, prior to her selection to stand in the 2010 General Election, that she had 'unparliamentary hair' (BBC 2015: n.pag.), and this is a trend that continues.

Rodgers identified forms of reclassification within the House of Commons as a strategy by male members of parliament to keep an understanding of the House as a male preserve despite the presence of women members of parliament. The two most common forms were reclassification as 'an honorary man' – as with Margaret Thatcher being described as the best man we have – or as a supernatural being – as with Nancy Astor's designation as a witch (Rodgers 1993: 54). A consequence of this reclassification for the clothes women wear is a need to adhere as close as possible to traditional masculine attire and to reflect the 'perennial strain of Puritanism long endemic in Englishness' (Pevsner's notion of 'truly English' is refuted in Ribeiro 2002: 23). That this Puritanism, and the requirement for female members of parliament to adhere to it, is relevant today can be seen when Theresa May herself became the centre of a media-feeding frenzy for wearing a red dress and jacket that showed cleavage during the 2016 budget debate (Bates 2016: n.pag.).

How then did Theresa May's choice of dress on her first day in Downing Street reflect this negotiation between becoming an honorary man, demonstrating western individuality and sexuality and projecting an English nationality based on tradition? In common with the female members of the Royal Family; Queen Elizabeth II, and Catherine, Duchess of Cambridge and Meghan, Duchess of Sussex, Theresa May makes a point of supporting British designers and manufacturers. Reflecting a position taken by Margaret Thatcher, who believed 'if anyone represents Britain, with our reputation for tailoring [...] they ought to turn out looking quite good' (Conway 2016: n.pag.). May's outfit upon becoming Head of Government was traditional in its tailored outline and block colours. She chooses to wear a dress rather than trousers indicating her femininity but the dress was styled to below the knee, with a shallow V-neckline and in dark navy. Her matching edge-to-edge coat, again in dark navy but with a strongly colour contrasting deep yellow hem was also tailored. The outfit was from British designer Amanda Wakeley, used by Catherine, the Duchess of Cambridge, whose designs also graced Diana, Princess of Wales. May chose to accessorize the dress and coat with—what *Vogue* designates the best power-dressing prop—a statement necklace (Sheffield 2016: n.pag.), also designed by Wakeley.

Kitten heels and leopard prints

Theresa May's shoes were the only unusual note in her ensemble, leopard-print kitten heels from British high street fashion retailer L.K. Bennett (see Plate xix). First attracting comment in 2002, when she wore the same leopard-print shoes with an all-navy dress to address the Conservative Party conference as Party Chairman (and famously informed her party that they were perceived as the nasty party). Theresa May's shoes, as well as her other clothing choices have continued to attract attention; she has become famous and/or notorious for them.

English shoe manufacturing is even older than the English tailoring tradition. The Cordwainers, established in 1272, are one of the oldest London Guilds and English shoes are another clear signifier of English dress to the world (Glenville 1996). However, even for men, a British politician's choice of shoes carries with it the possibility of transgression: 'it was widely considered that overstated designs in footwear were worn by those who were "cads", "bounders" and "gigolos".' Even such minor variations as the use of suede were usually regarded as unacceptable, to the extent of 'signifying homosexuality' (Glenville 1996: 171).

In May's case, it was her choice of glossy black, croc print patent leather over knee boots to a state event to greet the president of Mexico in 2015 that provoked outrage in some areas of the press: 'It's the high-shine patent that is particularly unflattering. It can look, dare I say it, a bit cheap. They don't really go with that coat and gloves either, which are actually very chic' (Glazin cited in Tweedy 2015: n.pag.).

The response to these boots demonstrates some of the problems of choosing suitable footwear. May wore them in Whitehall at Horse Guards Parade and with their to-the knee-sheath and over-knee flap in the style reminiscent of the boots worn by the Queen's Household Cavalry, a fitting militaristic reference for the situation. However, their glossiness and the faux crocodile pattern made these boots inauthentic and therefore unseemly. Also, their production by British high street stalwart Russell and Bromley and their price, far from being cheap at about £495, did not save May from appearing inappropriately dressed. Rather, the shiny leather material referenced aspects of kinky behaviour and sexual availability hints, revealed by comments such as 'kinky boots' and '[s]he always gives good boots' (Prince 2015: n.pag.).

Theresa May's choice of shoes on her first day as prime minister continues to reinforce her role in projecting British (English) national identity coming as they do from an important British retailer. However, in these shoes, May clearly steps away from the male puritanical precedent to something more feminine. The question here revolves around whether this step moves towards a form of everyday resistance and subversion, or towards a form of heteronormative sexual fantasy and reinforcement of the male dominance in the House of Commons. The discussion focuses first on these shoes as heeled footwear before considering the choice of leopard-print decoration and the two in combination.

The heeled shoe is the most clearly gendered object in western wardrobes (Riello and McNeil 2006). Originally, worn by both men and women through the course of the eighteenth century, but the rise of restraint in male clothing and the wish to distance themselves from aristocratic excesses, men abandoned the heel and it became an exclusively feminine accessory (Semmelhack 2006). One of the perceived advantages of the heel for women was that it reduced the apparent size of the foot, 'big feet [...] have always signified vulgarity, peasantry and poverty' (Pine 2006: 357). The Cinderella fairytale has this privileging of small feet at its heart, marking out their owner as unique and separating her from the ugly sisters with their oversized feet (see Grimm and Grimm 2013).

Heels with steel rods or 'stilettos', first created in 1951, had instant erotic overtones when pictured worn in the bedroom and through the translation of the name stiletto meaning 'little dagger'. The 10 cm full stiletto was associated with sexual availability (Semmelhack 2015) whilst the demure 5 cm kitten heel was associated with youth and inexperience (Bennett, L.K. n.d.). The day before May's appointment as prime minister, British newspaper *The Sun* ran the headline 'Heel Boys' clearly referencing the erotic nature of the heel and also invoking ideas of female domination that together referenced the fantasy of the dominatrix. The headline's reference to Maggie May clearly aligned May with Margaret Thatcher, a woman who was also portrayed as erotic in her domination of her all-male Cabinet as well as referencing the Rod Stewart single of the same name about a Liverpudlian prostitute. Conway (2016) identifies the Nanny aspect of this domination and the implied subtext of women as better managers because they are the ones who get everything done in the home. May's early depiction as 'the headmistress' dressing down the party in 2002 resonates with these understandings of woman as disciplinarians.

At this stage, May's choice of kitten heels on 13 July 2016 appears to be another traditional choice, conforming as they do to ideas of feminine display and infantilization; methods by which women have passed within environments understood as masculine. So how can an accessory so clearly connected to the sexual fetish (Steele

2006) and heteronormativity be attributed as resistant? The discussion of this possibility recognizes women in Parliament as a subaltern group and draws on the idea of 'everyday resistance,' to the dominant group (Haynes and Prakesh 1991) as expressed through the material culture of dress. This also aligns with the feminist position that women should be able to wear what they want without assumptions of their sexual availability or intellectual status; a position articulated by May as 'I know I have a brain and I'm serious so I can wear pretty shoes' (Retter 2016: n.pag.). The site of resistance is situated in the choice of 'fabric' for the shoe; a kitten heel in a plain leather would do no more than conform to the traditional codes cited above both as sign of national identity and as appropriate feminine attire allowing her to pass as an 'honorary male' on both the national and international stage. Women politicians who have followed this route are Angela Merkel, German Chancellor (2005–21) and Beato Szydło Polish Prime Minsiter (2015–17).

The reading of women members of parliament as a subaltern group derives from the mismatch between their number within the House of Commons and the proportion of women in the general population as discussed earlier. The work of James Scott (1989) on everyday resistance alongside de Certeau's theories of consumption (1984) expressed the practices of dominant cultures. Here, Vinthagen and Johansson build a framework for discerning actions by subaltern groups as resistant. Importantly, they identify the entangled nature of power and resistance and locate resistance in the specific act and context thus allowing for changing and contradictory acts of resistance by the same actor. As everyday resistance is more enmeshed with the dominant field than resistant behaviour and resisting only some actions and not all, 'everyday resistance is necessarily contradictory – both subordinate and rebellious at the same time' (Vinthagen and Johansson 2013: 37). Theresa May's choice of kitten heels (subordinate) in a leopard print (rebellious) sits within this enmeshed and contradictory field.

Vinthagen and Johansson propose the following criteria for identifying actions as forms of everyday resistance:

1. done in a regular way, occasionally politically intended but typically habitual or semi-conscious;
2. done in a non-dramatic, non-confrontational or non-recognized way that (has the potential to) undermine some power, without revealing itself (concealing or disguising either the actor or the act) or by being defined by hegemonic discourse as 'non-political' or otherwise not relevant to resistance and
3. done by individuals or small groupings without a formal leadership or organization, but typically encouraged by some subcultural attitude or 'hidden transcript'.

(2013: 37)

Prime Minister Theresa May's choice of shoes, the leopard-print kitten heels may be an example of 'everyday resistance' by considering the possible meanings and associations of fur in general and leopard print in particular and then placing those meanings within the wardrobe of the prime minister.

The wearing of fur and animal skins has a long history in human dress history and varies across time and cultures. From the twelfth century in England sumptuary laws were enacted by Parliament governing the use of luxury items by social hierarchy (Phillips 2007). Most of the items regulated are items of dress, and fur is mentioned in many, as most restrictions are associated with levels of yearly income. Most furs moved across income barriers; however, the use of ermine was restricted to the Royal family and their children. This understanding of ermine as the Royal fur is gloriously expressed in the 1701 portrait of Louis XIV of France by Hyacinthe Rigaud. Ermine also had associations with virtue, the 1585-'ermine' portrait of Elizabeth I is understood as an allegory of her virginity and chasteness. While in general, English sumptuary laws paid little attention to women's attire, one exception was the wearing of fur by prostitutes so that they would not be mistaken for virtuous female citizens (Phillips 2007). In the sixteenth and seventeenth centuries, the sumptuary discourse became less about social divisions and standing, and more a moral discourse on material excess and puritanical debates about the control of female sexuality (Bolton 2004). The wearing of fur became increasingly associated with prostitution and sexual fetish. In 1870, the publication of *Venus in Furs* upended the association of ermine with virtue when the protagonist Wanda dominates the male character dressed in an ermine-edged robe (Harper 2008). The association of fur and immorality continued through the twentieth century becoming associated with both the pimp and the prostitute. This link is seen in Annie Leibovitz's photo for Nija Furs of P. Diddy in a full-length white fur coat and Kate Moss in a leopard-print wrap (*c.*1999), and Helmut Newton's 1994 photo of Laura dressed in fur cape, on Avenue Georges V, 30 Paris (Bolton 2004). With technological advances in textile production, furs and faux furs have become lighter and more accessible; the middle-aged woman wearing her mink tippets to demonstrate the social advances of her life (Harper 2008) has been displaced by a younger, more sexually aware woman who negotiates a line between appropriate sexuality and vulgarity.

Leopard skin, or leopard print, has a long history of association with bravery, hunting and war. The wearing of the animal's skin was used variously to indicate power and status, as in Uganda, or to connect priests with a relevant god as in Egypt. Leopard skin was associated with fierceness in hunting and was particularly associated with women as the leopardess was known as the more deadly hunter. Thus, early artistic representations of women such as

Diana the Huntress and Amazonians depicted them wearing leopard skins. This positive association lasted well into the eighteenth century in Europe with representations of aristocratic women as Diana, such as Jean Marc Nattier's portrait of Madame de Maison Rouge as Diana (1756). Leopard skins formed part of the Hussar saddle furniture from the eighteenth century and simulated skins continue to be used by regimental horse bands to protect the saddles from damage (National Army Museum 2019). Alongside this, however, were less military associations such as the wildness associated with Bacchantes, the female adherents of the god Bacchus, who in their drink-induced madness would tear to pieces any man they came across. The leopard skin also became associated with enchantresses and witches such as Circe and Morgan Le Fey, the half-sister of King Arthur (see Raymond 2017).

Over time the association with dangerous women, the femme fatale and sexual availability became the dominant meaning. In the late eighteenth century, Emma Hamilton, Lord Nelson's mistress, became famous for her *tableau vivant*, striking poses of classical figures. Victorian artist Lawrence Alma-Tadema, along with others, became known for his depictions of the Roman Empire using archeological detail to surround images of decadence and luxury. His painting 'The Roses of Heliogalbus' (1885) shows the emperor of Rome smothering his guests with roses whilst listening to music played by a leopard skin-clad bacchante. Alma-Tadema's work was exhibited at the Royal Academy and was popular with Victorian society; however, his work also reached a far wider public, with his involvement in theatre design depicting the descendency into decay of the Roman Empire before its salvation by Christianity (Barrow 2010). Another figure beloved of painters such as Alma-Tadema and theatre producers was Cleopatra, Pharaoh and lover of Julius Caesar and Mark Anthony. Cleopatra, the last Pharoah to rule Egypt independently was represented as the ultimate exotic lover and femme fatale. Alma-Tadema painted the meeting of Antony and Cleopatra with the Pharaoh aboard her barge sitting on a leopard skin-covered stool. In Victorian theatres, in sharp contrast to Queen Victoria as the pattern of a female ruler, Cleopatra was played by Lillie Langtry, mistress of the Prince of Wales, and Constance Collier, both of whom were photographed in their costumes including leopard-skin cloaks (see Barrow 2010).

The association of leopard prints with actresses and performers and therefore sexual availability continued throughout the twentieth century. The emergence of jazz (McClendon 2015) in the early part of the century linked wearing leopardskin to exotic barbaric cultures in Africa, through the slave trade and further, the depiction of Negro men as barely contained animals (Guyatt 2000). In the 1920s Paris, Josephine Baker, the famous African American burlesque performer, was renowned for her pet leopard and her use of the print in her stage costumes (Alexander 2018). Hollywood actresses of the 1940s and 1950s, such as Jane Mansfield and Marilyn Monroe, often wore leopard-print bathing suits and evening dresses in films and publicity stills. Elizabeth Taylor, one of the most famous British Hollywood stars of this period, known for her lavish lifestyle and multiple marriages and whose scandalous affair with Richard Burton was ignited on the set of Cleopatra in Rome, often wore leopard print. Beyond this association with immorality, leopard print became increasingly associated with kitsch, popular culture and bad taste.

In 1973, when BIBA opened Big BIBA, its new London store in Kensington leopard prints were used liberally throughout the store (see Plate xx) and were scattered throughout the promotional store guide. Even the centre spread is a poster of a BIBA employee dressed as Cleopatra reclining on a leopard-covered bed, located in the 'Mistress' section of the 'men-only' third floor was entirely decorated in leopard prints (see Figure 7.1).

This confirms the long-standing association of female political power with leopard fur and print in both art history and popular culture that has become associated with dangerous female sexuality and immorality. Therefore, a female prime minister who chooses to wear leopard print, because she represents the British government, can be seen as a challenge to the institution itself.

FIGURE 7.1: Illustration advertising the 'Mistress' section of the third floor men-only department of Big BIBA, London, England. September 1973. Copyright Kasia Charko.

Conclusion

According to Vinthagen and Johansson's three criteria (2013) Theresa May's shoes rank as transgressive:

- May wears noticeable footwear and often wears leopard print – these kitten heels in particular – on significant occasions such as her first day as prime minister and when announcing the snap general election in May 2017.
- These shoes undermine the dominant clothing-society culture of the House of Commons in two ways. First, as introducing the system of change that is represented by fashion into the traditional and therefore more static clothing – the society of parliamentary dress codes and secondly by wearing a print with associations of female not male power. Both interventions reflect feminine characteristics and so disrupt attempts to reclassify May as an honourary man.
- May wears these shoes on her own cognizance with no 'official' remit. However, May, with Baroness Jenkin of Kensington, co-founded the group Women2Win to provide support and mentoring to women seeking election as Conservative candidates (see https://www.women2win.com/, accessed 15 October 2021). Moreover, she has consistently networked with women members of parliament across party lines to acknowledge their similar situation despite political differences. This is in contrast to Margaret Thatcher who did little to support or advance female conservative members of parliament and encouraged male colleagues' reclassification of her as a 'supernatural' being (Rodgers 1993).

The resistance signified by leopard-print shoes on the feet of the British prime minister becomes contradictory, as the print invokes fantasies of heteronormative female sexuality which challenges governmental authority. However, that contradiction is inherent within tropes of everyday resistance. The scale of the challenge is commensurate with the subaltern position that women still occupy within the House of Commons both numerically and ideologically. Their position limits the scope of everyday resistance to what is possible without retribution whilst still pushing and testing those limits. Theresa May's choice of these shoes, ones she returns for momentous moments (*Vogue* 2019), conflicts with the norm of British parliamentary dress for women. But in doing so, she balances out the wearing of traditional ministerial clothing with her expression of belonging to the subaltern group in Parliament. By invoking the feminist ideology of wearing what she pleases and with reference to the feminine sexuality and power associated with the leopard, these shoes represent a moment of rebellion by inserting fashion society into the everyday costume-society of British politics and in the House of Commons in particular.

REFERENCES

Alexander, Hilary (2018), *Leopard Fashion's Most Powerful Print*, London: Lawrence King Publishing.

Barrow, Rosemary (2010), 'Toga plays and tableaux vivants: Theatre and painting on London's late-Victorian and Edwardian popular stage', *Theatre Journal*, 62:2, pp. 209–26.

Bates, L. (2016), 'So Theresa May has breasts: Who knew?', *The Guardian*, 17 March, https://www.theguardian.com/commentisfree/2016/mar/17/theresa-may-breasts-home-secretary-cleavage-budget-sexism-westmins-ter. Accessed 13 January 2019.

BBC (2015), *Inside the Commons: Lifting the Lid*, BBC Two England, 1 October, https://www.bbc.co.uk/programmes/b05234h3. Accessed 3 March 2020.

Behnke, Andreas (2016), *The International Politics of Fashion: Being Fab in a Dangerous World*, London: Routledge.

Bennett, L.K (n.d.), 'Kitten heel', https://www.lkbennett.com/kitten-heel. Accessed 13 January 2019.

Bolton, Andrew (2004), *WILD: Fashion Untamed*, New York: Metropolitan Museum of Art.

Breward, Christopher, Conekin, Becky and Cox, Caroline (eds) (2002), *The Englishness of English Dress*, Oxford and New York: Berg.

Certeau, Michel de (1984), *The Practice of Everyday Life*, Berkeley: University of California Press.

Conti, Samantha (2016), 'Why everyone is talking about Theresa May's shoes', *Footwear News*, 13 July, https://footwearnews.com/2016/influencers/power-players/theresa-may-prime-min-ister-fashion-shoes-style-239518/. Accessed 13 January 2019.

Conway, Daniel (2016), 'Margaret Thatcher, dress and the politics of fashion', in A. Behnke (ed.), *The International Politics of Fashion: Being Fab in a Dangerous World*, London: Routledge, pp. 161–86.

Country Life (2017), 'Take the gentleman test', *Country Life*, 18 March, https://www.countrylife.co.uk/luxury/gentleman/the-39-steps-to-being-a-gentle-man-78780. Accessed 3 January 2019.

Cumming, Valerie, Cunnington, C.W. and Cunnington, P.E. (2010), *The Dictionary of Fashion History*, Oxford: Berg.

Flügel, John C. (1930), *The Psychology of Clothes*, London: Hogarth Press.

Gerard, Jasper (2009), 'The curious case of David Cameron's suit', *The Daily Telegraph*, 10 October, https://www.telegraph.co.uk/news/politics/david-cameron/6291362/The-curious-case-of-David-Camerons-suit.html. Accessed 3 March 2020.

Glenville, Tony (1996), 'Shoes', in A. De La Haye (ed.), *The Cutting Edge: 50 Years of British Fashion*, London: V&A.

Grimm, J.L.C. and Grimm, W.C. (2013), *The Complete Grimm's Fairy Tales*, New York: Quarto Publishing Group USA.

Guyatt, Mary (2000), 'The Wedgwood slave medallion', *Journal of Design History*, 13:2, pp. 93–105.

Harper, Catherine (2008), 'I found myself inside her fur', *Textile*, 6:3, pp. 300–13.

Haynes, Douglas E. and Prakesh, Gyan (eds) (1991), *Contesting Power: Resistance and Everyday Social Relations in South Asia*, Berkeley and Los Angeles: University of California Press.

Hobsbawm, Eric and Ranger, Terence (eds) ([1983] 2017), *The Invention of Tradition*, Cambridge: Cambridge University Press.

Jansen, M. Angela (2016), *Moroccan Fashion: Design, Tradition and Modernity*, London: Bloomsbury Academic.

Marzel, Shoshana-Rose and Stiebel, Guy D. (eds) (2014), *Dress and Ideology: Fashioning Identity from Antiquity to the Present*, London: Bloomsbury.

McClendon, Alphonso D. (2015), 'Subversive representation: Vernacular, dress and morality', *Fashion and Jazz: Dress, Identity and Subcultural Improvisation*, London: Bloomsbury Academic, pp. 91–102.

Mills, Eleanor (2016), 'The magazine interview', *The Sunday Times Magazine*, 27 November, pp. 14–21.

National Army Museum (2019), 'Online collection leopard-skin flounce, 15th (King's) Hussars, 1904 c', National Army Museum, https://collection.nam.ac.uk/detail.php?acc=1974-08-20-1. Accessed 3 January 2019.

Parkins, Wendy (2002), 'Introduction: (Ad)dressing citizens', in W. Parkins (ed.), *Fashioning the Body Politic: Dress, Gender, Citizenship*, Oxford: Berg, pp. 1–18.

Bloomsbury Fashion Central, http://dx.doi.org.ezproxy.uwe.ac.uk/10.2752/9781847888723/FASHBODPOL0005. Accessed 1 January 2019.

Phillips, Kim M. (2007), 'Masculinities and the medieval English sumptuary laws', *Gender and History*, 19:1, pp. 22–42.

Pine, Julia (2006), 'Sole representation: Shoe imagery and twentieth century art', in G. Riello and P. McNeil (eds), *Shoes: A History from Sandals to Sneakers*, Oxford and New York: Berg, pp. 352–71.

Prince, Rosa (2015), 'Theresa May wears thigh-high boots to greet queen and Mexican president', *Daily Telegraph*, 3 March, https://www.telegraph.co.uk/news/politics/conservative/11447119/Theresa-May-wears-thigh-high-boots-to-greet-Queen-and-Mexican-President.html. Accessed 6 November 2019.

Raymond, Dalicia K. (2017), 'Motives, means, and a malevolent mantel: The Case of Morgan le Fay's transgressions in Sir Thomas Malory's *Le Morte Darthur*', Claussen, Albrecht (ed), *Magic and Magicians in the Middle Ages and the Early Modern Times*, Berlin: De Gruyte, pp. 547–64.

Retter, Emily (2016), 'Theresa May: The vicar's daughter in kitten heels who will be our new prime minister', *The Mirror*, 11 July, https://www.mirror.co.uk/news/uk-news/theresa-may-vicars-daughter-kitten-8399895. Accessed 1 January 2019.

Ribero, Aileen (2002), 'On Englishness in dress', in C. Breward, B. Conekin and C. Cox (eds), *The Englishness of English Dress*, Oxford and New York: Berg.

Riello, Giorgio and McNeil, Peter (eds) (2006), *Shoes: A History from Sandals to Sneakers*, Oxford and New York: Berg.

Rodgers, Silvia (1993), 'Women's space in a men's house: The British House of Commons', in S. Ardener (ed.), *Women and Space: Ground Rules and Social Maps*, 2nd ed., Oxford: Berg, pp. 46–69.

Root, R. (2002), 'Tailoring the nation: Fashion writing in nineteenth-century Argentina', in W. Parkins (ed.), *Fashioning the Body Politic: Dress, Gender, Citizenship*, Oxford: Berg.

Ross, Robert (2008), *Clothing: A Global History*, London: Polity, pp. 71–96.

Scott, James C. (1989), 'Everyday forms of resistance', *The Copenhagen Journal of Asian Studies*, 4, p. 33.

Semmelhack, Elizabeth (2006), 'A delicate balance: Women, power and high heels', in G. Riello and P. McNeil (eds), *Shoes: A History from Sandals to Sneakers*, Oxford and New York: Berg, pp. 224–47.

Semmelhack, Elizabeth (2015), 'The allure of power', in H. Persson (ed.), *Shoes: Pleasure and Pain*, London: V&A.

Shapiro, Fred R. (ed.) (n.d), *The New Yale Book of Quotations*, New Haven: Yale University Press, p. 843.

Sheffield, Emily (2016), 'Meet the power dressing prop', *Vogue*, 5 June, https://www.vogue.co.uk/gallery/statement-necklaces-theresa-may. Accessed 11 January 2019.

Shinko, Rosemary E. (2016), 'This is not a mannequin: Enfashioning bodies of resistance', in A. Behnke (ed.), *The International Politics of Fashion: Being Fab in a Dangerous World*, London: Routledge, pp. 19–40.

Statista (2016), 'Population of the United Kingdom in 2016 by gender', https://www.statista.com/statistics/281240/population-of-the-united-kingdom-uk-by-gender/. Accessed 13 January 2019.

Steele, Valerie (2006), 'Shoes and the erotic imagination', in G. Riello and P. McNeil, (eds), *SHOES: A History from Sandals to Sneakers*, Oxford and New York: Berg, pp. 250–70.

Tweedy, Jo (2015), 'Leopard print kitten heels, hologram wellies and thigh- high boots to meet the queen: Inside Theresa May's fabulous collec- tion of flamboyant shoes', *Daily Mail*, 4 March, https://www.dailymail.co.uk/femail/article-2978868/As-Theresa-wears-thigh-high-boots-meet-Queen-Home-Secretary-s-outrageous-footwear-revealed.html. Accessed 13 January 2019.

Vinthagen, Stellan and Johansson, Anna (2013), '"Everyday resistance": Exploration of a concept and its theories', *Resistance Studies Magazine*, 1:1, pp. 1–46.

Vogue (2019), 'Theresa May: A political life in pictures', *British Vogue*, 11 January, https://www.vogue.co.uk/gallery/theresa-may-political-life-in-pictures. Accessed 13 January 2019.

Young, Kirsty (2014), *Desert Island Discs*, BBC Radio 4, 28 November, https://www.bbc.co.uk/programmes/b04pr6rz. Accessed 3 March 2020.

8

Felix Siauw, Storyteller, Preacher and Profiteer: Fashioning a New Brand of Islam in Indonesia

Rheinhard Sirait

Introduction

Since September 11, 2001 (post-9/11), the study of Islamic fashion has proved a fertile ground for scholars. Earlier, the role of the veil was investigated as mediating among the various tropes of 'modesty, privacy and resistance' (El Guindi 1999; Hassan and Harun 2016). Various journals, such as the *Journal of Islamic Marketing* began to interrogate the dynamics between consumption, women's choices and the rise of the veil as an integral part of a new Muslim-based fashion consciousness. The ethnologist Sandra Hochel suggests that scholars often ascribe meaning to women's head coverings from the outside to indicate Islamic radicalism, ignoring how women themselves conceive of their clothing choices. Further, 'to veil or not veil' presents a complex decision-making process that does not necessarily indicate either excess modesty or even religious beliefs (2013: 40). Elsewhere, scholars who consider Islamic fashion as an up-and-coming trend analyse the headscarf alongside a rise of consumerism and luxury consumption in veil purchases (Hassan and Harun 2016). Hassan and Harun have promoted this new form of purchasing power among women who wear the veil to title them 'hijabistas' borrowing from the familiar term 'fashionistas' or those who seek to wear the finest in fashion. They further state, 'The hijabista market segment can be considered as the fastest growing consumer segment in the world and [...] Muslim women have been observed to continue to explore fashion trends within the bounds of Islamic principles' (2016: 491). Other scholars have suggested that cultural elements of the veil are more significant than religious ones (Blommaert and Varis 2015).

However, the veil, while limiting the wearer's aspect, cannot be hidden from others (Brenner 1996).The wearing of the veil presents an overt indicator of the Muslim faith, almost signalling a 'red flag' to those who are concerned with radicalization within Southeastern Asian nations, such as Indonesia and Malaysia (see Othman et al. 2008). The nearby countries of Australia and New Zealand critically watch any rises of Islamic extremism during stress points such as the Lindt Cafe siege in Sydney (Ralston and Partridge 2014: n.pag.) and backlash terrorism such as the tragic mass shooting tragedy in a mosque in Christchurch, New Zealand on 15 March 2019 (see Chapter 2).

In this context, the charismatic figure of Felix Siauw presents the perfect case study to understand how one man through social media could reconfigure the veil, its relation to Muslim female propriety and its uptake with young women in Indonesia.

This chapter details the rise of Felix Siauw, who is an Indonesian-Chinese Muslim convert to his position as one of the most successful digital *ustadz* ('preachers')[1] in Indonesia. Siauw's journey to fame began with his membership in Hizbut Tahrir Indonesia (HTI), a branch of the pan-Islamic Party Hizbut Tahrir, that was banned by the government for purportedly endangering Indonesian democracy (see Baran 2004). Felix Siauw gained celebrity status as a preacher through his narrative as a *mualaf* or Muslim convert, and as a convert who redeemed himself through overcoming enormous challenges to become a Muslim. Siauw draws from his experience as an ethnic minority to connect to Indonesian Muslims who feel that they are marginalized by both the current global order and the Indonesian state. It is this narrative that overrides any criticism that Siauw receives from moderate religious authorities who mock him because of his lack of Islamic credentials and command of Arabic, and dubbed him a *ustadz dua ayat* ('two-verse preacher'). His conversion story would have been inconsequential without his grasp of the essential ingredient to his popularity through social media platforms to convey his messages to urban middle-class Muslims in Indonesia. Today, Siauw is one of the highest-ranked digital preachers in Indonesia with over 4.3 million Instagram followers and more than three million Twitter followers. The reach of Felix Siauw's online persona through his celebrity status has enabled him to commodify pious Islamic ideals through his commercial enterprises – the marketing and selling of veils – that have gained overwhelming popularity among young Muslim women.

First, the unique case of Felix Siauw needs to be understood within the context of a rise of Islamization of Indonesia's public life. Second, he was part of the changing guard of authority in Indonesia's cohort of preachers. Third, he capitalized on the disorienting effects of online technology that propelled new kinds of preachers and their ideology into the public sphere in Indonesia. Siauw's preaching then turns to profit (rather than prophet) by merging his promotion and commodification of the hijab through his various commercial outlets. While his influence is undeniable, sometimes his audience reacted unfavourably thus demonstrating that Siauw's celebrity and *ustadz* status can be challenged at any moment, a process that continues under negotiation.

Siauw the storyteller: His troubled identity

Felix Siauw or Siauw Chen Kwok was born into an Indonesian-Chinese family from Palembang, South Sumatra on 31 January 1984. His family became subject to President Suharto's Instructions for Population Registration of 27 January 1980, and was forced to choose one of the five official state-sanctioned religions within his New Order regime. Under the law, Chinese religions such as Confucianism were no longer officially recognized in Indonesia, and thus outlawed on one's national identity card (Suryadinata 2001). Siauw's parents chose to be Catholic, while in everyday life his family continued to practice Chinese rituals. He reports that his grandmother advised him that he could choose any state religion excepting Islam, because it was against Chinese culture and religion.

On YouTube, Siauw describes the tensions that surfaced in his family between the Chinese cultural traditions and Islam as a religion. Siauw's grandmother's attitude towards Islam is emblematic of the Indonesian society's discrimination toward Indonesian Chinese minorities, stemming from colonial settlement of Indonesia by the Dutch. The historian Christian Chua explains that the anti-Chinese sentiment resulted from general opinions that the Chinese collaborated in the 30 September 1965 movement/incident, which later restricted their involvement in politics, the military and the public service (2008). In order to prevent the influence of Chinese culture, Suharto's regime enforced an assimilation policy towards this populace by abolishing the three pillars of Chinese identity: the Chinese-language press, ethnic Chinese organizations and Chinese high schools (Setiono 2003; Suryadinata 2010). Meanwhile, the Indonesian-Chinese were given privileges in the commercial sector to expand the national economy, which led to a deepened animosity towards them as an ethnic group especially by the poor (Chua 2008).

Felix Siauw recounts his hardships of growing up as Indonesian-Chinese in Palembang. He was the victim of racism numerous times and was once assaulted by a group of Muslim boys who called him slit-eyed. He recalls that he felt under constant threat wherever he went in Palembang and would avoid riding public transportation. These experiences made him feel discriminated against and he developed a prejudice towards so-called *pribumi* ('Indigenous') Indonesians. When the May 1998 riots broke out, Siauw felt even more traumatized because Indonesian Chinese became the targets of the violence (Mydans 1998). Siauw recalls that he was also terrified by the fact that Islamic groups initiated terror campaigns and widespread bombings in Indonesia after the fall of Suharto. All of these events strengthened Siauw's view that Islam was a religion of terrorists who condoned violence.

As a result, Siauw's religious identity was in turmoil. He publicly acknowledges that from the age of 12, he began to question the concept of God. His religious beliefs in childhood were not from his parents or the priests but from PlayStation games such as *Final Fantasy*. These games build their own set of belief systems, where 'God' is irrelevant, and their construction consists of rules built of pure power as energy (see Washburn 2010). At a young age, he began to question Christianity and often thought about philosophical questions such as the origins of human existence, life's purposes and the afterlife. He questioned his priests about the concept behind the Holy Trinity that he struggled with and he grew even more discontent when he realized that the New Testament of the Holy Bible was written by the Apostles rather than God. At the age of 14, Siauw decided to become an atheist because he felt that no one could answer his questions and he considered Christianity to be irrational.

The conversion (mualaf) narrative

The main key to Siauw's success is his self-historization of his 'conversion' (*mualaf*) to Islam that has become his core 'trademark' while preaching in Indonesia. In 2001, just three years after the anti-Chinese attacks of 1998, Siauw began his study of agricultural cultivation at the Bogor Agricultural Institute (IPB) in West Java. His father owned an agrochemical business in Palembang and encouraged him to study at IPB, the most prestigious agricultural university in Indonesia. Alongside its educational reputation IPB was a well-known centre for Islamic revivalism in Indonesia. When Siauw enrolled, there were three Islamic organizations that dominated IPB: the Tarbiyah movement or *Ikhwanul Muslimin*, which later transformed into *Partai Keadilan Sejahtera* (PKS, Prosperous Justice Party), Salafist groups and *HTI* (Machmudi 2008).

At university, Siauw encountered his first HTI activists as they all lived in the same *kost* ('boarding house'). As Zeyno Baran explains, HTI is a branch of the international Islamic pan-organization Hizb ut-Tahrir (Liberation Party) established by Palestinian jurist and cleric Taqiuddin an-Nabhani (2006). The focus of HTI's movement was based on Nabhani's narrative about Islam's glorious past, which he contrasts with the present day where Muslims are seen as sufferers and are relegated to peripheral players in the eyes of the world. Nabhani's purpose in establishing the worldwide *Hizb ut-Tahrir* ('Party of Liberation') is to promote intellectual leaders who can rectify the failures of today's Muslims by reinstating the Islamic way of life among the *ummah* ('Islamic world') and establish an Islamic Caliphate that will guarantee the application of a *kaffah* ('full and comprehensive') set of Islamic laws (Baran 2004; Hanif 2012).

His growing friendship with HTI activists not only made him question his assumptions about Islam but also gave him a sense of belonging that he lacked previously in his life. Siauw recalls that he was impressed with HTI's methods in organizing routine public discussions on his campus and that the atmosphere was intellectual, polite and civilized. It was completely different from his previous impressions of Islam. Most important was that Siauw describes himself as 'feeling privileged' because he was accepted into the group like all the other participants. They were also not concerned about his physical appearance as a Chinese Indonesian. In a YouTube video, Siauw openly contrasts this feeling of acceptance with his traumatic adolescent experience of racism in Palembang.

Siauw describes his meeting with a young HTI activist called Fatih Karim as the turning point in his fascination with Islam. Karim was a young HTI *ustadz* ('preacher') who presented a public discussion at the Al-Hurriah mosque on the IPB campus. Siauw describes his attraction to Karim because he was an unusual *ustadz* who did not wear conspicuous Islamic, that is, Arabic-styled attire. He had a calm and patient temper and above all, he displayed a vast knowledge of Islam. In dramatic style Siauw describes his conversion to Islam after he confronted Karim in a continuous evening-to-daybreak debate after they ceased to argue just before the Mosque's dawn call to prayer. Siauw's romanticized this 'Road to Damascus' (*sic*) moment when the silent pause just at dawn finally convinced him to convert to Islam (Yaden and Newberg 2015). Karim had convinced and enlightened him about Islam's superiority over other religions. Consequently, Siauw formally joined HTI's movement.

The chance to convert a nominal Catholic, who was also Chinese by ethnicity to HTI's cause was mutually very beneficial. Despite Indonesian Muslims comprising 88 per cent majority of the population, they have often felt threatened by a Christian minority (see Aragon 2000; Mujiburrahman 2006). Therefore, a *mualaf* ('convert') is always special for the Muslim community as the conversion sparks a sensation of joy and triumph, and further a sense of superiority over other religions. The fact that Siauw is Indonesian of Chinese descent makes him a truly remarkable convert and HTI was quick to realize Siauw's 'star power' when compared to the average Muslim. As Siauw states, he was encouraged to start proselytizing immediately following his conversion despite his limited knowledge of Islam. Clearly, HTI needed Siauw not for his nascent religious learnings but as a demonstration of their recruitment success. HTI's campaign to establish the Caliphate and *sharia* (also *shariah*, *shari'a*), or Islamic religious law throughout

Indonesia was not too popular but Siauw's conversion communicated HTI's rhetoric by showing that both Muslims and *mualafs* ('persons who have embraced Islam') support their ideals (see An-Na'im 2008).

Again, there were benefits on both sides. After Siauw joined HTI, he acquired his significant 'backstory' detailing his self-legitimizing spiritual journey. It also legitimates his membership among the imagined *Ummah* ('transnational community of believers') in Indonesia, a new identity that gave Siauw his sense of true belonging and a 'real home' that he longed for in his early life. This feeling of 'home' was missing from his birth family's beliefs and culture, as well as in his imagined online fantasy life. This conversion story liberates him from carrying the burden of a double-minority identity as Chinese Christian. Siauw presented that his journey was arduous as he had to convincingly belie his physical appearance that represented a disliked ethnic group in Indonesia (Weng 2018a).

Siauw describes his life as spinning faster after he converted to Islam and joined HTI. His friends at the agricultural college were startled when they discovered that Siauw went to a mosque for the first time, and their response was cynical or even sceptical. It seemed improbable to them that Siauw would begin his 'preaching career' only three weeks after his conversion to Islam. This conversion also presented problems with his family, and his father accused him of being possessed by an evil spirit. Also, Siauw experienced significant financial hardship after losing his family's support. Later, in 2006 after Siauw decided to marry his friend Parsini from IPB he was able to repair his relationship with his father. As time went by Siauw's relationship with his family improved and eventually he was accepted back into the fold. Also, Siauw began to work as a marketing manager for the agrochemical company owned by his father, PT Biotis Agrindo. The *mualaf* story ended happily when his father sponsored Siauw and his wife on their first pilgrimage to Mecca.

Siauw's story, or his narrative about his conversion to a Chinese Indonesian *mualaf* ('believer') performs two important functions. First, it cemented his affiliation among the Muslim majority in Indonesia and second, it embodied him as an Islamic repentant. This repentance acquires symbolic force as it alleviates outside scepticism of his role as an *ustadz*. Therefore, Siauw's story functions to justify that he is more Islamic than the average Muslim, because he has been through this thorny spiritual journey.

From convert to Islam motivator

Felix Siauw's early days of preaching were a struggle as his credentials as a Muslim were constantly challenged. Particularly, his decision to retain his Chinese name after his conversion distinguishes him from other preachers. Yet, his trademark as Chinese *mualaf* was insufficient to accord him success in the long run; he needed to create his own personal 'brand' or style. For a start, while he needed to learn the Islamic texts, he also found them quite difficult. His teacher (*ustadz*) rejected his desire to study the Koran and other Arabic scriptures as he was not circumcised. Initially, on many occasions the audience would leave Siauw's sermons after they noticed that he could not read Arabic. Further, his connection with HTI complicated his route to success. Despite an extensive network across Indonesia, HTI had not yet produced a successful celebrity *ustadz* within the growing ranks of Indonesia's popular preachers. This is not too surprising since HTI's ideological stances included the promotion of an international Caliphate (Muslim state) and further, the implementation of sharia law, both largely unpopular with the majority of Indonesian Muslims.

For a long time, Siauw was cautious about how he promoted his Islamic credentials. Rather than the title of *ustadz*, Siauw chose to call himself an 'Islamic motivator', which circumvented his lack of Islamic credentials. This new moniker of Islamic motivator meant he was exempt from using Islamic texts as the sole materials for his preaching. So he chose to preach a bricolage or 'ready-to-hand' set of concepts that included Islam, science, history and personal stories to inspire his audience. In fact, combining Islam text and popular psychology (self-help) or motivational texts is not a new formula for the prominent Islamic preaching personalities in Indonesia. In fact, the Indonesian television superstar preacher, AA Gymnastiar used self-help guides and motivational techniques to attract larger audiences (Hoesterey 2015).

In this mode, Felix Siauw started to attract attention after he published two books titled *Beyond Your Inspiration* and *Muhammad Al-Fatih 1453* (Weng 2018a). These are two typical self-help books that encourage and inspire Muslims to embrace the religion of Islam, its past glory and its ideological goals. Both of Siauw's books employ the heroic narrative of Muhammad Al-Fatih (Mehmed II or Mehmed the Conqueror) whose army defeated the city of Constantinople, ending the long reign of the Byzantium Empire. Through the narrative of Mehmed the Conqueror, Siauw promotes his ideal Muslim man. Mehmed's status as a true believer with a strong and firm faith who had surrendered himself to God, respected the *ulemas* ('body of Islamic scholars'), and embodied a righteous family man. Siauw also highlights Mehmed's heroism through his courageous, goal-oriented and assertive military leadership. His first two books demonstrate Siauw's aptitude as a simple, but lucid writer who blended Islamic teachings, history and popular psychology. Consequently, these two books became bestsellers that promoted his name to the wider public beyond his original political network formed by HTI.

There was a gradual transformation as Siauw graduated from Islamic motivator to one of Indonesia's influential preachers by uploading his preaching materials to the Internet. In an online interview Siauw was quoted that he quickly realized the potential of social media as a space where many Muslims, especially young families and teenagers, accessed their information and religious guidance (see http://www.indochine.com, accessed 24 September 2021). In 2007, Siauw began his online preaching on Facebook, a year after he finished his college studies at IPB. But his preaching on Facebook was not the success he imagined, he recalled in an interview with *Tempo* (Anon. 2015). Siauw continued to tenaciously trial other social media platforms such as YouTube, Tumblr, Twitter and Instagram. He also maintained a personal blog until 2015, until it also outlived its usefulness in attracting an audience (see http://felixsiauw.com/home/, accessed 1 January 2015).

Online celebrity preacher

Here, the stars aligned for Siauw's success. In Indonesia, Siauw was an early adopter or pioneer in his utilization of social media for *dakwah* ('preaching') purposes in Indonesia. When he started preaching online the social media space was relatively unpopulated by preachers, despite their awareness of the rise of this new communications technology. Television remained the apex of one's popularity and very few preachers acquired regular programming. Celebrity preachers, such as AA Gym, Jefri Al-Buchori and Umar Mansyur anchored their popularity through national television broadcasts even though they employed social media as well. It seemed they could not harness the power of social media and chose to use it only as a one-way or broadcast method to post up advertising materials similar to street posters, without employing the tools required for audience participation. In contrast, Siauw chose to strategically nurture his online persona through managing his digital reputation (Marwick 2013). His perfect timing plus how he utilized this new environment for preaching cemented his dominant position in Indonesia's online preaching market.

By persistence, Siauw found his algorithm of success through Twitter's social media platform. He opened his Twitter account in 2010. Siauw's first tweet dated on 2 September 2010 quoted his hero Mehmed the Conqueror saying: '*Aku akan menaklukkan Barat, menyatukannya dalam 1 kepemimpinan, dan 1 aturan untuk seluruh dunia*' ('I will conquer the West, unite it under one leadership, and one [Islamic] rule for the whole world'). His use of Twitter mushroomed in 2012 after Twitter was hyped as 'the' platform in Indonesia. In fact, Indonesia's capital Jakarta shortly became the most active Twitter city in the world and was dubbed the world's 'Twitter capital' (Aly 2013). This platform dominated because it allowed quicker conversations with a wider range of participants compared to other platforms. The Twitter platform also recalls an open space, similar to an Indonesian *pasar* ('traditional market') whereby the public, despite their differences in background and social status can converse directly with others. Last but not least, this newly popular platform enabled those like Felix Siauw – from non-celebrity backgrounds removed from the broadcast mode of national television – to reach instant popularity and celebrity status. As a result, Siauw could navigate through Twitter in his online persona and quickly became a 'micro-celebrity' in the online space (Senft 2008), in Indonesian, a *celebtwit* (Twitter celebrity).

Siauw's tweet on 19 January 2015 promoted his main strategy in social media, that is, to produce controversial comments that are not normally voiced out loud in Indonesia. To build his online reputation, he placed himself at the centre of controversial issues to develop his online persona as a hub for preaching. He continually chose to address the various social tensions that lay dormant in Indonesian society. His controversial figure allowed him to garner a large 'followership' composed of his fans, his haters and even bystanders who enjoyed the excitement offered during the online argumentation. Siauw delivered content from the HTI teaching and doctrinal materials, but with a masterly finesse. However, HTI's teachings were not often so acceptable in the online forums, while Siauw's popularity grew from his tweets that depicted everyday life themes.

In Siauw's first year on Twitter he gained a massive audience of more than 250,000 followers, which ranked him as fourth among the most followed *ustadz* in Indonesia in 2015. Further, the mainstream media outlets started to quote him publically, and he became a national celebrity after he and his family made appearances on prime time television talk shows, where his conversion story became widely publicized. Two trends assisted the growth of Siauw's popularity in a relatively short time. First, the emergence of pious urban middle class (Hadiz 2016) that began to adopt Islamic habits in their lives within Indonesian society (Fealy and White 2008). Second, the ubiquity of digital technology and social media platforms in Indonesia enabled religious people to personalize their own religiosity through their adherence to specific online discussions (Hoover 2006).

Islamic youth and their fashions

Siauw's success depended on his strategy to target his audience and/or followers, and he tried to bridge the gap that existed between Indonesia's young people and religion. Through his own experience with the failings of Christian theology, Siauw realized that young people in Indonesia were searching for their religious identity, but they did not yet understand Islam. This age group was also the largest consumers of online content coupled with their vulnerability as seekers of faith. Therefore, his most-popular tweets and preachings or lessons addressed themes that were popular among teenagers. Topics including Islam's prohibitions on dating, the wearing of the hijab for young women and his controversial ban of taking 'selfies' were widely discussed.

His online appearance was calculated to appeal to a young audience and his bald head projected the appearance of a Buddhist monk. He presents himself as cool *ustadz,* a free-spirited man who enjoys travelling and is fond of nature, sport, coffee and culinary delights. He also did not adopt the traditional Arabic style of clothing or adornments. His signature is sporty, with a backpack and SLR camera draped over his shoulder as his official online costume. Instead of Arabic vestments he wears shirts in the Indonesian national cloth called *batik* ('traditional block-printed fabric'), or a plain t-shirt or casual outfit. He communicated that casual clothing was the norm for the young males that he was addressing online while communicating his Islamic principles.

For Siauw, there is a special link between the wearing of batik and its popularity in Indonesian culture. In his Facebook page on 18 January 2018 titled '*Mengapa Batik?*' ('Why *Batik?*') Siauw explains that his choice of wearing *batik* provides a latent social communication (see Achjadi 1999). He felt that the Indonesian cultural trope is gentle and sensitive, therefore, his lessons must instruct by gentle attraction. His use of *batik* as a national message was emphasized by the use of *wayang* ('stick puppets') to convey Islam across the archipelago. According to Siauw, both *wayang* and *batik* became established as symbolic expressions of Islam. Later, Siauw compares the use of *batik* with most common Islamic attire such as *surban* ('turban'). He says that Muslim men are not required to wear either the turban or *jubah* cloak. It is more important is that their deeds and speech must be based on Islam. He criticizes those Muslims who 'dress up' in turbans, cloaks and *peci* ('hat') if their lifestyles are liberal and not adherent to the Islamic creed. While he often addressed young men to expand their faith, it is his interest in young women and their behaviour that came to the fore in his preachings.

Young women and the hijab

In marked contrast to his easy-going approach to young men's clothing, Siauw promoted strict guidelines for young women both in dress and manners, or decorum. Posted in this online website, Siauw revealed that from the beginning his aim was to influence teenage girls with his online lessons, whom he regarded as neglected by other Islamic organizations (see https://tabloidbintang.com, accessed 5 August 2021). Siauw based his lessons around female piety derived from HTI's purist Islam ideas. His considerable talents lay in extracting and recontextualizing the HTI doctrines and the HTI leader's work such as 'The social system of Islam' into a number of *kultwits* ('culturally based tweets'). He borrowed heavily from Taqiuddin an-Nabhani's interpretation of Islamic rules and regulations about relationships between men and women (2006). Here, an-Nabhani argues that meetings between men and women were the cause of social unrest in Indonesian society, and abiding by his doctrines would fix these problems. It is curious that Siauw never mentions this text as the source of his tweets or lessons, therefore giving an impression that these constituted his original thoughts about male–female relationships.

Therefore, Siauw established his authority among his followers by combining a strict interpretation of Islamic texts alongside his provocative statements. For one example, he upheld the prohibition on Muslims to acknowledge non-Islamic religious celebrations, including Valentine's Day. He gained popularity because these questions persist in online debates among young Indonesian Muslims. His *kultwits* employed hashtags such as #UdahPutusinAja to explain that Islam prohibits dating that shocked and created controversy among teenaged girls. Despite these disruptive messages Siauw continued to adapt his online skills so he could convey very serious religious messages wrapped up in a 'lighter' package to suit his young female followers. When delivering his tweets Siauw was adept in employing jokes, slang and elements of pop culture to make his preachings both memorable and even thrilling to a young audience.

For young women, wearing the hijab, veil or headcovering became Siauw's most popular kind of *dakwah* or religious lesson. In 2012, he published four *twitseri* ('a series of tweets') about the hijab and its importance for women. The tradition of wearing the hijab has a long history in Indonesia, but Siauw's teachings assign a moral burden for any Muslim women who do not wear it properly. From Siauw's study of Islam, adopted from the ideology voiced by HTI through their founding Palestinian clerics he crafted his interpretation of women and their bodies. He promoted the view of women's bodies are jewels which must be covered from the outside world. He then condemns Muslim women who wear ordinary clothing on the street as actually 'naked' as they reveal sacred parts of their bodies to unrelated men. Further, he imposes more guilt on these women because under HTI's ideology, they will not be accepted into heaven. In many interpretations of Islam, women can decide to wear the hijab when they are mentally ready (Kusumawati et al. 2019), but according to Siauw, women should wear it regardless of whether they are 'ready' or not.

So Siauw's *kultwits* promote the way women should wear hijab. For example, the usual Indonesian headdress still reveals a women's *aurat* (taboo body parts) or the outlined form of a woman's body. To correct this, Siauw introduced the concept of *hijab syar'i*, which consists of three different pieces of attire (the *khimar* or veil, *jilbab* or long dress and *tabbaruj* or socks) that cover the entirety of a woman's body (see Plate xxi). Siauw goes into great detail to describe how women should wear the hijab in terms of its length, shape and form. Siauw's *kultwits* on hijab have been extremely popular with massive re-tweets. Part of the reason why the *kultwits* are popular is because it clearly outlines how women should wear the hijab. His *kultwits* employed a Q&A style approach to cover the general questions that hindered women from wearing their hijabs correctly.

Hijab as high fashion

The hijab, and its uptake as a high fashion item by Islamic women has attracted much scholarly research. It is important to note that there are many differences between Islamic interpretations of the proper dress for women from the Arabic, Persian and archipelago perspectives, including Malaysia and Indonesia (for Indonesia, see Kartajaya et al. 2019). Kartajaya et al. found many differences within clothing choices among Indonesian women. Factors can include age, religiosity and even public expression of social identity rather than just religious beliefs. In the online space, Siauw's rhetoric was designed to reach teenagers and young women who first, had funds available to purchase headwear, and second, sought to be seen as popular with their peers (Sirait 2017).

Siauw's success in promoting anti-dating and wearing hijab is indebted to a female visual designer, Emeralda Noor Achni, nicknamed Benefiko. She was a former band member and a student of visual communication design from a prestigious university in Indonesia. She met Siauw during one of his sermons while she was having a crisis in her life. He was attracted to Benefiko's graphic skills, so he asked her to illustrate his ideas to appeal to young girls' tastes. In 2013, Siauw published two visual books titled #*UdahPutusinAja* (*Just Breaking Up*) and #*YukBerhijab* (*C'mon Wear a Veil*) and both became bestsellers for young Muslims in Indonesia. He constructed the titles from series of tweets, which then snowballed into a popular Twitter hashtag. Their popularity was driven by their visual appeal, which then generated an entire new look for Islamic publications. As a result, Benefiko became an integral part of Siauw's success and she continues today as his business partner.

Through Benefiko's ability to appeal to young women, Siauw enlarged his trajectory in his online mission: to promote the *hijab syar'i* (proper hijab) not just through his preaching but also through his commercial enterprise. Even before Siauw started to preach about *hijab syar'i* in the online space in 2011, he and his wife, Parsini, ran a hijab business called *Hijab Alila*, named after their 4-year-old daughter. His wife, Parsini offered her sewing skills, and it was clear that the prospective market for *hijab syar'i* was viable, as in Indonesia, Muslim women had not yet participated in *fashionable* veil shopping (Hassan and Harun 2016). Consequently, Parsini started to sell her own product online with Siauw's assistance. Later, Parsini invited Benefiko to become co-owner of Hijab Alila as well as her partner in managing the store. The store was successful and their business expanded to many cities in Indonesia.

The establishment of *Hijab Alila* was not just a retail store but played a key role in marketing Siauw's lessons for female piety. This amalgamation of business and preaching was promoted through the store's Hijab Alila events that targeted young Muslim women. These events evolved as talk shows or public lectures with Felix Siauw and his *ustadz* colleagues from HTI networks and sometimes included Muslim celebrities as the main guest speakers. Participants bought tickets for admission to these functions and the tickets often came with additional offers, such as discounts for hijab garments or Siauw's books. The store became a 'full-service' hub to provide the latest branded designs from *Hijab Alila* but also established a sense of community among young Muslims in Indonesia and became a fashionable place to engage with HTI's teachings on women's dress and other Islamic doctrines.

In the online environment, *Hijab Alila* online shop promoted the concept of *hijab syar'i* (religious or 'proper veil') to young women and displayed the 'correct' types of hijab in a youthful style that could appeal to young women. Overall, the *Hijab Alila* online store offers a two-tone colour style, mixing pink and purple colours (see Plate xxi). Siauw's business partner Benefiko explains this two-tone colour style communicates a firm, bold and focussed outlook for 'good' young Islamic women (see https://www.facebook.com/BenefikoJunior, accessed 5 August 2021). Benefiko's designs also employed a unique typeface for *Hijab Alila* with a 'casual and youthful' flavour that suited this younger market. *Hijab Alila* also promoted video channels in YouTube that show young girls role-playing 'good' girls while wearing the more restrictive *hijab syar'i*. They demonstrate online through their pious choices how to be good and moral Muslim girls. Here, the promotional materials focus less on the up-to-date hijab fashions, but rather encouraged moral standards for young girls on a range of issues. These items included cheating on school exams, promulgating the prohibition of befriending the opposite sex and rejecting the vocal singing of or listening to love songs. These lessons were designed to play on young women's insecurities, while also addressing their parents' concerns about what is required for their daughters to present as 'good' Indonesian Muslims. Through his YouTube lessons, Siauw is able to exploit the general populations' fear that they were somehow behaving improperly in their day-to-day lives, which would condemn them to the consequences of living in sin. His overall message was to ensure that his viewers will live their lives in adherence to HTI's stricter Islamic principles and therefore would reach heaven.

The selfie backlash

In January 2015, Siauw hit an unexpected backlash from his followers after the *kultwits* that he released about taking 'selfies' (photos of one's self-posing, some-times with friends, usually taken with a smartphone). He published seventeen tweets that urged young women not to take selfies. He said that taking photos of oneself is boastful, ostentatious and arrogant, and questioned a woman's purity when taking a selfie. In Indonesia, the rising popularity of Twitter meant that taking selfies had become a routine activity, and a way for young people to express and represent themselves online (Aly 2015). Siauw's statements forbidding the taking of selfies immediately attracted criticism from his followers, and they reacted as if he had banned their existence in cyberspace.

Siauw's declaration against the selfie proved a failure: immediately a number of people mocked him as *ustadz dua ayat* or two-verse preacher. This was one of many terms such as *ustadz dadakan* ('instant preacher'), *ustadz sosmed* ('social media preacher') that came to epitomize those *ustadz* who did not have a background in Islamic education or lacked family ties to proper Islamic credentials. Ahmad Sahal, an activist from the *Liberal Islamic Network*, argued that Siauw's statement was flawed because Islamic teachings do not condone boastfulness, ostentatiousness or arrogance whether or not a *selfie* is involved. Siauw also received strong criticism from an online audience who said that Siauw's statement was a sign of his hypoc-risy as his online persona was loaded with photos of himself(!). Five hours after Siauw's first tweet on 19 January 2015 prohibiting the selfie, a Twitter account @dianparamita posted a selfie with the caption: '#Selfie4Siauw Have a nice day!' In her photo @dianparamita showed the top half of her body as she was lying back in a car. Her facial expression is filled with ridicule and she has wrapped her long hair around her face, suggesting this is her hijab. Her caption #Selfie4Siauw went viral and people rushed to make their own selfies to satirize Siauw's prohibi-tion. For three days #Selfie4Siauw became a trending topic throughout Indonesia. #Selfie4Siauw also attracted the attention of netizens and news services from around the world (Weng 2018b).

In response, Siauw cleverly employs a disengagement or avoidance strategy when encountering his audiences' online critiques (see Kumar et al. 2018). Siauw's approach was similar to other celebrity preachers when he avoided confrontation or disputation with his followers. Rather than address the #Selfie4Siauw with a direct reply, Siauw produced new *kultwits* or simply tweeted his critics with a humourous post. In this instance, he had to take a break from Twitter and let his followers cool down before he responded. Years after the hashtag #Selfie4Siauw peaked in popularity, it will still resurface in new posts despite its declining relevance to Siauw's more recent topics.

Therefore, the example of the hashtag #Selfie4Siauw remains as a cautionary tale for celebrity preachers and their precarious status as micro-celebrities. Here, Siauw underestimated his audience and failed to comprehend the significance to young Indonesians of their right to represent themselves visually online. In the case of #Selfie4Siauw his audience demanded their rights by rejecting and satirizing Siauw's statement on selfies. This undermined Siauw's credibility as an *ustadz* and challenged his authority. Finally, #Selfie4Siauw demonstrates that young Indonesians are not just passive consumers of online preachings, but will react swiftly to messages that threaten their online activities (see Plate xxii). Siauw's status as an *ustadz* is not guaranteed, so he must continue to renegotiate his status with his audience and the wider *ummah* ('community').

Conclusion

This chapter has traced the rise of Felix Siauw, the Indonesian-Chinese *mualaf* who became the Hizb ut-Tahrir's (the HTI, or The Liberation Party) most successful online preacher in Indonesia. Siauw's success was due to a combination of different skills. First, he was able to craft his narrative as a double-convert, coming to Islam from both a Chinese-Christian family background and to rebrand himself as a Muslim preacher. His popularity allowed Siauw to publicize HTI's principles that were often unpopular with the rest of the Indonesian populace. He promulgated quite controversial topics such as rejecting the Indonesian party line – which has not supported HTI's goals of an Islamic state – by repackaging the state's political ambivalence by highlighting the narratives of repentance, heroism and restoration of the former glory of Islam. At the same time, his troubled background and Chinese appearance allow the Indonesian populace to question his Islamic credentials and authority to produce *fatwa* ('Islamic statements') (see Hosen 2008). Contrary to any criticism, Siauw's identity coalesces on his heartfelt quest for belonging, and after his conversion he discovered and could celebrate the concept of the Muslim community (*ummah*).

Second, Siauw explored a variety of social media platforms to carry his message. Since 2016, Siauw moved his preaching platform from Twitter to Instagram. He explained that Instagram is more suitable for his target audience since interaction within the platform is softer than Twitter. The very terseness of Twitter posts often lends a harsh tone to the messages (Weng 2018a). On Instagram, Siauw organizes his persona through a combination of photos and text. He developed a unique style of posting where every photo, text or caption that he posts are not interrelated, which allowed him leeway to appear non-confrontational towards any followers who disagree with a given topic. This style of posting allows Siauw to continue his previous practice of text-based preaching. His posts are designed to maintain his image as a courageous preacher who is critical of the government and most importantly, continues to construct his authority within the Islamic community in Indonesia.

In a similar vein, the content of his photos (despite preaching against them) continues to construct new layers in his online persona by letting his audience view his life experiences. This allows his followers to 'know' him better through the photo streams of his everyday life. He curates his photos to be visually appealing, so his preachings about anti-dating and wearing hijab are illustrated in romantic images of himself and his wife in different parts of the world. Further, he introduces *halal* ('permissible') dating as opposed to pre-marriage dating. His harmonious family photos guide his followers to approve of him an ideal family man. The photos of his worldwide travels also fulfill the fantasies of the younger middle-class Muslims in Indonesia, who cannot afford his lifestyle. Both the text and the photos he posts on Instagram contribute to strengthen his persona as a credible preacher.

Third, his utilization of popular social media platforms is linked to his commercial enterprises and the organization of offline Hijab Alila events. Here, Siauw meets his followers in person through events such as book launches, hijab promotions and seminars. One of his latest initiatives was a comprehensive programme called #YukNgaji or C'mon Study the Koran. The programme was designed through social media to target young people to build a new Islamic community in Indonesia. These programmes seek to deconstruct commonly held ideas among young people that Islam is a tedious and rigid religion (see Wilson 2013). Through the programme, Siauw and his *ustadz* colleagues introduced a different face of Islam that was both fun and cool but pious at the same time. Besides creating community events, #YukNgaji shares its message by including HTI leaders as speakers. Through #YukNgaji, Siauw can construct his own ideal imagined Islamic community in Indonesia.

In conclusion, Siauw was strategic, employing his charismatic popularity and micro-celebrity status to solidify his credentials as an *ustadz*. His online persona links him into the wider networks of the televised celebrity preachers throughout Indonesia. Here he fostered friendships within the HTI's party network, and employed online channels to increase his popularity as a motivator and preacher. Consequently, he turned these teachings into profitable stores and online businesses with his wife Parsini and business partner Benefiko to promote and sell the 'proper' hijab to young women in Indonesia.

NOTE

1. All translations included in this chapter are the author's own.

REFERENCES

Achjadi, Judi (ed.) (1999), *Batik: Spirit of Indonesia*, Jakarta: Yayasan Batik Indonesia.

Aly, Waleed (2013), 'Welcome to Jakarta, the world's number one Twitter city', ABC (Australian Broadcasting Corporation), 29 May, https://www.abc.net.au/radionational/programs/drive/social-media-in-indonesia/4720678. Accessed 29 March 2020.

An-Nabhani, Taqiuddin ([2001] 2006), *The Social System in Islam*, 4th ed., New Delhi: Milli Publications.

An-Na'im, Abdullahi Ahmed (2008), *Islam and the Secular State*, Cambridge: Harvard University Press.

Anon. (2015), 'Felix Siauw interview', *Koran Tempo*, 18 April, https://nasional.tempo.co/read/2065/kejagung-telah-mengirim-surat-panggilan-ke-akbar-tandjung. Accessed 21 March 2020.

Aragon, Lorraine.V. (2000), *Fields of the Lord: Animism, Christian Minorities, and State Development in Indonesia*, Honolulu: University of Hawaii Press.

Baran, Zenyo (2004), *Hizb ut-Tahrir: Islam's Political Insurgency*, Washington, DC: Nixon Center.

Blommaert, J. and Varis, P. (2015), 'Culture as accent: the cultural logic of "Hijabistas"', *Semiotica*, 203, pp. 153–77.

Brenner, Suzanne (1996), 'Reconstructing self and society: Javanese Muslim women and "the veil"', *American Ethnologist*, 23:4, pp. 673–97.

Chua, Christian (2008), 'Capitalist consolidation, consolidated capitalists: Indonesia's conglomerates between authoritarianism and democracy', in M. Bünte and A. Ufen (eds), *Democratization in Post-Suharto Indonesia*, New York: Routledge, pp. 221–45.

El Guindi, F. (1999), *Veil: Modesty, Privacy and Resistance*, New York: Berg.

Fealy, G. and White, S.E. (2008), *Expressing Islam: Religious Life and Politics in Indonesia*, Singapore: Institute of Southeast Asian Studies.

Hadiz, V.R. (2016), *Islamic Populism in Indonesia and the Middle East*, Cambridge: Cambridge University Press.

Hanif, N. (2012), 'Hizb ut Tahrir: Islam's Ideological Vanguard', *British Journal of Middle Eastern Studies*, 39:2, pp. 201–25.

Hassan, Siti Hasnah and Harun, Harmimi (2016), 'Factors influencing fashion consciousness in hijab fashion consumption among hijabistas', *Journal of Islamic Marketing*, 7:4, pp. 476–94.

Hochel, Sandra (2013), 'To veil or not to veil: voices of Malaysian Muslim women', *Intercultural Communication Studies*, 22:2, pp. 40–57.

Hoesterey, J.B. (2015), *Rebranding Islam: Piety, Prosperity, and a self-Help Guru*, Redwood City: Stanford University Press.

Hosen, Nadirsyah (2008), 'Online Fatwa in Indonesia: From Fatwa Shopping to Googling a "Kiai"', in G. Fealy and S. White (eds), *Expressing Islam: Religious Life and Politics in Indonesia*, Singapore: Institute of Southeast Asian Studies, pp. 159–73.

Hoover, S.M. (2006). *Religion in the Media Age*, London: Routledge.

Kartajaya, H., Iqbal, M., Alfisyahr, R., Deasyana Rahma Devita, L. and Ismail, T. (2019), 'Segmenting Islamic fashion lifestyle on Indonesian woman', *Research Journal of Textile and Apparel*, 23:4, pp. 306–22.

Kumar, R., Ojha, A. K., Malmasi, S. and Zampieri, M. (2018), 'Benchmarking aggression identification in social media', *The First Workshop on Trolling, Aggression and Cyberbullying* (TRAC), Proceedings of the 27th International Conference on Computational Linguistics, Albuquerque, New Mexico, 26–28 August, pp. 1–11.

Kusumawati, Andriani, Sari Listyorini, Suharyono and Yulianto, Edy (2019), 'The impact of religiosity on fashion knowledge: consumer-perceived value and patronage intention', *Research Journal of Textile and Apparel*, 23:4, pp. 269–90.

Machmudi, Y. (2008), *Islamising Indonesia: The rise of Jemaah Tarbiyah and the Prosperous Justice Party (PKS)*, Canberra, Australia: ANU EPress.

Marwick, A.E. (2013), *Status Update: Celebrity, Publicity, and Branding in the Social Media Age*, New Haven: Yale University Press.

Mujiburrahman (2006), *Feeling Threatened: Muslim-Christian Relations in Indonesia's New Order*, vol. 3, Leiden: Leiden University Press.

Mydans, Seth (1998), 'Jakarta reports of numerous rapes of Chinese in riots', *The New York Times*, 10 June, https://www.nytimes.com/1998/06/10/world/in-jakarta-reports-of-numerous-rapes-of-chinese-in-riots.html. Accessed 28 March 2020.

Othman, N., Puthucheary, M. and Kessler, C. (2008), 'Religion, citizenship rights and gender justice: women, Islamization and the Shari'a in Malaysia since the 1980s', *Sharing the Nation: Faith, Difference, Power and the State*, 50, pp. 29–58.

Ralston, Nick and Partridge, Emma (2014), 'Martin place siege being treated as terrorist attack, police confirm', *Sydney Morning Herald*, 15 December, https://www.smh.com.au/national/nsw/martin-place-siege-being-treated-as-terrorist-attack-police-confirm-20141215-127mh5.html. Accessed 20 March 2020.

Senft, T.M. (2008), *Camgirls: Celebrity and Community in the Age of Social Networks*, New York: Peter Lang Publishing, Inc.

Setiono, B.G. (2003). *Tionghoa dalam pusaran politik*, Jakarta: Elkasa.

Sirait, Rheinhard (2017), 'Online Khilafah and Micro-Celebrity' presentation to: Bridging Gaps: National Identity in Persona, Branding and Activism: Centre for Media and Celebrity Studies, University of Western Australia, Perth, WA, 8–10 December.

Suryadinata, L. (2001), 'Chinese politics in Post-Suharto's Indonesia: Beyond the ethnic approach?', *Asian Survey*, 41:3, pp. 502–24.

Suryadinata, L. (2010), *Etnis Tionghoa dan Nasionalisme Indonesia: Sebuah Bunga Rampai, 1965–2008*, Jakarta: Penerbit Buku Kompas.

Washburn, Dennis (2010), 'Imagined history, fading memory: Mastering narrative in final fantasy X', *Mechademia*, 4, pp. 149–62.

Weng, Hew Wai (2018a), 'On-offline dakwah: Social media and Islamic preaching in Malaysia and Indonesia', *Mediatized Religion in Asia*, 1, pp. 89–104.

Weng, Hew Wai (2018b), 'The art of *dakwah*: Social media, visual persuasion and the Islamist propagation of Felix Siauw', *Indonesia and the Malay World*, 46, pp. 61–79.

Wilson [Bilal], Jonathan A.J. (2013), 'Emo-Indonesian youth – a new school culture of dual-cool', *The Marketeers*, April, pp. 82–87.

Yaden, David Bryce and Newberg, Andrew B. (2015), 'Road to Damascus moments: Calling experiences as prospective epiphanies', in D.B. Yaden, T.D. McACall and J.H. Ellens (eds), *Being Called: Scientific, Secular and Sacred Perspectives*, Santa Barbara: Paeger, ABC-CLIO, pp. 27–46.

9

All Dressed in Black: The Gendered Appearance of Protest

Anne Peirson-Smith and Jennifer Craik

To be peaceful or 'valiant': a day in the life of a [young woman] Hong Kong protester.

(Omar 2019: n.pag.)

Introduction

Women have protested across the ages and played essential roles in many political movements while often using materials that they have to hand. In the American Civil War, patterned quilts were sewn by women in the North embroidered with secret signposts to the Underground Railway, a route whereby Southern slaves could escape to freedom (Tobin et al. 1998). These journeys were long and perilous and fraught with the possibility of capture, torture and death for those who undertook the journey. More than 200 years later, the rise of 'craftivism' (Greer 2007: 401; 2014), or 'DIY' (do-it-yourself) became integral to women's protest (see Rall and Costello 2010). On 21 January 2017, over 1 million women knitted and collected 'pussy hats' to wear as they marched in the streets of Washington DC to protest sexist comments by the then President-elect Donald Trump (Gökarıksel and Smith 2017: 631). These hats were knit from patterns passed along broad-based social media networks all over the world to women's knitting circles that also extended to some male knitters (see https://www.pussyhatproject.com, accessed 3 August 2021).

These are just two examples of how 'women's work' created expressions of activism. Recently, the street protests in Hong Kong indicate the significance of women's representation within the realm of public protest. Here, issues of attire are paramount, as protest clothing worn by women at demonstrations in the public sphere serves to communicate discontent with the social order. It is important to analyse the symbolic aspects of HK's female dissident dress through its rationale, communicative impact and gender implications during large-scale protests from 9 June 2019 to 21 March 2020. Street protests appeared as early as May while protesters struggle to continue after the onset of the COVID-19 pandemic (Birtles 2021). HK's female protestors present the opportunity to examine embodied dress codes, uniforms and materiality, identity presentation and explore how dressing-up can transformatively and mimetically invest the wearer with individual agency. This agency then promotes female protestors to build a collective consciousness – by dressing up in shared uniforms and how these are discursively framed as radical or seditious in the street – within this newly situated cultural context. Here, protest clothing serves to enhance, neutralize or negate individual identity when operating amongst the liminal zones of an open street protest. Clothing, as uniform addresses solidarity to a political cause in multiple ways: to communicate an ideology, to reinforce personal anonymity, to evade surveillance and thereby offers protection against retaliation (Friedman 2019).

The argument here is that the black clothing has manifested in Hong Kong as the go-to uniform of resistance for young women.

In the recent HK street battles, female protestors presented themselves through donning black clothing, accessories and face masks. Here, the adoption of black[1] offers an embodied dress that negotiates ideological boundaries by both individuals and groups as divisions that impact on identity, emotion and behaviour. It is argued that this strategic choice for young HK women protestors in their dress and accompanying objects became collectivized, and realigned their appearance within a socio-cultural context that links clothing to political resistance in order to effect societal change. These garments offer the chance to reassign the expression of individual, collective and gendered power within a given 'style tribe' (see Maynard 2006).

Background for the HK protests

The organized mass protests from May 2019 to March 2020 began after a proposed criminal extradition bill that would allow any HK citizen suspected of a misdemeanour to be sent for trial to mainland China (the People's Republic of China, PRC) (Robles 2019). Currently, sporadic protests continue as HK citizens have issues following the COVID-19 pandemic based on the perceived mishandling by delaying the border closures with China and the location of virus quarantine sites (Birtles 2021). Likewise, protests are held to mark certain anniversaries involving violent clashes with HK's riot police resulting in protestor injuries (see Rose 2020). The social protest movement also rumbles on via online activities and through commemorative artwork circulated on social media platforms. Collective tactics also include boycotting brands, restaurants or stores perceived to support the pro-Beijing, anti-protest stance. As many of the 7,000 plus arrested HK protestors are still awaiting sentence on rioting or illegal assembly charges, in detention or imprisoned, these issues maintain a visible and/or invisible public concern for HK residents (Creery 2019).

The territory of Hong Kong has been occupied over the last 20 years. In July 1997, the British colony's 99-year lease expired, and HK was handed over to the sovereignty of mainland China (PRC). As a former British colony for over 150 years, Hong Kong was returned to the PRC's administration under the auspices of the mini-constitution, known as Basic Law that guaranteed under a 'one country, two systems' arrangement, as a Special Administrative Region (SAR). This SAR region suggested that HK's status quo would be preserved for 50 years with its existing indigenous laws and freedoms, including protections for freedom of speech and assembly, which was hoped to open the door for the implementation of universal suffrage for Hong Kong (Chan and Lee 2015); but this was not to be.

In fact, much of the population, particularly in areas such as politics, journalism and publishing, the arts and academia feel their rights to expression have been eroded. Rather than a more democratic political system, their rights to elect their leader and legislators have been curtailed, and from 2014, candidates are now chosen with a pro-Beijing orientation. This provoked HK's protestors to 'occupy' the city centre that crippled the city over a 79-day occupation from October 2014 onwards, or the so-called Umbrella Movement (Kaiman 2014). This Occupy protest followed after world-wide Occupy movements that began in New York City's Wall Street in September 2011. As with the other Occupy movements, this protest gradually faded away, yet many activists at that time vowed that they would return to the streets. The umbrellas, most often bright yellow, but sometimes black, could hide the protestors' identities as well as offer protection from pepper spray used by police.

The 2019 protests also decried this erosion of Hong Kong's Indigenous rule, first through the introduction of the extradition to China bill, and then spurred on by the government's mishandling of the proposed 'Article 23', the anti-subversion bill from 2003 that threatened civil freedoms by amending the Basic Law and introducing legislation to deal with treason, sedition, subversion and so on against China's central government (Anon. 2003). In June 2019 the protestors took up the baton again when thousands of people marched peacefully on subsequent Sunday. The attempted introduction of the extradition bill into the Legislative Council on 17 June resulted in heated confrontations between police and protestors outside the Legco building. These protests spread into the city and the central business district (CBD) thereby framing the urban battle lines for the violent and public nature of the political unrest that followed. Protests occurred across the territory almost each day from 17 June resulting in violent clashes between riot police invariably resulting in tear gas, pepper spray and water cannon directed crowd dispersals. The HK airport was closed by protestor occupation on 19 August (Regan et al. 2019). By December 2019 the crackdown by the authorities resulted in over 7,000 citizen arrests of all ages with retaliatory damage to China-linked property such as banks, shops and restaurants, shopping malls, university campuses and the airport and mass transit railway system (Creery 2019).

Significantly, this evolving politicized, post-handover landscape has resulted in the search for, and a crystallization of the Hong Kongers' identity as being distinct and different from Mainland Chinese citizenship in terms of values and culture, despite the majority of inhabitants being ethnic Chinese in origin (Abbas 1997). As above, cultural differences are reflected in the preferred dialects, where especially the Cantonese script is distinct from that of Mandarin and spoken throughout HK, with inclusions of many foreign language words adopted from the eras of British and Portuguese rule (Lui 2017). This identity search is reflected in protestor demands and a general antipathy to the Chinese central government's increasing attempts to control the territory, particularly amongst the younger demographic. Consequently, the rise of 'localism' appears in the emergence of democratic-leaning political parties, often well supported and headed by younger millennial leaders such as Joshua Wong and Agnes Chow with their Demosistō political party. This party openly champions to increase the territory's self-determination and even moots independence from mainland China (PRC).[3]

Here the HK protest movement can be viewed through the lens of street clothing as garments can enhance, neutralize or negate expressions of identity when operating in the liminal zones of a protest.

Clothing and the body

Clothing across time, space and place has often been used to signal difference and belonging. Foundational fashion theorists attributed to clothing the capacity to signal the stratification of society based on levels of wealth (Veblen 1899) and leading to mimetic efforts to attain social status (Simmel 1957). Other scholars stressed class-based consumption practices (Bourdieu 1984). More contemporary accounts focus on the 'embodied exercise' of dressing up or modifying the body with a range of coverings and assemblages (Roach-Higgins and Eicher 1995: 7). In 2000, Diane Crane introduced three requirements for clothing, first, to modify biological body processes; second, to offer protection from external environmental conditions and third, to dress for an aesthetic effect while overall conforming to the social norms of acceptable dress guided by society's prevailing situated value systems. Although these three purposes of functionality, protection and aesthetics are logical, they largely fail to explain the reasons for dress as a totality. Clothing as signifier depends on the situation or context and its intent is expressed non-verbally by individuals and their group affiliations.[1] This operates alongside other lived experiences based on clothing's expressive ability, allied with the human need to communicate ideas, knowledge and beliefs in everyday life, as a way of sense-making when creating, contributing to or challenging the social order (Leach 1976).

The material layering of dress and accessories transforms the appearance of the wearer and visually imparts new meaning for the 'presentation' of self and others (Goffman 1959). Subsequently, twentieth-century theory turned to technology to express the metaphor of the body as a machine or a form of technology, the way that the body is trained, performed and perceived enables identity construction as when making fashion choices,

> a person is animating (making alive, activating, performing) her or his body by imposing on it a social veneer that permits it to perform in specific desired ways and to be interpreted in the intended manner by others. In their choice and mode of wearing clothes and accessories.
>
> (Craik 2009: 3)

The precepts that govern material culture allows for the deliberate creation of differentiated identities, and these embodied personas created through certain types of apparel facilitate the dressing 'into or out of' group identities. According to Marcel Mauss, the body is produced through the coalescence of three modalities of bodily training namely physical and biological (as manifested in outward corporeal enactment); cognitive (found in internalized norms and behaviour); and social (in sense-making based on collective roles and habits) (1973). Further, this performance and projection of the contextualized body using embodied techniques is dynamic and fluid, and always in a process of evolving, adapting to the varying norms and behaviours considered appropriate and later framed by the physical and social context or 'habitus' in which they exist (Mauss 1973). Material and visually oriented technologies of clothing deliberately envelop bodies and prime them for public display. Further, the kinetic technologies of body, performed through movement, gestures and actions crystallize individual identities that is positively or negatively evaluated in the social collective where they appear. In this way, 'body techniques are internalised or naturalized to the point where we do not perceive them as learned or arbitrary but simply *the* way to do something specific to the social milieu' (Craik 2009: 137). Hence, the formation of identity become an amalgam of recognized cultural capital, knowledge capital and acquired embodied practices that either support or transgress social norms and the status quo (McCracken 1990). In this way, the clothed body enabled by embodied techniques do not provide the unitary result proposed in Crane's theory (2000). Rather, dress codes as the habitus of self-operated technical strategies that afford the body's performance of 'display, presentation, representation and ritual' (Craik 2009: 139). This activation by both garment and recognised visual codes conveys meaning and elicits responses for the self and others.

Body techniques are seemingly influenced by broader structural forces and direct power relations expressed through gender, ethnicity, class and race, for example, thereby adding a political dimension to the technical and social aspects of bodily appearance, given that:

> [d]ress is a significant material practice we use to signal our cultural boundaries social separations, continuities and, for the present purposes, political dissidences [...] Beyond offering physical protection clothes have many functions, not least of which is attractive body covering. More significantly, clothing can inform us of national or ethnic belonging, and significantly relations of power, along axes of class, religion, gender and race.
>
> (Maynard 2006: 103)

Protest dress as communication

By extension, dress can be used to regulate or rebel through clothing, adornment and performance that conveys affinity and connection with groups, style tribes and ideological positions, as with many dissenting groups across history (see Bartlett 2019). In their dress, as 'the materialisation of political consciousness' protestors can create a distinct identity (Yangzom 2016: 630). Dress has occupied a significant role in the symbolic expression of protest and dissent with long-standing precedent 'for social protest to be written on the body' (Torrens 1999: 77) highlighting the entwined relationship between the technologized body, dress, power and protest (Rubinstein 1995). The ability of the technologized body to convey both belonging to a like-minded style tribe and/or a collective visual becomes a unifying principle (Peirson-Smith 2013). Clothing becomes indispensable when proclaiming dissent from historic political movements to contemporary sub-cultural tribes (Evans 1997). This involves utilizing clothing as powerful or extraordinary visual statements of solidarity with the collective in opposition to the mainstream ways of being and appearing

(Peirson-Smith 2019a and b). Dissident dress has been documented across time, space and place in terms of defining political or ideological positions using 'clothing as an argumentative sign of movement membership in identifying individuals who dissent, resist or protest' whereby 'individuals make claims about their affiliations and loyalties through their clothing' (Torrens 1999: 77). Fashion becomes argumentative by provoking ruling elites, dominant discourses or political regimes, as

> [f]ashion has always provided rich visual, material, symbolic and narrative spaces within which to articulate, negotiate and perform political issues and there is ample historical research that examines the many links between fashion and politics.
>
> (Torrens 1999: 77)

Throughout history, clothing has played a role from French Revolution's *sans-culottes* (Landes [2003] 2018) to the present day, where the farmers' yellow-vests (*gilet jaune*) protests arose after a fuel tax hike in France. In Poland, the colour orange triggered the worker's formation of an 'Alternative Orange' party protesting Soviet rule in 1987 (Ost 1990). Closer to the complex issues in the Chinese sphere of influence, in Tibet the practice of wearing traditional clothing on Wednesdays indicated support for the Tibetan Freedom movement (Yangzom 2016). Such examples of protest dress demonstrate how clothing and artefacts can visually and non-verbally communicate political consciousness, while sartorially performing dissent, discontent, difference and division. Further, women have employed handicrafts for centuries to enact protest, from women's rights to health activism, to highlight environmental degradation (see Costello and Rall 2013). The highly visible exhibition of all shades of pink as women and their families in 'pussy hats' marched on Washington DC to protest then President-elect Donald Trump's videotaped comments, 'grab 'em by the pussy' as revealed by the transcript published in the *New York Times* (Bullock 2016: n.pag.). This later spurred on the virtual movement for women during the #metoo movement and the ultimate conviction of serial sex offender Harvey Weinstein in 2020 (Aratani and Pilkington 2020).

Therefore, it can be argued that dress has always played a communicative role, and the reading of clothing as text is highly complex. If an outfit expresses an open or under-coded text (Lurie 1981, see also Barthes [1967] 1990) multiple readings will occur, given that 'fashion communicates not in the way of speech, but by conveying social and political identities that frame and reflect contextual cultural values' (Evans and Peirson-Smith 2018: 8). This is particularly apposite for contemporary protest clothing which appears in public settings where the act of protest is mediated multi-modally in word, image and sound through mainstream press and social media. Here, clothing comprises open texts as, 'dress does not speak to a single cultural audience. It is variously decoded by those of different political persuasions, and certainly further reinterpreted or reframed by the media' (Maynard 2006: 103). This negotiation for meaning through colours and clothing styles are deliberately employed by the protestor to create social cohesion among followers by encoding and narrativizing their viewpoint through either overt covert 'cultural work in creating a coherent narrative' such as that presented by the #metoo movement (Yangzom 2016: 623).

HK's female protest outfit: The tripartitie view

The leaderless, organic movement that galvanized the 2019 HK protests was a deliberate strategy after the arrest of leaders during the 2014 Occupy or Umbrella movement (Kaiman 2014). Here, the 2019 protests are driven by a countless, largely anonymous army of supporters who tend to connect up and plan operations on social media sites such as *Telegram*, as Wong explained in a recent media interview:

> We have a lot of facilitators in this movement and I'm one of them [...] it's just like Wikipedia. You don't know who the contributors are behind a Wikipedia page, but you know there's a lot of collaboration and crowdsourcing. Instead of just a top-down command, we now have a bottom-up command hub.
>
> (Wong 2019b: n.pag.)

This online army also appears in material form in regular street protests. When doing so, they generally wear black outfits comprising jeans, t-shirts, leggings and sports shoes, face masks, goggles, arm and leg padding, hard construction hats carrying large dark umbrellas (see Plate xxiii). The uniformity of this outfit among the protestors is a visual display of solidarity for the same cause, while simultaneously assuring a collective anonymity that is sealed and secured by the wearing of a face mask – often black. The protesters' black gear is not gender-specific and signals a collective presence and support while hiding individual identity; both challenging authority and protecting compatriots by their numerous mass. This combination of the displayed body in a massed context affords a powerful visual assertion of resistance.

Physical performance and training

The black protest outfit described above signals the physical evidence of a protestor on HK's streets and at designated protest sites, officially sanctioned or otherwise. In effect, these black outfits from June 2019 onwards increasingly became associated with protestation and a reminder of the deepening civil unrest enveloping the territory. The initial mass gatherings with an estimated one million plus protestors (Lam 2019) first instructed participants to wear white Chinese garments traditionally associated with death and funerals. From mid-June 2019 onwards and notably on the day that the HK (SAR) government attempted to pass the extradition legislation, black became the dominant colour of HK protest dress (see Plate xxiii). The colour black has often signified resistance towards dominant regimes. In the nineteenth century, the fascist 'black shirts' in Italy controlled textile production (Paulicelli 2004) and black is worn to support current movements such as Black Lives Matter, #BLM that emerged in the United States but figured in protests around the world.

The counter-attack came after black clothing was worn by the elitist police special forces unit or the 'raptors' who dispersed and arrested protestors. Their adoption of black meant they could operate undercover by blending in with protestors and often blamed for their brutal treatment on surprise arrests (Lo et al. 2019). The black-covered protestors also contrasted with the green camouflage-clad, helmeted, shield-wielding riot police, some of whom are female officers and against the standard blue uniform of the regular HK police force. Further, the pro-Beijing/anti-HK protestors' contingent alleged participants in triad gangs appeared in pale blue or white t-shirt uniform of the anti-protesters. These violent gangs 'attacked and injured over 45 civilians' that they claimed were returning from the protest in a Yuen Long train station in mid-August 2019 (Lo et al. 2019: n.pag.). This deployment shows that even 'everyday dress has political import, for it is clothing defined in relation to its dramatic obverse' (Maynard 2006: 112). Piles of clothing were even used to build temporary barricades of worn and tear-gassed clothing, the torn clothing of official police uniforms, riot police fatigues as well as leftovers from black-clad protestors. Here, clothing presents its 'combative and divisive' or connective characteristics (Barnard 2013: 40), and protest outfits can either represent 'bridges' by connecting shared identities or as 'fences' in differentiating social groupings through the concept of 'lifestyle' (Klein 2009: 23). In military language, clothing that challenges those in dominant political positions acts 'as weapons and defences in that they express ideologies held by social groups which may be opposed to the ideologies of other groups in the social order' (Barnard 2013: 41). Cultural fashion theorist Jo Turney noted that during the UK riots in 2011, the UK's press reported the public's concern with the looters ubiquitous wearing of 'the hoodie' where the 'sweatshirt with a hood became the symbol of social disobedience' (2014: 128).

From June 2019 onwards black clothing became an implicit message of support by the wearer for the anti-extradition protests. As black came to dominant the social landscape, one of the authors here, when wearing her black leggings, t-shirt and trainers en route to an exercise class was asked, 'where the protest was taking place today'.

Besides the contentious extradition bill, HK protestors added associated grievances: an independent enquiry into alleged police brutality, a rescinding of the classification of protestors as rioters and an automatic amnesty for all arrested protestors and universal suffrage (Rourke 2019). These five demands appeared visibly and symbolically by extending five fingers of one hand whilst marching in protests and chanting or singing 'Do You Hear the People Sing?' from *Les Miserables* or the 'Glory to Hong Kong' protest anthem. Often, citizens quickly become protestors and bustling streets of shoppers would melt away into a tense protest stand-off only to return to normal urban activities of working and shopping within hours. This off/on switch revealed how these fluid social arrangements turned the streets into a liminoid/liminal, transitory zone (Turner 1982).

The entire protest movement became colour-coded in terms of their roles an occupational role and/or an ideological stance. Hence, the frontline press corp wore a yellow vest marked 'PRESS', gas masks, visors, goggles and protective builder's helmet. The volunteer medics in the combat zone wore yellow tabards bearing a red cross and 'FIRST AID' labels on front and back. Even these explicit labels sometimes offered little protection as the protests became more violent, both local and international reporters were caught up in the tear gas, water cannon or bean bag volleys. Note that the colour yellow also reflected the previous 2014 Yellow Umbrella protests in HK (Steger 2019) (see Plate xxiii). In two separate incidents, a female volunteer first aider and an associate editor of Indonesian *Suara Hong Kong News* were both shot in the eye, the latter resulting in the permanent loss of sight in one eye, when riot police fired bean bags and rubber bullets, respectively, at close range into the press and medical corps covering the protests (Graham-Harrison 2019; Ho Kilpatrick 2019).

Significantly, injured female faces became defiant symbols of the protest struggle. Protestors quickly added eye patches and bloodied bandages covering one eye to their protest outfits as further statements of discontent against perceived acts of police brutality and regularly added chants of 'an eye for an eye!' or painted eye-patch slogans on banners and graffiti (Chui 2019: n.pag.). Further, female protestors are estimated to constitute half of the body of dissent and one-third of all arrests and those charged or admitted to HK's hospitals (Xinqi 2019), reinforcing women's activity in the 2019–20 street protests (see Plate xxiv). Unlike the Occupy Movement in 2014 where women played supporting roles of handing out water, food or information leaflets, while male protestors battled it out with the authorities and the riot police on the frontlines. Rather, recent female protestors are consciously taking a hands-on role alongside their male compatriots, even taking part in training sessions. As a recent news article noted in an interview with female HK protestor Aria:

Over months of recent pro-democracy demonstrations [...] the 25-year-old Hong Konger marched to the front lines cloaked in black with her hair tucked into a helmet while wielding a wrench and a Swiss Army knife. She regularly joined a team of 30 people for physical training drills, and listens to aggressive Cantonese rapcore music.

(Banjo and Wong 2020: n.pag.)

Items of clothing protect the body with goggles, face masks, hard hats and thermal gloves and limit the physical impact of tear gas, rubber bullets, sponge rounds and pepper spray. Further, baseball hats and face or surgical masks also conceal individual identities. These items aided to protect protestors from surveillance systems geared to identify and punish through collecting 'image events' (Delicath and DeLuca 2003). At the height of the protests, even peaceful activists were often branded as 'rioters' in some sectors in the official discourse (Wu et al. 2019). In October 2019, the HK government resurrected a colonial-era Emergency Regulations Ordinance (ERO) banning the wearing of face masks by all HK citizens. This legislation was defied by protestors alongside citizens in general, who routinely don masks to prevent flu and other seasonal illnesses. This anti-mask legislation implied imposition of boundaries (Douglas and Isherwood [1979] 1996) echoed in physical barricades erected against the advancing riot police. Here, face masking once normal became separated from socially acceptable ways of dressing, which emphasizes how the gaze is 'monitored and regulated' (Tseëlon 2012: 3). The wearing of face masks challenges an 'authentic' self in the public perspective and creates a private space for the masked self.

The umbrella likewise functions to buffer the physical body from view and prevents the identification of individual protestors. The umbrella symbol has also surfaced on bodies as tattoos, alongside images of bauhinia flowers and bleeding eyes whereby, the 'protest-themed tattoos act as public statements of dedication and belief – particularly striking when most demonstrators are trying to conceal their identities' (Yeung 2019: n.pag.).

Collective role play

Many Asian societies are structured with gendered expectations of the roles that males and females should play in society through a stereotyped domestic division of labour (Lee 2002, Choi and Chung 2012). In Hong Kong males do dominate in most aspects of public and private life. Scholars often overlook the presence of 'mono-masculinity' but some see the need to recognize the existence of multiple masculinities (Tam et al. 2009). It can be argued that multiple femininities have also been overlooked in this socio-cultural space and place. But the 'Kong' girl emerging from these protests challenges normative female roles in the territory.

Social media discussions and/or media interviews have highlighted female involvement, as expressed here by female protestor Jordyn:

> Hong Kong youngsters tend to be a bit passive, mostly because of our education system [...] I feel more empowered now. Not sure if that relates to my gender. But I have grown as an individual [...] Some are now realizing that Hong Kong girls are not afraid of getting their hands dirty.
>
> (Carvalho 2019: n.pag.)

From the 2000s, young HK females have been stereotyped by their 'penchant for luxury goods, insistence on a boyfriend who pays, and any opportunity to be the centre of attention' (Kang and Chen 2014: 205). This distinctly contrasts with a serious-minded, 'brave fighter' seen in the streets:

> In recent months [...] many have watched in awe as a new type of Kong Girl emerged out of this year's protests, as women lobbed back tear gas grenades, built heavy-duty barricades, and stood in the frontlines to face an arsenal of increasingly powerful police weapons such as rubber bullets and bean-bag rounds [...] In short, Hong Kong's women have thrown themselves into the ranks of what's known as the 'brave fighters' segment of the protesters, marking a significant escalation from the roles played by women in the 2014 Umbrella Movement protests.
>
> (Steger 2019: n.pag.)

These interpretations of HK women as 'brave fighters' are polarized into positive and negative readings that generate shorthand diagnostics. These diagnostics become reinforced as stereotypes about this dynamic community of protestors and their detractors. These readings of HK female protestors underscore the power of dress. Here, those who don specific attire can assume roles and practice multiple variations of identities that are subsequently acknowledged and debated in the public domain and through social media.

Further, as the protests from June to December 2019 became increasingly violent and confrontational, participants attending those protests that lacked official sanctions were sometimes advised on social media sites such as Telegram to 'dress like tourists' to hide 'in place'. Such changes in attire offer a chance to shape-shift one's identity. Protestors often shed their black outfits worn in protests for everyday casual wear before boarding public transport to travel home. As the protests evolved over six months, those wearing black garments could be stopped and searched by the police on the streets, on buses and metropolitan trains. In the early days, anonymous donors would leave piles of coloured t-shirts and other garments in the mass transit railway concourse to enable protestors to change their outfits before embarking on their trip home, thereby enabling them to shift in appearance from dissenter to normal daily citizen.

On 1 October 2019, an unofficial protest occupying the Central and Admiralty districts of HK island was staged by the Civil Human Rights Front (CHRF) to coincide with China National Day resulting in fierce clashes between protestors and police. Following this event, discarded piles of black t-shirts, hats, leggings and sweatshirts and umbrellas were abandoned on the streets or in refuse bins. Protestors had shed their 'second protest skins' to change their sartorial identities while making a hasty getaway from riot police armed with tear gas and water cannon (Tsung-gan 2019: n.pag).

For HK's pro-democracy protestors, wearing ordinary clothes allowed them to hide 'in plain sight'.

Intrinsic individual identity

If we regard the body as the site where the social is inscribed through bodily performances (Mauss 1973), then clothing and how it is worn, presented, represented, mobilized and ritualized comprise individual identity. Within protest or dissent, normal practices are challenged by the bodily techniques of dress and its kinetic engagement with the environment. Female protestors, by wearing a black Nike t-shirt, exercise leggings and trainers and armed with black umbrellas could engage at the front line of the conflict. Over the initial 17 weeks of protest, an interview with 'Charlie' (a pseudonym) helps to clarify the zones of protest. As she reports, 'then I go out [...] and depending on where we have the protest I would decide what role I want to take' (Omar 2019: n.pag.). Here Charlie divides the protestors into two groups:

> During this whole movement there are the Yong Mo Pai, known as 'the valiant bunch' – who are more at the forefront [...] They're more daring [...] they are more of the people you've seen them rush into the legislative complex on July 1, they also make road blockages. Then there are the peaceful protesters, right, we call them the Wo Lei Fei – which means 'peace', 'rationality' and 'non-violence'.
>
> (Omar 2019: n.pag.)

In addition, these younger protestors have been joined by both male and female yellow-vested 'silver-haired' protestors affectionately named 'grandpa' and 'grandma' who often try and protect the young frontline protestors from police aggression (Omar 2019).

Beyond the black clothing and mask the female dissenters on the streets often engaged in active techniques of moving, singing, interacting, participating, protesting and defending as part of their role play (see Rühlig 2016). For young women, this recalibrates Asian social conventions about gender-oriented behaviour as well as assumptions about how citizens should behave in relation to authority. In retaliation, arrested female protestors were publicly frisked by male officers and had their pants removed during or after arrest by their captors as a form of humiliation (Amnesty International 2019) to reveal their gender, consciously or otherwise. It was reported in the newspaper that:

> In the course of arresting a female protester, her clothing was lifted up and her underwear dislodged; she was then carried into the police station in such a way that her private parts were exposed to the press and the public. We believe the arrest was made using excessive force, which resulted in damage to the dignity of the protester and deprived her of her right to bodily autonomy, constituting an act of sexual violence.
>
> (Wong 2019b: 3)

By extension, other allegations emerged across the latter half of 2019 of arrested female protestors being stripped, brutalized or even raped in detention by uniformed police or riot officers (Lau 2019). In this instance, the 'masculine' or non-gendered traits invested by the black uniform of the protestors and its symbolic power were physically stripped away and 'neutered' by police. Many female protestors reported that they were being harassed online by trolls when showing support for the pro-democracy movement or protest events with online photographs being altered, sexualized and re-posted as a weapon against them (Troup Beuchanan 2019). These accusations triggered thousands of female protestors to rally in Central Hong Kong Island on 28 August 2019 against such alleged abuse (Wong 2019a). Police and pro-establishment supporters have consistently denied these claims while accusing the women of weaponizing their gender.

In their collective role play, women could confidently use these body techniques after adopting a uniform associated with the inherent behaviour of protest, where, 'the uniform, like any other form of dress, makes the body culturally visible' (Black 2014: 93). HK's young women who chose to enact this role in the streets linked themselves to dichotomous codes of authority, hierarchy, conformity, status, discipline and punishment versus opposition, difference, disruption, dissent, deviance and anti-authoritarianism.

Protest dress as a feminist object

Four main classifications of objects – corporeal things; world-making things; knowledge and communicative things; and protest things are identified by Bartlett and Henderson when defining the material culture of female political dissent: items that are created, assembled, worn and used by female protestors to highlight their cause. They are also invested with feminist agency (Bartlett and Henderson 2016) in the way that all objects are endowed with social agency (Gell 1998).

The potential of 'corporeal things' to technologize the body is evident, as they signify identity, belonging and convey an ideological position given that they 'highlight the feminist use of the body to promote feminist issues, rework codes of femininity, and attempt to refuse sexual objectification' (Bartlett and Henderson: 163). Equally, associated items – banners, flags, badges or flowers can facilitate protests. For the purpose here, the use of black objects and garments clothing employed to technologize the female body as a protest object then acquires a symbolic feminist or quasi-feminist purpose. Female protestors through their appearance and actions lead to feminist interpretations of their role as dissenters. Wearing the black costume de-emphasizes the feminine body through an androgynous uniform and even more undifferentiated anonymity comes with wearing a face mask. Similar 'blackness' in attire and flags were taken up by female protestors supporting the HK women world-wide (see Plate xxiv).

These everyday objects, such as t-shirts, face masks and umbrellas, circulate messages of political rhetoric that are anchored to the bodily sphere through visual and textual designs of banners and posters and broadcast by the vocalization of chants and songs.

This political corporeality displays a 'sign of allegiance to a type of camouflage' (Bartlett and Henderson 2016: 164). Protest dress as uniform offers both explicit and implicit meanings, because:

> Uniforms are all about control, not only of the social self but also of the inner self and its formation. Uniforms send out mixed messages [...] a combination of 'not' statements (rules of wearing and not wearing that are often unstated or partially stated – or arbitrarily applied) and transgressive messages.
>
> (Craik 2009: 4)

The uniform brings to the fore 'sameness, unity, regulation, hierarchy, status, roles' (Craik 2009: 5). Underneath the exterior, wearing a uniform offers a covert role for the self, as directed by the individual experience and interpretation of the wearer. Covert meanings could include subversive or rebellious expressions and a chance to demonstrate uniqueness within the overall uniformity. The body techniques of wearing uniforms that employ the colour black can communicate ambivalence and even dissent.[2] Here, black protest uniforms represent solidarity, not purely by colour or their construction, but rather, 'the fact that group of people, united in a common cause are united in a common shade. It's a joint identity that stands out: the casual expression of a voluminous force' (Friedman 2019: n.pag.).

Concluding thoughts

The black protest dress of HK's female pro-democracy dissenters from 2019 to 2020 and beyond operated to perform a role-based adherence to their cause. As their street appearances became altered through body techniques, these protesters then morphed into a technologized body by use of material shapes and colours signalling 'visual and physical boundaries' expressed outwardly by weapons or barricades (Barnard 2013: 40). These technologized masses could resist social control and surveillance on HK's physical/public and perhaps more importantly, the underlying ideological/private battlegrounds. In HK female protestors materialized their beliefs visually by marking out their identity/ies within the dissenting collective of mass protests to challenge and resist the social order.

By extension this presentation of self in 'black' alongside the physical, often violent and disruptive performance of protest appeared in the shifting and liminal zones of urban streets and modern structures, aided by protest props. The tripartite modalities of training through physical action, thought and role performance enabled a blurring of gender. These collectivized performances offered momentary empowerment and agency for the women thereby challenging traditional power relations (Hao 2019). Through their actions female HK protesters have also redefined gender discourse and perceptions across social media. Here, their situated involvement has begun to dismantle cultural stereotypes normally ascribed to women as carer, mother or cute daughter to aggressive and committed activist. As one Twitter post put it: 'There's this strange belief from the other side that a woman's role is domestic [...] HKers and our art says "eff" that. Mothers, nanas, aunties – they are on the streets, raging against power' (uwu_uwu_mo 2019: n.pag.).

The argument offered here that protestor as technologized body with its supporting accessories is always ambivalent and subject to the complex and contradictory webs of multivalent meanings exercised among players, props and the liminal sites that they inhabit. In Hong Kong, her use of black signals both allegiance to cause and disguise from the police and anti-protestor gangs. The performance of female protestors, while consistent in its visual, non-verbal display of resistance can assume many functional roles. As 'Charlie' explains:

> I feel like that role does not necessarily have to stay the same. Sometimes I will go to the front, I will help with tying the blockages. I will help shelter, if you have long umbrellas, I help shelter those who are trying to hide from surveillance cameras.
>
> (Omar 2019: n.pag.)

The question posed here, 'will I be valiant today?' shows how the female protestors' self-awareness of the importance of their struggle is set in the context of a newly differentiated role when they choose to take overt action wearing 'black' and accompanied by accoutrements including umbrellas, banners, hard hats, masks, face painting, tattoos and so on. Taking these actions all serve to highlight the transformed internalized state of each individual woman, as protestor, and subsequently places this new identity amongst the streams of past and present Asian femininities. At the same time, this offers an emergent state for female protestors' various interactive roles within HK's recent divisive street battles to reclaim their denied freedoms. As one protester said: 'We're no longer weak, or the ones with "princess syndrome". So I think now, we are evolving like Pokémon, we're on another level. We're different' (Yui 2020: n.pag.).

NOTE

1. Note: The biological argument takes the genotype as a determinant and individual variations within groups as expressed within the phenotype (Sproles and Burns 1994).
2. Note also that the recent Black Lives Matter movement starting in the United States and spreading around the world as #BLM also centres protest dress around the signifiers of black dress and masks to protest mistreatment of people through their skin colour.
3. As of January 2021, leaders of the Demosistō party, a total of 53 activists have been imprisoned.

REFERENCES

Abbas, A. (1997), *Hong Kong: Culture and the Politics of Disappearance*, Hong Kong: Hong Kong University Press.

Amnesty International (2019), 'Sexual violence against Hong Kong protesters – what's going on?', AI Blog, 20 December, https://www.amnesty.org/en/latest/news/2019/12/sexual violence-against-hong-kong-protesters/. Accessed 28 January 2020.

Anon., (2003), 'Q&A: HK's anti-subversion bill', BBC News, 1 July, http://news.bbc.co.uk/2/hi/asia-pacific/3035226.stm. Accessed 12 April 2020.

Aratani, L. and Pilkington, E. (2020), 'New York judge imposed 20 years for a first-degree criminal sex act and three years for third-degree rape, to run consecutively', *The Guardian*, 12 March, https://www.theguardian.com/world/2020/mar/11/harvey-weinstein-sentenc ing-rape-conviction. Accessed 12 April 2020.

Banjo, S. and Wong, J. (2020), 'Hong Kong women upend gender roles in democracy fight', *Bloomberg News: Politics*, 7 February, https://www.bloomberg.com/news/articles/2020-02-06/women-hong-kong-protesters-upend-gender-roles-in-democracy-fight. Accessed 10 March 2020.

Barnard, M. (2013), *Fashion as Communication*, London: Routledge.

Barthes, Roland ([1967] 1990), *The Fashion System*, (trans. M. Ward and R. Howard), Berkeley: University of California Press.

Bartlett, A., and Henderson, M. (2016), 'What is a feminist object? Feminist material culture and the making of the activist object', *Journal of Australian Studies*, 40:2, pp. 156–71.

Bartlett, D. (ed.) (2019), *Fashion and Politics*, London: Yale University Press.

Birtles, Bill (2021), 'Under the cloak of COVID-19, China has turned Hong Kong from a city of protest to a city of prosecution', 7 January, https://www.abc.net.au/news/2021-01-07/beijing-effectively-outlaws-hong-kong-opposition-parties/13036292. Accessed 16 March 2021.

Black, P. (2014), 'The discipline of appearance: Military style and Australian flight hostess uniforms 1930–64', in D.N. Rall (ed.), *Fashion and War in Popular Culture*, Bristol: Intellect, pp. 93–105.

Bourdieu, P. (1984), *Distinction: A Social Critique of the Judgement of Taste*, (trans. R. Nice), Cambridge: Harvard University Press.

Bullock, Penn (2016) 'Transcript: Donald Trump's taped comments about women', *New York Times*, 8 October, https://www.nytimes.com/2016/10/08/us/donald-trump-tape-transcript.html. Accessed 14 June 2021.

Carvalho, R. (2019), '#ProtestToo: the women at the forefront of Hong Kong's anti-government movement', *South China Morning Post* (SCMP), This Week In Politics/Asia, 31 August. https://www.scmp.com/week-asia/politics/article/3025146/protesttoo-women-forefront-hong-kongs-anti-government-movement. Accessed 12 March 2020.

Chan, J. and Lee, F.L. (2015), 'Media and social mobilisation in Hong Kong', *The Routledge Handbook of Chinese Media*, London: Routledge, pp. 145–60.

Choi, S.Y.P. and Cheung, F.M. (2012), 'Introduction', in S.Y.P. Choi and F.M. Cheung (eds), *Women and Girls in Hong Kong Current Situations and Future Challenges*, Hong Kong: Hong Kong Institute of Asia-Pacific Studies, The Chinese University of Hong Kong, pp. 1–20.

Chui, A. (2019), 'Journalist says she was blinded in one eye by police rubber bullet', *Asia Times*, 3 October, https://asiatimes.com/2019/10/indonesian-journalist-blinded-by-police-bullet/. Accessed 12 March 2020.

Craik, J. (2009), *Fashion: the Key Concepts*, Oxford: Bloomsbury Academic.

Crane, D. (2000), *Fashion and Its Social Agendas: Class, Gender, and Identifying Clothing*, Chicago: University of Chicago Press.

Creery, J. (2019), 'Hong Kong protesters rack up "enormous" vandalism repair bill incl. HK$10.5m in property maintenance costs, gov't says', *Hong Kong Free Press*, 7 November, https://www.hongkongfp.com/2019/11/07/hong-kong-protests-rack-enormous-vandalism-repair-bill-incl-hk10-5m-property-maintenance-costs-govt-says/. Accessed 14 March 2020.

Delicath, J.W. and DeLuca, K.M. (2003), 'Image events, the public sphere, and argumentative practice: The case of radical environmental groups', *Argumentation*, 17:3, pp. 315–33.

Douglas, M. and Isherwood, Baron C. ([1979] 1996), *The World of Goods: Towards an Anthropology of Consumption*, Milton Park: Routledge.

Evans, C. (1997), 'Dreams that only money can buy [...] or the shy tribe in flight from discourse', *Fashion Theory*, 1:2, pp. 169–88.

Evans, S. and Peirson-Smith, A. (2018), 'The sustainability word challenge: Exploring consumer interpretations of frequently used words to promote sustainable fashion brand behaviors and imagery', *Journal of Fashion Marketing and Management*, 22:2, pp. 252–69.

Friedman, V. (2019), 'The color of protest: Banning the import of black clothing to Hong Kong misses the point when it comes to clothing and opposition', *The New York Times*, 30 October, https://www.nytimes.com/2019/10/29/style/29china-ban-black-clothing-hong-kong-protests.html. Accessed 14 February 2020.

Gell, A. (1998), *Art and Agency: An Anthropological Theory*, New York: Clarendon Press.

Graham-Harrison, E. (2019), 'Hong Kong protests: journalist blinded in one eye amid mounting violence', *The Guardian*, 3 October, https://www.theguardian.com/world/2019/oct/03/hong-kong-protests-journalist-blinded-in-one-eye-as-attacks-on-media-escalate. Accessed 28 February 2020.

Goffman, E. (1959), *The Presentation of Self in Everyday Life*, New York: Anchor Books.

Gökarıksel, B. and Smith, S. (2017), 'Intersectional feminism beyond US flag hijab and pussy hats in Trump's America', *Gender, Place & Culture*, 24:5, pp. 628–44.

Greer, B. (2007), 'Craftivism', in G.L. Anderson, K.G. Herr (eds), *Encyclopaedia of Activism and Social Justice*, vol. 1, Sage: London, p. 401.

Greer, Betsy (ed.) (2014), *Craftivism: The Art of Craft and Activism*, Vancouver: Arsenal Pulp Press.

Hao, A. (2019), 'Young women are front and center in the Hong Kong protests', *Teen Vogue*, 6 December, https://www.teenvogue.com/story/hong-kong-protests-young-women. Accessed 29 February 2020.

Ho Kilpatrick, R. (2019), '"An eye for an eye": Hong Kong protests get figurehead in woman injured by police', *The Guardian*, 16 August, https://www.theguardian.com/world/2019/aug/16/an-eye-for-an-eye-hong-kong-protests-get-figurehead-in-woman-injured-by-police. Accessed 18 October 2019.

Kaiman J. (2014), 'The story behind the Hong Kong pro-democracy protests', *The Guardian*, 30 September, https://www.theguardian.com/world/2014/sep/30/-sp-hong-kong-umbrella-revolution-pro-democracy-protests. Accessed 12 April 2020.

Kang, M.A., and Chen, K.H. (2014), 'Stancetaking and the Hong Kong girl in a shifting heterosexual marketplace', *Discourse & Society*, 25:2, pp. 205–20.

Klein, N. (2009), *No Logo: No Space, No Choice, No Jobs*, New York: Picador.

Lam, J. (2019), 'Why did Hongkongers join million-strong march to protest extradition bill? It's about protecting freedom, and it's in their DNA', *South China Morning Post*, 10 June, https://www.scmp.com/news/hong-kong/politics/article/3013758/why-did-hundreds-thousands-hongkongers-take-streets-protest. Accessed 28 February 2020.

Landes, J.B. ([2003] 2018), *Visualizing the Nation: Gender, Representation, and Revolution in Eighteenth-Century France*, Ithaca: Cornell University Press.

Lau, C. (2019), 'Hong Kong student who accused police of sexual violence against protesters has taken legal advice and plans further action', *SCMP*, 11 October, https://www.scmp.com/news/hong-kong/law-and-crime/article/3032610/hong-kong-student-who-accused-police-sexual-violence. Accessed 28 February 2020.

Leach, E. (1976), *Culture and Communication: The Logic by Which Symbols are Connected – An Introduction to the Use of Structuralist Analysis in Social Anthropology*, Cambridge: Cambridge University Press.

Lee, W. K. (2002), 'Gender ideology and the domestic division of labor in middle-class Chinese families in Hong Kong', *Gender, Place and Culture: A Journal of Feminist Geography*, 9:3, pp. 245–60.

Lo, C., Cheung, E. and Lau, C. (2019), 'Elite police "raptor" squad went undercover to target radical Hong Kong protesters, insiders say', *SCMP*, 12 August, https://www.scmp.com/news/hong-kong/politics/article/3022457/elite-police-raptor-squad-went-undercover-target-radical. Accessed 13 April 2020.

Lui, J. (2017), 'Cantonese v Mandarin: When Hong Kong languages get political', BBC News, 29 June, https://www.bbc.com/news/world-asia-china-40406429. Accessed 12 April 2020.

Lurie, A. (1981), *The Language of Clothes*, New York: Random House.

Mauss, M. (1973), 'Techniques of the body', *Economy and Society*, 2:1, pp. 70–88.

Maynard, M. (2006), 'Dress for dissent: Reading the almost unreadable', *Journal of Australian Studies*, 30:89, pp. 103–12.

McCracken, G.D. (1990), *Culture and Consumption: New Approaches to the Symbolic Character of Consumer Goods and Activities*, vol. 1, Bloomington: Indiana University Press.

Omar, D. (2019), 'To be peaceful or "valiant": A day in the life of a Hong Kong protester', SBS (Special Broadcasting Service), 28 August, https://www.sbs.com.au/news/to-be-peaceful-or-valiant-a-day-in-the-life-of-a-hong-kong-protester. Accessed 30 September 2019.

Ost, D. (1990), *Solidarity and the Politics of Anti-Politics: Opposition and the Reform of Poland Since 1968*, Philadelphia: Temple University Press.

Paulicelli, E. (2004), *Fashion under Fascism: Beyond the Black Shirt*, Oxford: Berg.

Peirson-Smith, A. (2013), 'Fashioning the fantastical self: An examination of the cosplay dress-up phenomenon in Southeast Asia', *Fashion Theory*, 17:1, pp. 77–111.

Peirson-Smith, A. (2019a), 'Fashioning the embodied liminal/liminoid self: An examination of the dualities of cosplay phenomenon in East Asia', *Asia Pacific Perspectives*, 16:1, pp. 65–92.

Peirson-Smith, A. (2019b), 'Fashion communication: Introduction', in J. Hancock and A. Peirson-Smith (eds), *The Fashion Business Reader*, London: Bloomsbury Visual Arts, pp. 315–21.

Rall, D.N. and Costello, M. (2010), 'Women, craft and protest – yesterday and today', *Australian Folklore: A Yearly Journal of Folklore Studies*, 25, pp. 79–96.

Regan, H., Westcott, B., Griffiths, J. and Yeung, J. (2019), 'Hong Kong grounds all flights as protest paralyzes airport', *CNN*, 19 August, https://edition.cnn.com/asia/live-news/hong-kong-protests-airport-intl-hnk/index.html. Accessed 13 April 2020.

Roach-Higgins, M.E. and Eicher, J.B. (1995), *Dress and Identity*, New York: Fairchild Publications.

Robles, J. (2019), 'Hong Kong Protests: Key events from Hong Kong's anti-government protests', *SCMP*, 9 December, https://multimedia.scmp.com/infographics/news/hong-kong/article/3032146/hong-kong-protests/index.html. Accessed 29 February 2020.

Rose, J.J. (2020), 'Coronavirus and the Hong Kong protest movement: COVID-19 may have put a damper on pro-democracy street demonstrations, but the spirit is very much alive', *The Lowy Institute*, 23 March, https://www.lowyinstitute.org/the-interpreter/coronavirus-and-hong-kong-protest-movement. Accessed 12 April 2020.

Rourke, A. (2019), 'What do the Hong Kong protesters want?', *The Guardian*, 13 August, https://www.theguardian.com/world/2019/aug/13/what-do-the-hong-kong-protesters-want. Accessed 29 February 2020.

Rubinstein, G. (1995), 'Right-wing authoritarianism, political affiliation, religiosity, and their relation to psychological androgyny', *Sex Roles*, 33:7&8, pp. 569–86.

Rühlig, T. (2016), 'Do you hear the people sing "lift your umbrella"?, Understanding Hong Kong's pro-democratic umbrella movement through YouTube music videos', *China Perspectives*, 4, pp. 59–68.

Simmel, G. (1957), *Fashion*, Champaign-Urbana: University of Illinois.

Sproles, G.B. and Burns, L.D. (1994), *Changing Appearances: Understanding Dress in Contemporary Society*, New York: Fairchild Publications.

Steger, I. (2019), 'How Hong Kong's female protesters are reclaiming the "basic bitch" stereotype', *Quartz*, October 7, https://qz.com/1716703/hong-kong-female-protesters-challenge-pampered-stereotype/. Accessed 1 March 2020.

Tam, S.M., Fung, A., Kam, L. and Liong, M. (2009), 'Re-gendering Hong Kong man in social, physical and discursive space', in F.M. Cheung and E. Holroyd (eds), *Mainstreaming Gender in Hong Kong Society*, Hong Kong: The Chinese University Press, pp. 335–65.

Tobin, J., Dobard, R.G. and Wahlman, M.S. (1998), *Hidden in Plain View: A Secret Story of Quilts and the Underground Railroad*, New York: Anchor Books.

Torrens, K.M. (1999), 'Fashion as argument: Nineteenth-century dress reform', *Argumentation and Advocacy*, 36:2, pp. 77–87.

Troup Beuchanan, R. (2019), 'Rape threats, body-shaming and doctored photos: Hong Kong women protesters facing troll army', *Hong Kong Free Press*, 2 September, https://www.hongkongfp.com/2019/09/02/rape-threats-body-shaming-doctored-photos-hong-kong-women-protesters-facing-troll-army/. Accessed 30 September 2019.

Tseëlon, E. (2012), 'Fashion and the orders of masking', *Critical Fashion Studies in Fashion and Beauty*, 3:1&2, pp. 3–9.

Tsung-gan, K. (2019), 'October 1 in Hong Kong: Solidarity, resistance and the kindness of strangers', *Hong Kong Free Press*, 7 October, https://www.hongkongfp.com/2019/10/07/october-1-hong-kong-solidarity-resistance-kindness-strangers/. Accessed 2 December 2019.

Turner, V.W. (1982), *From Ritual to Theatre: The Human Seriousness of Play*, New York: Paj Publications.

Turney, Jo. (2014), 'Battle dressed – clothing the criminal, or the horror of the "hoodie" in Britain', in D.N. Rall (ed.), *Fashion and War in Popular Culture*, Bristol: Intellect, pp. 125–38.

uwu_uwu_mo (HongKongProtests#) (2019), 'A Women's Place in is the Resistance', Twitter, 30 September.

Veblen, T. (1899), *The Theory of the Leisure Class*, New York: Macmillan.

Wong, S.L. (2019a), 'Hong Kong police's indecent arrest of a female protester raises questions about the force's conformity to its own rules', *Letters, South China Morning Post (SCMP)*, 16 August, https://www.scmp.com/comment/letters/article/3022698/hong-kong-polices-indecent-arrest-female-protester-raises-questions. Accessed 2 December 2019.

Wong, S.L. (2019b), 'We used to play laser tag. Now we face real bullets', *Financial Times, Lunch with the FT*, 9 November, p. 3.

Wu, J.K.K., Lai, R., and Yuhan, A. (2019), 'Six months of Hong Kong protests: How did we get here?', *New York Times*, 18 November, https://www.nytimes.com/interactive/2019/world/asia/hong-kong-protests-arc.html. Accessed 28 February 2020.

Xinqi, S. (2019), 'Female frontliners upend Hong Kong gender stereotypes', *Hong Kong Free Press*, 11 December, https://www.hongkongfp.com/2019/12/11/female-frontliners-upend-hong-kong-gender-stereotypes/. Accessed 27 February 2020.

Yangzom, D. (2016), 'Clothing and social movements: Tibet and the politics of dress', *Social Movement Studies*, 15:6, pp. 622–33.

Yeung, J. (2019), 'Permanent protest: Demonstrators in Hong Kong are getting tattoos', *CNN Arts*, 21 August, https://edition.cnn.com/style/article/hong-kong-protest-tattoo-intl-hnk-trnd/index.html. Accessed 26 February 2020.

Yiu, P. (2020) '"Evolving like Pokemon"': Hong Kong women step up to protest frontlines', Reuters, 7 March, https://www.reuters.com/article/us-womens-day-hongkong-protester-idUSKBN20U08J. Accessed 14 March 2020.

Contributors

SARAH BAKER is a senior lecturer in the School of Communication at Auckland University of Technology, New Zealand. She is the co-founder of the AUT Popular Culture Centre and a member of JMAD and the AUT Media Observatory Group. She is the secretary of GANZA (The Gothic Association of New Zealand and Australia). She is a senior fellow of the Higher Education Academy. Her research interests include political economy, current affairs television programmes and popular culture focusing on the Gothic, sexuality and gender. As well as examining current affairs and broadcasting; other research interests include the analysis of gay characters in Hollywood film, apocalypse in popular culture, the quality of television in 'House of Cards' and borders and boundaries in popular culture. She has presented at many international conferences. Current projects include organizing an edited collection on horror in film and writing a book on current affairs television programmes.

* * * * *

PRUDENCE BLACK is a research associate in the Department of Gender and Cultural Studies at the University of Sydney and the School of Humanities, University of Adelaide. Her award-winning book relating to uniforms and the aviation industry *The Flight Attendant's Shoe* was published by NewSouth Press, 2011. She has published mainly in the areas of design, modernism, fashion, aviation and workplace culture. Her latest book, *Smile, Particularly in Bad Weather* (UWA Publishing, 2017) is about the gendered and industrial relations history of flight hostesses and flight attendants.

* * * * *

ANNITA BOYD is an adjunct senior lecturer at Griffith University, in Australia, where she lectured in programmes including screen studies, cultural history and fashion and film. Her research interests include the intersection of fashion theory with film and television and its uptake in various sites in popular culture. She has written on the Kennedy family, including Little Edie (Bouvier Beale) of *Grey Gardens* fame and designers Elsa Schiaparelli and Oleg Cassini, who dressed the US First Lady Jacqueline Lee Kennedy Onassis.

* * * * *

JO COGHLAN is a senior lecturer in the School of Humanities, Arts and Social Sciences at the University of New England in Armidale, New South Wales. Her research examines the media and popular culture through a sociological and political lens to understand the hegemonic power of representations and framing. Drawing on theorists from Gramsci and Foucault to Entman and Chomsky, her research critically examines contemporary and historical news, film and television. Other research interests include representations of political fashion and social and political debates about death and euthanasia. This research compliments scholarly interest in a range of social policy issues, particularly regulatory social policy and its impact of human agency, especially on the role of women. Jo has published various books on Indonesian and Australian politics and on the treatment of asylum seekers. She regularly publishes in *On Line Opinion* and *The Conversation*.

* * * * *

JENNIFER CRAIK is an adjunct professor of fashion at the Queensland University of Technology in Brisbane, Australia. She researches cultural understandings of the meaning of fashion and dress. Her internationally renowned publications include *The Face of Fashion*; *Uniforms Exposed*; *Fashion: The Key Concepts*; *Modern Fashion Traditions*; and *Re-visioning Arts and Cultural Policy*. Her publications are routinely cited as an authoritative source for fashion scholars around the world.

* * * * *

RACHEL EVANS is a senior lecturer at Bath Spa University, lecturing in historical and critical studies. A design historian, her research interests centre on everyday material culture, with a particular interest in reading against the grain of accepted understandings of design history. Recent research has considered Agatha Christies' Marple as fan fiction, Muriel Cooper's use of white space in the design of Learning From Las Vegas and the use of novel pedagogical methods in the 'Britain Can Make It Exhibition Design Quiz of 1946'.

LISA J. HACKETT is an academic at the University of New England in Australia where she lectures in popular culture and Australian sociology. As a sociologist and historian, Lisa's research interests include social and historical examinations of clothing use, the material culture of fashion and contemporary understandings of historical artefacts and events. Her Ph.D., 'Curves & A-Lines: Why contemporary women choose to wear nostalgic 1950s style clothing', focused on the sociological and material culture foundations of wearing 'retro' fashion, from the historical foundations of the style through to contemporary social practices.

*****

EMERALD L. KING is a lecturer in Japanese at La Trobe University, in Melbourne, Australia. She studied in Australia and Japan before receiving her Ph.D. in Japanese literature from the University of Tasmania in 2012. She worked at Victoria University of Wellington from 2013 to 2018 and was appointed head of Japanese in 2016. Emerald's research interests include violence in text, masochistic theory, kimono in Japanese literature, costume representation in anime and manga and cosplay in Japan and Australasia. In 2009–10, Emerald completed a Japan Foundation Doctoral Fellowship to conduct research at Ochanomizu University (Tokyo, Japan) for 11 months under Dr Satako Kan and Dr Kazuko Takemura. As part of her cosplay research, she has competed in and won a number of prizes, most notably winning the 2016 finals of the Madman National Cosplay Championship (MNCC), placing in 2012 and 2018, and placing third and second in the 2018 and 2019 heats of the Australian selection round of the World Cosplay Summit (WCS).

*****

AMANDA LAUGESEN is a historian and lexicographer, and currently Director of the Australian National Dictionary Centre at the Australian National University. She is the author of numerous books, book chapters, and articles on Australian and US history, as well as chief editor of the *Australian National Dictionary: Australian Words and Their Origins*. Amanda's research includes numerous books and articles in the areas of historical memory, the history of reading, libraries and publishing, cultural history (with a particular interest in the cultural history of war), the history of Australian English and lexicography. Her chapter, 'Models, medals and the uses of the military in fashion' was published in the edited collection, *Fashion and War in Popular Culture* (Rall, 2014). Recent books are *Furphies and Whizzbangs: Anzac Slang from the Great War* (2015) and *Rooted: An Australian History of Bad Language* (NewSouth Publishing, 2020). Her current research areas include cultural history of Australian English and slang; cultural history of war; and the global history of publishing, libraries and literacy. The monograph *Taking Books to the World: American Publishers and the Cultural Cold War*, a study of American publishers in the developing world, was published in 2017. She is currently completing a book on the history of bad language in Australia.

* * * * *

ANNE PEIRSON-SMITH is a senior lecturer and the course leader in fashion management, marketing and communication in the School of Art and Design, Nottingham Trent University in England. She teaches and researches fashion studies, fashion communication, popular culture and the creative industries. She is the co-author of *Public Relations in Asia Pacific: Communicating Effectively Across Cultures* (John Wiley, 2010) and *Planet Cosplay: Costume Play, Identity and Global Fandom* (Bristol: Intellect Books, 2019). She is an associate editor of the *Journal of Fashion, Style and Popular Culture* (Intellect Books) and *The Journal of Global Fashion Marketing* (Taylor & Francis) and is co-editor of *Global Fashion Brands: Style, Luxury & History* (Intellect Books, 2014), *Transglobal Fashion Narratives: Clothing Communication, Style Statements and Brand Storytelling* (Intellect Books, 2018), *The Fashion Business Reader* (2019, Berg/Fairchild); *Creative Industries in Flux in Hong Kong: A Critical Investigation into the Challenges, Agency and Potential of Cultural and Creative Workers* (Routledge, 2020).

* * * * *

DENISE N. RALL is an adjunct fellow (Research) in humanities and social sciences in the Faculty of Business, Law and the Arts at Southern Cross University, Lismore, New South Wales, and an adjunct lecturer in the School of Humanities, Arts and Social Sciences at the University of New England, Armidale, New South Wales, Australia. She currently researches the social and cultural meanings embedded in clothing and textiles. Her edited collection, *Fashion and War in Popular Culture* was published by Intellect in 2014. She has lectured in the critical sociology of clothing, and the relationships between craft and wearable art at Southern Cross University, Curtin University, the University of Adelaide, Auckland University of Technology and at conferences throughout Australia and New Zealand. Her current projects include exhibitions of her textile artworks and wearable art, and further research on how women employ dress, craft and art in political protest.

MEGAN ROSE is an adjunct associate lecturer in Sociology, Social Research and Policy at the School of Social Sciences, UNSW Sydney, Australia. She specializes in gender and sexuality in the Japanese context, with a specific interest in *kawaii* culture. Her work explores the creative capacity of women in Japan in their everyday lives, focusing on grouping such as feminist activists who use *kawaii* imagery, alternative *kawaii* fashion communities associated with *Harajuku* and doll makers and collectors in Tokyo. She considers the playful and performative nature of gendered presentations of the self, as well as affect and the relationships we form with objects in our everyday lives.

* * * * *

MADELEINE SEYS is a writer, researcher, curator and tailor from Adelaide, South Australia. She was awarded a Ph.D. with Dean's Commendation for Excellence by the University of Adelaide in 2015. She is a visiting research fellow and lecturer in the Department of English and Creative Writing at The University of Adelaide, where she teaches English literature. Her book *Fashion and Narrative in Victorian Popular Literature: Double Threads* was published by Routledge in 2018. Madeleine has also published on fashion, nineteenth-century museum culture, embroidery and literary censorship. She collaborated with Associate Professor Mandy Treagus (The University of Adelaide) in *Looking Back at Samoa: History, Memory and the Figure of Mourning in Yuki Kihara's Where Do We Come From? What Are We? Where Are We Going?* (Asian Diasporic Visual Cultures and the Americas, 2017). Working in both words and threads, Madeleine's research explores material, sartorial and literary cultures and practices in the nineteenth century and beyond. Interwoven into all of her work is Madeleine's abiding interest in gender, sexuality and the history of feminism. Madeleine also works as a consulting curator with the History Trust of South Australia and is involved in their 'Queering the Museum' Project.

* * * * *

RHEINHARD REIDOLF SIRAIT has graduated from the University of Western Australia, Perth, Australia. His research interests include social media, politics, activism, popular culture and Islam in Indonesia and maintains an active profile on Instagram to discuss issues affecting Asian popular culture and politics. He has lectured at Walailak University in Thailand and worked for the International Labour Organization, Indonesian Legal Aid and the Alliance of Indigenous Peoples of the Archipelago, Aliansi Masyarakat Adat Nusantara (AMAN).

JO TURNEY is an associate professor of fashion at the Winchester School of Art at the University of Southampton, United Kingdom. Her research interests extend from the manufacture of textiles (*The Culture of Knitting*, 2009, Berg) through to their consumption, display and use (*Floral Frocks, Antique Collector's Club*, 2007 and *Images in Time, Wunderkammer*, 2011). She is particularly interested in the ways in which users/wearers respond to and re-appropriate clothing and this is explored by her research into menswear and deviant behaviour, from the sub-cultural 1980s Casuals to today's 'hoodies' and tracksuit wearing youth (*Fashion and Crime*, 2017, IB Tauris), and her chapter, 'Battle-dressed – clothing the criminal, or the horror of the "hoodie" in Britain' in *Fashion and War in Popular Culture* (Intellect, 2014). Her research also encompasses analyses of garments hitherto marginalized from dress history, such as the cardigan, and, the white singlet or 'wife beater' vest. From this interest in casual clothing, she is currently seeking to publish a book that will offer a more thorough investigation into non-formal or 'comfortable clothes'. She is co-editor of the journal *Clothing Cultures* (Intellect). Her current project is a social history of fashion in the 1970s and plans to extend this historical focus to 'In Private', a book that considers the cultural significance of 1970s domestic interior design in the United Kingdom and the United States.